The Church
and the Relentless Darkness

The Church
and the Relentless Darkness

ROBERT THORNTON HENDERSON

Bob Henderson

2/20/13

WIPF & STOCK · Eugene, Oregon

THE CHURCH AND THE RELENTLESS DARKNESSS

Wipf & Stock
An Imprint of Wipf and Stock Publishers
199 W. 8th Ave., Suite 3
Eugene, OR 97401
www.wipfandstock.com

ISBN 13: 978-1-62032-549-0

Manufactured in the U.S.A.

I dedicate this book to the memory of my wife, Betty: my encourager, my intercessor, and my dearest friend for fifty-eight years, . . . whose last spoken words were her prayer for the completion and fruitfulness of this very book. What a gift she was to me, and to so many.

Contents

Acknowledgments

I HAVE NOT WRITTEN this without the much-appreciated ministry of so many others to me. Primary among these would, of course, be my own wife Betty, but I also need to remember my own mentor Susan E. Beers and the Peniel Bible Conference saints, who first tuned me in to the reality of the spiritual warfare. But much more recently, I need to express my appreciation of some really wonderful young friends who have tried to keep me knowledgeable about generational culture, and the appraisal of this whole subject by their acquaintances who inhabit their very real daily world. I would mention Erik Vincent, Sherri Hutter, David and Reagan Charney, Fidel Agbor, Rene and Seth McLaughlin, Bobby Gross, and Shayne Wheeler. Then there are those helpful staff folk across the country at Wifp and Stock, whom I never see, but who are certainly a gift to me in this project.

Foreword

H AVING TEENAGERS IS FUN . . . and more than a little scary! It can
be difficult to discern what is going on in their lives when their
communication with you is reduced to short phrases or monosyllabic
grunts.

But you learn a lot when they don't think you are listening: while
driving them and their friends to the movies, or when they are talking
excitedly on the phone. You learn what they really think about things
and sometimes it is not very encouraging.

Have you ever wondered what we must sound like to God? If he
were listening in on our conversations about who (or what) we think
God is, would God be encouraged or would he think we have completely
missed the point? After all, there is a lot of pseudo-religious God-stuff
out there, and some of it is even coming from within the church! And
it's all pretty crazy.

In the movie *Out on a Limb* (1987), Shirley Maclaine swirls around,
chanting, "I am God. I am God." Really?

Following the terrorist attack of September 11, 2001, more than
one television preacher publicly proclaimed that it was God's judgment
because there were homosexuals in the building. Hmmm.

We have grown accustomed to politicians labeling the political en-
emies of the United States as being part of some nebulous "evil empire."
The clear implication being that we are the holy and righteous ones.
God is on our side because we are a free and democratic country, as if
Christianity and the American Dream are one in the same thing.

If that is how God really is, I don't know that I could believe in him.
The world I live in is much more nuanced and complex than that. The
God who must have created that world and created me must therefore
be much more complex than the reductionistic, passive, anemic, indifferent, or outright bigoted deity that is often presented to us by well-
meaning but tragically misguided quasi-religious leaders.

If Shirley Maclaine is God. And you are God. And I am God. As Donald Miller says, "It all gets pretty boring."

If God kills three thousand people just because of a few gay folks, then there is no hope for me.

If Christianity is reduced to having the economic freedom to have a bigger house or a new car, well: been there and done that. And it leaves me no more satisfied in my soul than folks who love Jesus in Rwanda, Russia, or Iraq.

Let us be clear, the mission of God in this world is not to make you a mini-deity. It is not to wipe out every person you find disagreeable. It is not to make your life more comfortable and worry free. The mission of God is to remedy the damage, top to bottom, of sin and evil in this world, done at the hands of the great deceiver, Satan. The hope of the gospel is that God, in Christ, is putting the world to rights, and this has always been his mission.

In Genesis 12, when God calls Abraham to follow him, he says, "I am going to make you into a great nation and I will bless you." This is the beginning of a group of people being called out to be a distinctive gathering of God followers. But—and this is important—they weren't called out just to have their own private religious club. They were called, gathered, equipped, and blessed in order to *be a blessing*. God said it clearly: "All peoples on earth will be blessed through you."

This is nothing short of earth shattering for those of us who call ourselves Christ followers, who are the inheritance of the family of Abraham and a part of this thing we call: "the church." Are we fulfilling that mandate? Are we a blessing to the nations? Are we actively resisting the influence of sin and evil in our lives, our communities and, yes, even in our churches?

We are a people who are called to the mission and purposes of God for this world. We are called to resist what Bob Henderson so aptly calls the "relentless darkness" that sneaks into our lives and even our churches in the Trojan horses of apathy, comfort, and abject spiritual ignorance and laziness. Will we equip ourselves, and our people, with the spiritual armor of grace, truth, peace, righteousness, and faith? Will we remember that we are the children of God, filled with the Holy Spirit, who nevertheless "are residing in rebel-held territory" and living as subversives against a dominant culture of darkness? Beloved, this is who you ARE and this is your mission! It is not a job that is reserved for the professional clergy or the uber-spiritual elite. It is a job for all of us and not only can we do it, but this is where the real work of God's kingdom happens—not in the padded pews or perfected programs, but in the daily (dare we say ordinary?) lives of God's people as we confront the relentless darkness with the transforming light of Jesus Christ!

Our effectiveness in this mission will require some of us to radically rethink the way we view such basic things like faith and church.

In the consciousness of most Christians, church is the building we go to for a couple hours on a Sunday morning in order to listen to a sermon, sing some songs, and, if we are lucky, have a cup of coffee. But this is not how the Bible conceives of the church. As Bob puts it in this book, the church is a "visible, Spirit-created, new humanity, which is created to be the demonstration of the communal formation of the kingdom of God. It can gather anywhere: in a living room, on the seashore, in the park, in a ballroom, in a prison, around a table at the neighborhood pub—in the most unlikely places." Such a vision reminds us that church is not a destination, it is a movement of people hell-bent on bringing the healing and grace of the gospel of Jesus Christ to bear on a world that has been ravaged by the prince of darkness.

Likewise, it is imperative for us to see that Christianity is more of a *reality* than it is a *religion*. It is an invitation to join in God's purposes of making all things new in Christ. It is your invitation to be light in the midst of the darkness, to resist evil and be an agent of hope, healing, and renewal. Christianity is being empowered by the Spirit of Christ himself to stand for what is good, beautiful, and true. If we are content to merely "go to church," we miss our invitation to "walk as children of the light." Even worse, in our contentedness to be comfortable with the church as a mere institution in which we can hide and be religious, we actually let the darkness invade the church itself. Spiritual apathy, religiosity, and indifference to the mission of God invite the darkness to walk right in through the front door.

But, friends, it does not have to be this way in your church or in mine. There is hope! In fact, the Scriptures tell us that it is *through the church* that the wisdom of God is to be made known! That's your church and mine! God has equipped us with the armor to do this. Our lives as Christians have a greater purpose and power than most of us have ever dared to imagine! Christ gives us all we need to join his work. You don't have to be a spiritual superhero. You only need to be a faithful follower of Jesus, who has secured victory over the evil one on the cross.

So, will we get out of our pew and follow? Will we take the light of Christ into the streets of our cities and neighborhood as we stand against the very tangible darkness of injustice, suffering, and oppression? Will we dare to love the marginalized with the same radical love we have received in Christ? My prayer is that we will be a generation that grasps the fullness of the gospel of Jesus Christ—that God is not just saving a few souls for heaven, but is rather destroying the entire dominion of darkness, here and now, and putting the world to rights.

My earnest desire is that the Christian church will recover the core message of Jesus Christ and his mission of healing in the world, and lose our infatuation with flashy religious experiences and worry-free and comfortable lives where our faith is reduced to a ticket out of hell and makes little difference to the world we inhabit now. May we recover the news that is truly GOOD NEWS: Jesus Christ has come to destroy the dominion of darkness and make all things new and has called us to join him in that mission!

Such a calling cannot be contained in the title of a few ecclesiastical elites, or well-oiled church programs, or Wednesday night potlucks. It cannot be contained within the four walls of a church building! It is a calling that goes deep into the identity of every Christian and compels them to go into their communities and workplaces to be a blessing to the nations, making the light of the kingdom of God a *reality* (not a *religion*) that pushes back the darkness and fearlessly proclaims that Jesus is truly good news for the world!

And be assured, we can do this because, as Bob reminds us, "darkness is no match for the community of the kingdom of God, the church, as it heralds the gospel of the kingdom unto every people group in the world before the Lord returns."

May it be so.

Shayne Wheeler
Author of *The Briarpatch Gospel*
Decatur, Georgia
August 2012

Preface

WHEN THE DOMINION OF darkness inhabits the church . . . and the church inhabits the dominion of darkness . . . what then?

Does that sound like a weird sort of question?

Okay, if the church (the Greek word meaning something like: an assembly *called out* for some specific purpose) is a community of folk ostensibly called out of the dominion of darkness (or, of Satan) and *called into* the dominion of God's dear Son[1] (or the kingdom of God) . . . then one would assume that the church community, and those who compose it, would have some basic awareness of what they had been called *out of*, as well as that *into* which they had been called . . . and with the character and implications of such a calling, right?

Wrong!

Twenty years ago, in the pastoral agony that I was (and so many other friends were) enduring while seeking to be faithful teaching shepherds in difficult (and often dismal) congregational settings, I wrote a book entitled *A Door of Hope: Spiritual Conflict in Pastoral Ministry*,[2] which became a resource for many and required reading in a few seminaries that I know of.

But so much has transpired socially, culturally, generationally, and ecclesiastically in the intervening years . . . plus, my own engagement with the church has shifted from the formal role of a teaching shepherd (pastor-teacher) to that of a (clandestine?) mentor, big brother, or maybe a wisdom figure to some remarkable young friends who are serious in their discipleship and ruthless in their honesty and inquisitiveness. The church for them is not some *sacred cow* exempt from their own probing (and sometimes wicked) sense of integrity. With these friends and

1. Col 1:13
2. Still available in reprint from Wipf and Stock Publishers.

their probing minds before me I have written two books: *Enchanted Community: Journey into the Mystery of the Church* (about the *what* of the church), and *Refounding the Church from the Underside* (about the *why* of the church).[3] In so doing I created, as a literary device, a single composite person (to include all of these young friends) to whom I have given the name of Alan. Alan, then, is my attempt to portray the thinking and question of a group that includes something like a dozen much younger and very gifted friends from many professions, including a couple of pastors and church planters.

In my former writings I have focused on the non-professional, or the non-clergy, folk who were stumbled by the whole church scene. I was, admittedly, a bit hard on clergy, naming them as one of the subversions imposed on us by the whole Christendom phenomenon (even though I am one of them—but that's a whole other story). Now, I want to take a half-turn back toward my clergy friends since I have a couple of them as part of my Alan composite person. The other young adult friends come from such varied professional vocations, and their daily ministry is in law, architecture, education, affordable housing, nutrition, coaching, information technology, etc.

But my ultimate goal in what follows is to lift up the very much-avoided biblical theme of our *warfare with the dominion of darkness*. When one struggles with the integrity of the church, and with its authenticity as a community of the kingdom of God . . . sooner or later one comes up against the sobering reality that our context here is not in any sense a neutral one, but rather that there is something subtle and corrosive and dark and utterly resistant, even though it may be cloaked in very familiar, (and on the surface) normal, and pleasant religious, spiritual, and ecclesiastical settings.

What's behind this? What's going on that we don't see?

At the same time I do not want to lose my focus on that company of devoted disciples of Jesus Christ who take their obedience to him, his Word, his mission with utter seriousness . . . yet are so often stumbled, or led astray by the ecclesiastical darkness, and who, inadvertently, become conformed to that darkness simply because they know of no other viable alternative (other than to drop out).

What is one to do when the ecclesiastical darkness is deeply entrenched? If we are serious in our intent to be positive influences in

---

3. Both also published by Wipf and Stock.

this scene of darkness, what will be required on our part is patience, perseverance . . . but with hope. Plus, dusting off the church's ancient and formidable traditions, liturgies, hymns . . . can give to subversive pastor-teachers and to disciple makers (along with that underside cabal of faithful men and women who are so frequently the authentic heart of the church) . . . an awesome potential.

To engage in such an encounter with the darkness is not a calling for the faint of heart. It is, albeit, awareness that one of Satan's cleverest wiles is the assumption that the context of our Christian calling is *neutral.* No, such an engagement is probably not everyone's calling, but it must be intentional and alert to the potential. We are living in a period of cultural and ecclesiastical *liminality* where what were once, perhaps, scenes of missional faithfulness are now in the throes of some kind of a *cultural whitewater* moving ineluctably, and with breathtaking rapidity, into a cynical post-Christian culture that has no patterns, but . . . where God's design to have the gospel of the kingdom proclaimed to every national and people group is *still* our calling. This creates for us a fascinating and hopeful potential.

MY OWN CREDENTIALS

It will be important for my readers to know of my own credentials in addressing such a subject, since the book contains some challenges to some of the embedded and prevailing ecclesiastical assumptions and the *ecclesiology* of the church that has been in place for a millennium and a half. This will be, obviously, a bit controversial. But it will, hopefully, provoke thought and conversation, as well as being encouraging and equipping for my young friends. I trust, also, that it is profoundly biblical, since I would not want to stray from that authority.

I was a pastor-teacher within the Presbyterian church for forty years in four congregations. I also served as a denominational staff person in the field of its mission of evangelism. That part of my career involved me in several ecumenical agencies where I interacted with my counterparts from many traditions. In all of those capacities I did leadership training, or was a consultant of one sort or another in of scores of congregations. I was also invited to lecture and lead discussions in a number of seminaries. This is not to mention conferences of many sorts. In all of this, my integrating theme, which I articulated, was that the gospel of the kingdom of God is the essence of the New Testament message.

Upon formal retirement from my more formal pastoral role of some forty years, I was for ten years on the staff of a denominational renewal organization (Presbyterians For Renewal) as director of its ministry to seminarians, to both faculty and students. This took me into numerous theological schools and engaged me nationally with the theological training schools of the church.

During that period I also was a participant in the Gospel and Our Culture Network (the think tank of those engaged with Lesslie Newbigin's missiology), the American Society of Missiology, and other stimulating missional conversations.

In this post-retirement passage of my life (as an author, mentor, etc.), I have been an ordinary participant (without credentials) in a substantial old congregation with which I have had meaningful ties for over half a century—only this time I have not had any ordained role in its leadership, only a "coffee-cup conversation partner" with many of its members, some of whom are, in fact, its leaders. They have taught me much. At the same time my (late) wife Betty and I found ourselves to be something like mother/father figures or wisdom figures (or something) to the above-mentioned set of remarkable and gifted and inquisitive and refreshingly honest younger adults.

Put all of these together and it provides me with a provocative mix, and a context of ecclesiastical reality that is the matrix out of which this present book emerges. Actually, as I have noted above, this is the third book that has been provoked out of these several strands of my experience. Together the three of them compose something of a trilogy on missional ecclesiology. This present one in many ways presupposes the previous two books.

At its heart is the whole much-avoided reality that the Scriptures absolutely do *not* avoid, namely, the reality of Satan, the roaring lion (of Peter 5:8), the beast of the Book of Revelation, the liar, the father of lies, the murderer . . . and his dominion of darkness. This book is about how this ominous reality is actually the very context into which Christ calls his church and invests it with his power and authority over Satan's malice . . . only, the whole subject is too generally avoided (or consigned to authors who do melodramatic interpretations that are more incredible than convincing).

I am also, admittedly, writing especially to a *particular segment* of the church, particularly (or primarily) to those disciples who inhabit older Christendom church institutions that are wedded to passing patterns, forgetful, bewildered . . . yet somehow bearers of remnants of glory. There is a huge host of such, being swept along in the whitewater of this liminal period between Christendom and whatever is to follow in the cynical post-Christian era now becoming dominant, what with its hostility to the whole Christian reality.

I am indebted and fully appreciative of the fruitful works of the Gospel and Our Culture Network, of the many wonderful writers who are proposing creative approaches, such as Michael Frost, Brian McLaren, Hugh Halter, Matt Smay, Alan Roxburgh, and that whole syndrome of provocative persons who have enriched my thinking.

But, at the same time, as I am provoked by their creative and compelling insights, I do not find them speaking to those of us who inhabit so many of the venerable old (but forgetful and drifting and culturally out of touch) church institutions. It is to the faithful disciples inhabiting such that I write. At the same time, as I weekly discern in my conversation with my friends engaged in new church plants, this relentless darkness from the outset demonstrates its subtle assaults against every witness to the light of the gospel.

I want to lift up this whole reality of spiritual conflict, of the reality of the *dominion of darkness*, out of which we are called—even as we are called by Christ into his salvific dominion. I want to portray this as a thrilling and demanding and hopeful dimension of Christ's calling and purpose for us. I want to confess that the church far too often inhabits the cultural darkness and allows the religious darkness to inhabit its communal life. The church even reinterprets and accommodates its self-definitions, its rites, and liturgies in order to make them aesthetically pleasing, and in so doing reduces them to *merely human* religious expression that is no threat to the gates of hell.

That's one piece . . .

Another would be all of those great hymns that I love, that stir the blood and speak of such things as "Lead On, O King Eternal," or "Onward Christian Soldiers, Marching As to War," or "Who is on the Lord's side, who will face the foe?," or ". . . though this world with devils filled, should threaten to undo us" . . . which are such a rich part of the church's musical heritage, and yet seem so totally unreal when we are sitting in the ambience and soft light of church sanctuaries, with the socially congenial folk in St. John's-by-the-Boulevard Church, and reciting familiar Christian creeds . . . or maybe the local megachurch with all of its colorful attractions and institutional successes.

I confess that I fall back here on the notions of *ambiguity* and *complexity*, given the infinite variety of church expressions to which I might be writing. Satan has, according to the apostle, so often clothed himself as "an angel of light" (2 Cor 11:13–15). Even that raises questions about whether true believers can be used by Satan so that they appear to be authorized leaders, while complicit in the drift into darkness.

So many questions. And our adversary is brilliant, sophisticated, and utterly malicious in his wrath toward the Bride of Christ.

I invite you into a journey with me. I acknowledge resources I have read over many years that have at least given me clues, which have alerted me to this conflict. I could name the Puritan William Gurnall's *The Christian in Complete Armour*, or F. J. Huegel's *That Old Serpent the Devil*, or Michael Green's short *I Believe in Satan*, or Walter Wink's provocative three volumes on *the powers*, or especially Gregory Boyd's profound two-volume study, *God at War* and *Satan and the Problem of Evil*. Perhaps most helpful for me, in a unique way, would be C. S. Lewis' science fiction trilogy,[4] and the subtle and sophisticated way in which the forces of evil infiltrated the acceptable academic culture. I can only ask of my readers your kind understanding at my hermeneutic on this large part of the biblical story and the church's mission.

But again, my basic thesis is that the cultural setting of our calling to be Christ's church is not in any way neutral. Rather, we are called *out of the dominion of darkness, and into the kingdom of God's dear Son.* That reality informs our continual repentance and faith as the people of God. It must require that we continually renounce any affinity to the dominion of darkness, and give ourselves to our Lord Jesus and to his kingdom. By his grace we are saved. So join me in what follows.

By way of explanation to my readers, there will be considerable dialogue in a few of these chapters, sometimes with just "Alan" and myself, and in Chapter Four with a third party: "Lucy." Dialogue can be a bit confusing, so I will put my participation in the dialogue in simple quotation marks, but with Alan and Lucy I will use italics in quotation marks to

---

4. *Out of the Silent Planet, Perelandra,* and *That Hideous Strength.*

indicate their words. In the first chapters, where it is just Alan and myself it will be obvious. In Chapter Four I will indicate who is speaking at the beginning of their contribution, and their contribution will be indented. I hope this helps.

PART 1

When the Church Inhabits the Darkness,
and the Darkness Inhabits the Church . . .
What Then?

1

Conversation at the Trackside Tavern

"Okay, Bob, here's my cut-to-the-chase question: Can Satan, can the gates of hell, actually prevail against the church after all?

"All right, let me finish. I know that Jesus said that the gates of hell would not prevail against the church . . . but is it just possible that Satan can so hoodwink a particular church community, can so blind its participants, that it can just cruise along doing 'churchy' stuff and not even see or understand what the church is all about . . . or even especially care what its God-given mission is?

"Or maybe another question: Do you think that some pernicious, supernatural personality could so take captive the very imagination of the church's inhabitants, so that those folk wouldn't have any capacity to even imagine anything other than the pleasant church traditions that they were presently, and quite happily, experiencing?

"Or worse . . . wouldn't even care?

"I mean, hey! The folks in my North Park Church can go on mission trips to Nicaragua . . . while at the same time being totally oblivious to the sojourners next door, or the Hindu family down the street, or the compelling justice issues on the doorstep—or relate any of that to what goes on in their so-called worship services.

Something doesn't fit. Is it all some kind of a subtle counterfeit that is so pervasive and profound that it all seems normal . . . like, acceptable church life to most?

"Bottom line: Do you think Satan and the gates of hell are real, and if they are, are they even the least bit intimidated by our North Park Church?

"Is that enough for starts?"

Alan and I had been in an ongoing conversation about his (and our) struggle with the whole concept of the church since shortly after he had come to faith in Christ some five or six years previous to this conversation. His cynicism about it all was so healthy and provocative. He and I had spent months working on the essence (or the why?) of the church as we explored scriptures on the concept. He initially wanted to know if North Park Church was an authentic Christian scene, and should he take seriously the pastor's 'full-court press' on him to join the congregation. We worked out some signs of authenticity, and I had persuaded Alan that there was probably enough authenticity in North Park for him to take the plunge.

So he did.

It was a warm October afternoon, and the maples were a blaze of bright yellow around the patio of the Trackside Tavern where Alan and I had landed. The two of us had been on an odyssey together for six years or so. His was a quintessentially probing and mildly cynical but also positively pragmatic mind, so typical of his twenty-something generation (though he was now in his early thirties). When we had first met (almost by accident, in a coffee shop) he was a graduate student in bioengineering, blond, ponytailed, and bespectacled. The two of us had bonded immediately—whatever constitutes that chemistry between persons. I was by then a septuagenarian, formed by a whole other culture. But I had a long career as a pastor-teacher-author in the church, and had been around the block in the church scene, and it was that which provoked his initial questions to me about the place of the church in his newfound faith, and about its authenticity.

I had always loved his relentless, insightful, and probing questions. We had spent many, many hours working on the purpose of the church in the mission of God in all kinds of venues. He had pushed me to get honest about a whole lot of the mindless acceptance of so much of the Christian church scene, things to which I had hardly ever given a thought.

Now, Alan was in his early thirties, looking a bit more mature and professional. By this time he was also one of the founders of a consortium of bioengineers engaged in research that is beyond my capacity to even remotely understand. At the same time he had plunged into North Park Church with a vengeance, and had been recruited to do some teaching and to lead some discussion groups (I'm not sure that the folk at North Park knew what they were getting themselves into!). It was from those experiences that he had texted me, out of the blue, and asked me if we could meet and pick up our conversation, which conversation had been on hold for at least six or eight months.

So here we were. We spent a little time reconnecting and filling each other in on what had been going on in our lives since our last time together. But as soon as our server had delivered us a couple of pints of Guinness, he wanted to get to the above questions.

I had to chuckle a bit. "Yeah, I think that's enough. I'm not the least surprised at your questions. I've been the victim of your questions often enough. I think I would have been disappointed if you had something bland and simple to ask me.

"So, what's behind these? Sounds like you've got some kind of a bone stuck in your teeth. Fill me in."

"No, you're not going to get off that easy. Can the gates of hell (whatever they are) prevail against the church? Or maybe, do you really believe that there is a Satan who is relentless in his attempts to emasculate the church and render it impotent in the mission of God?

"Or, maybe: Can the church itself really be a mission field?"

I responded, "My immediate abbreviated answer is: yes, no, sometimes, or maybe . . . but ultimately, *no!* The gates of hell will not—cannot—ultimately prevail, yet at the same time, some expressions of that church will in fact go dormant, or forsake the battle, or drift away, or forget the message, or revert to conformity to the world, or redefine themselves into merely human religious institutions . . . but the gates of hell are not going to *ultimately* prevail.

"And, yes, some church communities are most definitely mission fields themselves . . . but carry on and tell me what's provoking all of this."

"Bob, where does the drag come from inside the church—the unconscious drift away from kingdom authenticity? What's behind the scenes that, somehow, seems to be a neutering influence, some negating presence, some sophisticated something that reduces and redefines it all into some kind of comfortable religion, or spirituality. It is so pervasive and profound that it all seems quite normal.

"I mean, just stop and look at it: with North Park Church we get all the traditional church stuff, like liturgical seasons. We get what are called 'worship services'—great performances, admittedly . . . but with no real passion for Christ, or the gospel, and certainly no transformational encounter with a holy God—just music and nice, listenable sermons, with no particular expectation. You know, all the expected traditions of most typical church institutions. And we all sit there as passive recipients.

"Then, we have a continual array of ever-changing church activities being promoted to keep the folk engaged in the institution . . . and, activities that, in themselves, are quite commendable. But nothing connects. It's all sort of a grab bag of in-house churchy programs. And . . . we're supposed to accept all this uncritically, even mindlessly, what with all of these things that come down from on high (wherever that is) as though they were important to our Christian welfare. I mean, come on Bob, this kind of safe, predictable religious stuff can't be what we are called to be witnesses to . . . can't be the content and essence of the mission of God, can it?

"Deliver me!

"Sound familiar?

"To me, any clear sense of gospel, of purpose, of transformational discipleship, of mission is so obfuscated that my kingdom calling all becomes fuzzy, what with all of these expected church pieces that, to me, have no discernable importance, or relatedness to my 24/7 focus on the people I live and work with—not to mention the complex political and social culture I live in.

"The image I get of the church at our North Park is some kind of (what I call) 'Thomas Kinkaid ecclesiology' . . . you know? Bucolic, soft light, sort of a romanticized view of life without conflict, and hardly related to my life. And certainly with no reference to any calling to a spiritual warfare! So, what's going on? Am I expecting too much? Or is it just my perfectionist personality getting pissed by my frustration with the pervasive indifference to all these things that seem like such a contradiction to me?

"Or is something darker at work?

"Make sense? Got the question? Is the question out of bounds?"

I took a couple of sips on my drink to give me time to digest what he was asking.

"Alan, it's a fascinating set of questions and well worth exploring if you want to go there. But first, let me ask you a question: When you speak of North Park Church, *whom* are you talking about? I mean: we're talking about real people who are our friends. Who are these church folk? What's their story? How do you think they *imagine* the church? What do you think this collection of persons thought they were 'joining' when they joined North Park?

"What did *you* think you were joining? Even after you and I spent many months processing the essence of the authentic church, you were still entering into a whole composite of unknowns. Do you think it occurred to all these familiar friends of ours in North Park that God's design for the church was that it is to be a *supernatural* community?

"I probably need to remind you (as I have to frequently remind myself) that most of these folk have never known anything else—their whole experience of church has been in some form such as they experience with North Park. This may even be true of the pastoral staff. They have no other image. That's going to be a critical factor in answering the questions you are raising.

"My point is just this: I don't want us to get too far out into a critique of churches such as North Park, and forget that we're dealing with real people who are the objects of God's love. Oh, as far back as the first-generation Christian communities there were, evidently, those who had no 'ears to hear' what the Spirit was saying to the churches (Rev 2:17ff.). Yet these are the sincere, real, and without-a-clue folk who find refuge in Christian communities for whatever reason. Okay?

"But, back to your question: I guess I don't need to remind you that there could be some uncomfortable consequences of probing into the source of whatever darkness may be an influential and clandestine force in creating the 'drag' you ask about. If the church were only designed to be a merely human religious institution, then we could easily write off your drag as simply that of typical human nature, which human nature easily forgets, or gets distracted. But you and I have long been convinced that the church is not a merely human institution, but is actually to be 'the dwelling place of God by the Holy Spirit' (Eph 3:19–22)."

"I'm ahead of you. You're assuming that there really is a Satan, and that whatever, or whoever, that Satan is . . . that he is not some myth, which we use as an excuse for our human tendencies, but is a real and supernatural reality, or something like that. That's either a quaint cop-out . . . or a reality of ominous consequences. Right?

"But before we tackle that one, let me add in some context of my own thinking and evaluation which evolves out of my several years of significant involvement with North Park. I think, maybe, I look at what I experience as three disparate dimensions—or maybe three different facets or levels, which interact and influence each other. First, (and because of the conversations that you and I have engaged in over these past six years) I operate with a biblical-theological-missional and christocentric set of assumptions. I see that Jesus intends the church to be his agent in heralding the joyous news of the kingdom of God, of his new creation, to every corner and ethnic group in the world. Okay?

"Have I learned well, or what?

"And, happily, I find within North Park other informal networks and cohorts of those who operate primarily out of this same dimension. The fact is, interestingly, that many of these cohorts are also overlapping with similar hearts and minds in other Christian communities and congregations, so that they are not at all confined to the dynamics only of North Park. This seems to be a fairly common pattern among the folks I am close to.

"Secondly, however (and this is the distressing part), there is that more traditional and social dimension—that Christendom institution—which is the one I am struggling with. How to define it? It comes down to some kind of image of the church as being merely a part of their social network, where folk feel safe and in some contact with transcendence. But the folk who are defined by this dimension hardly seem to be formed by anything biblical or theological or missional. That may be unfair and too broad of a brush—but it is something like an ecclesiocentric dimension. The church is a place and an organization that you go to, where you engage in religious rites and activities—but most of which probably have nothing to do with the gospel of the kingdom of God.

"Plus, Bob, it certainly does not do much to equip me, week by week, to function fruitfully as a kingdom person in my daily routines and relationships and responsibilities.

"There seems to be a total absence of any kingdom consciousness, or any sense of the church being the community of God's new creation in Christ. In other words, I struggle with how this came to be. Where is the breakdown with what seems to me to obviously be the whole reason for the existence of the church? Why don't so many of these folk seem to have any capacity to wonder about it? This is where my 'drag' question comes from.

"As I read my New Testament, it would seem to me that those folk who come to faith in Christ should be growing in knowledge, and becoming more mature and obedient, more into the image of Christ, like: 'from one degree of glory to another' (2 Cor 3:18) as Paul speaks of faith in Christ in his second Corinthian letter. So why does the faith, rather (conversely?), seem to deteriorate from generation to generation? Why do folk who populate churches not seem to tune in to the agenda of Christ? How can they be so easily led away from the awesomeness of our calling to be new creation folk? . . . Or, even more disturbing, how can they be so casual about the huge implications of the life, death, and resurrection of Jesus, the Lamb of God, whose bride the church is?

"Something like that.

"Which brings me to my third dimension, which is the question: Is there something significant and negative going on here, some relentless darkness? Does the drag have a source? And if so, why is it never mentioned? What is it? Who is it? And as garbled at that question may seem to you, it is why I needed to spend some time with you, and what is behind my initial question about the gates of hell. Do you really believe that there is a supernatural and malicious personality called Satan who is alive and active and intent on immobilizing the church . . . incapacitating the whole mission of God?

WHAT BIBLE DO YOU READ?

"Alan, for the sake of our discussion . . . and before I respond to what you are questioning, let me direct a question to you: If there were some such malicious supernatural, clever personality out there, who doesn't like what's going on, where do you think he would begin? Where would *you* begin if you were that malignant force? And to what end? How do you think he would accomplish his goal of immobilizing or incapacitating the church . . . like: How would he *try* to prevail against the present day church? Do you think he would come on brazenly like some Voldemort in the Harry Potter stories? Or like some Sauron the Sorcerer from the *Rings* trilogy? Or, maybe, like Mephistopheles from Faust?

Or would that personality be much more subtle and clandestine, somewhat like our present international intelligence communities, who infiltrate and subvert—something like that?"

Alan chewed on that one in silence for a few minutes, and then, typical of his mind, he came up with this answer:

"*That's simple. I'd go for the nerve center.*

"*Go for where it is all formed and initiated, where decisions are made, where images come from, where community formation originates, where directions are chosen and self-image is formed. Go for the strategic source of all that determines the life and character of the church. Get at the nerve center and control that . . . and everything else follows.*

"*That may not be all that obvious, so let me toss in a few dimensions of this.*

"*I think, maybe, if I were some dark lord, some Satan (whoever he/she/it may be), I would tamper with the church's imagination, with its cognition—maybe even more with its metacognition (its capacity to even think about thinking differently about the church). If I could attempt to so capture the imagination of the folk who make up the church community so that they wouldn't expect anything other than a humanly explainable religious institution, then I would have accomplished my goal.*

"*That much for starts.*

"*It wouldn't take much . . . just recalibrate its sense of purpose and mission ever so slightly and imperceptibly off on a tangent, which tangent would ultimately take it out of any contention in the warfare. Like: obfuscate or redefine its self-understanding, then distract it with other really good activities and commendable agendas that have nothing to do with the church's divinely given mandate. Along the way, let essentials of the gospel fade into the secondary, into liturgical nostalgia . . . or be forgotten altogether.*

"*Then populate the community with non-expectant religious folk who've never been discipled into kingdom understanding, or behavior. Recruit members who've never renounced the dominion of Satan, nor intentionally entered into God's radical newness in Christ—and probably don't really expect anything remotely like a church engaging the darkness in a holy war . . . but only want to be identified as members in a safe and successful (and prestigious?) church institution. Then make it all seem so normal, so 'spiritual.'*

"But first go for its leadership and those who have influence.
"How does that sound? Am I close?"

"Spoken like a true bioengineer. It's what I would expect of you. I hope you realize the implications of what you are proposing. You're putting the finger on the church's influence holders, on leadership, on pastors, on theologians, on the elders of the church who form the mind and image of the church and—in our contemporary ecclesiastical patterns—on the agencies or schools, or curricula, that pertain to equipping church leadership."

"Bingo!"

"But, hold that, and let me propose another question to you: What Bible do you read?

"Already in my Bible's opening pages there are portrayed a couple of realities that will determine the whole of the rest of the biblical narrative. The first, and most essential for our understanding, is that the eternal God created the whole of the universe, and of its constituent parts . . . from the rolling spheres of space to the minutest detail of this world (the Higgs boson and all). He also created, as the crown of his creation, the human community to dwell within the embrace of, and in communion with, the Trinitarian community. All of this he created (as we learn in the biblical narrative) to be a radiant display of his own divine nature, what with all of the beauty, splendor, joy, love, and attention to detail that would reflect that divine nature.

"The other reality is a bit more complicated, and can only be extrapolated from the narrative, but it is what is behind your dilemma with the church, Alan.

"Right away there appears on the scene a figure portrayed only as a serpent. His immediate intention is to cast doubt, to enlist in a cosmic rebellion, and to usurp the prerogatives of deity for himself. Who is this figure? Where does he come from? As the biblical narrative unfolds it becomes clear that there is actually a whole other *world in between*, a layer of created beings called 'angels.' Angels are given supernatural powers, and are those who are to be the servants of the creator in the stewardship of the creation.

If Eve had not fallen would Satan have been defeated, stymied

"The biblical narrative also reveals that there was a rebellion in heaven. One of those angelic beings was a leader in that rebellion. He will later be revealed as one *Satan*, who is the serpent in the Genesis account. As he rebelled against his creator, he evidently also became the leader of this cosmic rebellion, and evidently enlisted some other angelic beings to join him. Through him, then, *evil* and *darkness* came into the pristine creation, as Satan initiated his design to subvert it and to usurp glory for himself. (This becomes most obvious in his temptations of Jesus in the fullness of time.)

"Satan is exposed in the biblical narratives as the prince of darkness, the god of this world, and as the enemy of God in every way, as he seeks to usurp the glory for himself. The church has, tragically, become embarrassed to accept such a possibility . . . and has done so to its own diminished effectiveness, as it has sought to marginalize this mysterious and somewhat ambiguous reality.

"Let me repeat: Satan is portrayed as an alien presence, a serpent figure, who *has it in* for God the creator. Satan is obviously not of the created human order of Adam and Eve. He simply appears from some realm that is not described, and he lies and distorts God's pure intent, and seeks to defame God's character with misinformation and doubts.

"This Satan obviously wants to usurp God's glory and initiate a rebel order that is autonomous, and in which he—not God—is the one to be followed. He wants to suggest an alternative view of creation that does not at all reflect the glory of the creator or extol the divine nature. That accuser of God then recruits our first human parents to be a part of his cosmic rebellion. All this in the first three chapters of the Bible!

"That episode exposes the reality of a whole mysterious angelic layer of beings, some of whom are servants of God the creator, while others are part of the cosmic rebellion. Some are servants of God's glory, but others use their God-given powers as weapons against God. These dark personalities keep mysteriously cropping up all through the pages of Scripture as a given. This same Bible ends with that serpent (by then identified as the devil), and all of those who are his legions of hell, ultimately being cast into total destruction—into the lake of fire.

"In between the first pages of the Bible and the last, you have periodic references all the way through the biblical narrative of the malicious activity of the minions of this evil one, appearing in various guises. Most dramatically, at the coming of Jesus, Satan obviously sensed that the true

Lord was invading his world with the eschatological (ultimate and ir-revocable) purpose of ransoming and recreating the whole of creation.

"Satan, more than others, knows that Jesus is the eternal Son of God and the world's true Lord. This being so, Satan is determined that this plan shall be thwarted by whatever means. Watch as this unfolds. Immediately after Jesus' nativity, this destroying spirit seeks to have Jesus destroyed through Herod's massacre of all the male children under two years old. He fails. Satan then personally confronts Jesus in the wilderness after his baptism and offers him three easier alternative plans—plans that would avoid the cross—and would enlist Jesus in the rebellion.

"Again Satan fails.

"Jesus introduced his brief public ministry by challenging all of the devastations of the dominion of darkness: hopelessness, guilt, demon possession, sickness, hunger, imprisonment, and so much more . . . with the thrilling news of God's design to make all things new. The joyous announcement that Jesus heralds (and demonstrates with miraculous signs) is that he himself has come from God to inaugurate just such a new creation. Jesus brings a message of true hope.

"Alan, how blithely we pray: 'Thy kingdom come, thy will be done on earth as in heaven,' without stopping to think of the implications of that prayer, namely, that there is already an alien kingdom present, and that there is an alien will at work bringing all kinds of darkness into the human community and beyond. Then how mindlessly we close that prayer by praying, 'Deliver us from the evil one,' again mouthing familiar words and never stopping to consider the captivating work of an ever-present evil personality—as though the context of our church life were in some neutral or merely human religious context.

"Quite the opposite. There is an energized darkness that is at once subtle, sophisticated, religious, even *spiritual* . . . that so effectively takes up habitation within the church that hardly anyone even notices. This is so obviously taught in the New Testament documents, yet so routinely ignored, that it is frightening.

"Remember, too, that as Jesus approached the cross he saw the re-sults of what lay before him and said: 'Now is the judgment of this world; now will the ruler of this world be cast out' (John 12:31). But the *clincher* (to my mind) is in the passage where John records: 'The reason the Son of God appeared was to destroy the works of the devil' (1 John 3:8). As if that were not quite enough, let me add Paul's commission from the risen Lord: 'I am sending you to open their eyes, so that they may turn from darkness to light and from the power of Satan to God' (Acts 26:18). Or Paul's word to the Colossians that God 'has delivered us from the domain of darkness and transferred to the kingdom of his beloved Son' (Col 1:13).

"Let's come at this from another angle, Alan.

"This is such a critical dimension of our biblical understanding of Christ's work and of the mission of God in the world that it is uncanny that it has become so eclipsed. Think of the apostle John's candor in ending his first letter: 'We know that we are from God and the whole world lies in the power of the evil one' (1 John 5:19). Or, one of Paul's many references to Satan's workings that come when he describes Satan as 'the god of this world' (2 Cor 4:4).

"So much is this so that in our ancient and classical baptismal vows there was included the *renunciation* of Satan's dominion, which renunciation was renewed each time the community gathered around the Eucharistic table. The baptismal questions are: 'Do you renounce Satan and all the spiritual forces of wickedness that rebel against God?' 'Do you renounce the evil powers of this world which corrupt and destroy the creatures of God?' 'Do you renounce all sinful desires that draw you from the love of God?' 'Do you turn to Jesus Christ . . . ?'[1]

"Makes one think that one of Satan's cleverest schemes is to see that this baptismal renunciation is conveniently either revised out or forgotten, and is hardly ever mentioned in conjunction with the Eucharist, right?

"So, in answer to your question, and in short: yes! There's a cosmology here in the Bible that includes a malicious darkness that has personality. There is unmistakably a holy warfare going on here clandestinely in the very setting of our pilgrimage. The present setting in which you and I operate is not at all neutral territory. This enemy, our enemy, is determined to make it all look neutral and natural and normal—even 'spiritual'—and in so doing to be able to work unseen and unsuspected. There is, right there in the opening pages of the biblical narrative, one who violated God's pristine creation, and who incited a cosmic rebellion in the primordial human community, and who continues his malice down to this day. It is to this that (I intentionally and deliberately repeat)

1. Proposed *Book of Common Prayer* of the Episcopal Church, 1977, p. 302.

John makes it quite plain that 'The reason the Son of God appeared was to destroy the works of the devil' (1 John 3:8).

"So, my friend, get it straight: the context in which we live is not neutral. The ultimate battle was decisively won on the cross (and that is a whole study in itself) . . . but our dethroned and defeated enemy still rages, and especially against Christ's church, so much so that Jesus taught us to pray regularly: 'Deliver us from the evil one.' So much is this so that you do not even begin to understand the church, or its mission, apart from this huge reality of the malice of Satan toward God's people. All you have to do is to look at the last book in the canon of Scripture to see this cosmic battle between the Beast and the Lamb . . . and to understand the outcome of it all . . . and be thrilled with our hope of glory.

"But meanwhile, in our context, in North Park Church and its kind across the globe . . . *the darkness is relentless.*

"So, can the gates of hell prevail against the church? Make no mistake, Alan, Satan is going to try every trick in the book to prevail, and will frequently appear to have succeeded, but ultimately the battle is already won (Jesus' triumph over Satan on the cross is, as I have just noted, a whole fascinating subject in itself, but for another time). But, meanwhile . . . Satan rages against the church. This can get sticky, really confusing, and full of dark challenges. I think the Bible adequately warns us of this inescapable reality."

"Why isn't this reality ever surfaced in our church conversations at North Park?"

"Go figure."

"That would mean that the nerve center of most of our church institutions might even be the church professionals, the clergy, the pastoral staff . . . or perhaps influential leaders within the community? The mission field would then be in-house, and would hardly be detected. Is that really a possibility?

"That's scary!"

"Absolutely. And what makes it even more ambiguous and complex is that these very folk who are the nerve center are not some ominous non-Christian agents, necessarily, but are probably actually well-meaning, respected and tenured believers, but who are still significantly influenced by the darkness out of which they have been somewhat (or only partially) delivered. Remember that Jesus called Peter 'Satan' at one point when Peter sought to dissuade Jesus from the cross.

"There are mentioned in Paul's writings those 'false prophets' and satanically inspired 'angels of light.' Does this mean they are not believers? I don't think that's necessarily so, but they are certainly being used as Satan's agents within the new creation community to mute or eclipse its essence and teachings. Believers (such as you and I) can 'give place to the devil' when we engage in thinking or behavior that is out of sync with the teachings of Jesus.

"The clergy folk, and other church leaders and teachers, would be the obvious targets for Satan's wiles, since (in your words) they are the 'nerve center' out of which the church's new creation life is to be formed. And when these men and women are asleep to the holy war in which the church is engaged, or are unequipped, or ill-equipped, in the use of spiritual weapons, then they themselves become a strategic mission field in their own right.

"Which is also to say that whenever you or I are *not* formed in the mind and the behavior of the kingdom of God, when we are *not* formed by the word of Christ . . . then we are also exhibiting the residual habitation of darkness in our lives, rather than of our calling to be children of the light. When the darkness inhabits the church, and the church inhabits the darkness, it means that somewhere and somehow our individual and corporate minds have become captive to a *merely human* (without the Spirit[2]) understanding and image of the church, and as such are no real threat to the 'gates of hell.'

"Is that a beginning of an answer to your *angst* about North Park?"

"That seems pretty grim.

"It would seem to almost make the church something less than good news to folk whose lives are pretty fragmented to begin with. How do you think this would go down with our North Park scene? Doesn't that sort of qualify our good news, make it something a tad more negative and a little threatening, so that it would be a community with which one would hesitate to identify?"

"*Au contraire!* It is at the very heart of our gospel.

2. The Greek word psukikos (ψυχικος), is used in the New Testament to denote "life without the Spirit" or "merely human," or is sometimes translated simply as "flesh."

"We are those who have been rescued out of captivity to Satan's darkness and his malignant redefinitions, from his blindness to the meaning of our humanity and servitude to what is false . . . and delivered into the dominion and the freedom and joy of the family of God—into 'the glorious liberty of the children of God' (Rom 8:21).

"So, only *if* and *where* the church is built on 'wood and hay and stubble'—where it is built on merely human definitions, or on the accepted redefinitions imposed upon it by the darkness—could this dimension be in any way dismaying, or anything other than God's thrilling design. For those who have been turned from darkness to light, it is the dimension of the *gospel* that is to be reflected and celebrated in the community of those who have been set free to know true freedom and high joy in God.

"The problem comes when Satan (as in the parable of the wheat and the tares) sows religious counterfeits in among that which is authentic, so that it all looks the same. It is only where the thinking and the behavior of the church are formed by the Word of Christ that the reality of God's new creation reality is demonstrated.

"But we always live with that complexity and ambiguity inside the church."

TO SAVE US ALL FROM SATAN'S POWER
WHEN WE WERE GONE ASTRAY

"Did you ever realize that the church has actually celebrated this joyous dimension of God's rescuing us from Satan's dominion, in song? Take, for instance, the familiar old English Christmas carol that opens with the line: 'God rest ye merry [translate: "happy" or "joyous"] Christian gentlemen, let nothing you dismay, remember Christ our Savior was born on Christmas Day; *to save us all from Satan's power when we were gone astray.*' So it's not at all an alien theme for the church; rather, it is a genuine cause for song.

"One is reminded that the 'singers of Israel' were sent out ahead of the armies of Israel in order to defeat the enemy. I want to propose that, rather than being embarrassed, or intimidated, or defensive about our *warfare worldview* pertaining to this dark lord . . . we rather sing of his defeat at the cross.

"The church—in the awesome design of God for new creation—is to be where this warfare worldview is heralded in our understanding of the church as the community of those liberated *from* death, from fear of rejection, *from* hopelessness and meaningless lives in the dominion of darkness, both individually and corporately by Jesus Christ, who came to destroy Satan and his dominion. Jesus came to deliver us *from* Satan's counterfeits.

"So, for Satan to clandestinely redefine the church from within and so create what is essentially something of a *church counterfeit* based on some kind of merely human religion, should call forth from us all of our missional fervor to refound the church as a true kingdom community, a community of true faith, hope, and tangible love in relationships—and so to expose Satan's redefinition."[3]

"Okay, but what do we do with this at North Park? Who begins to implement such an understanding? How would one go about subverting Satan's subversions in such a scene as ours? Who will initiate this? Who even has ears to hear such an 'outrageous' proposition?"

"Mission begins at home, like with you and me, and those other disciples who are intentional in being formed by the Word of Christ. Back to our previous point: the very fact that Satan has so redefined it all to be congenial to his darkness means that many (or maybe even most) people in many churches (including well-meaning leaders), sadly, have never known anything else. All of which reinforces our conclusion that the church itself is a primary mission field in need of being delivered . . . so that those spiritually hungry folk who identify with it, really seeking new life . . . will not be disappointed.

"Maybe a couple of wonderful biblical models would be Aquila and Priscilla, those two remarkably fruitful and self-effacing figures who seem to follow Paul around, or turn up in strategic places, and to nail down the details of so much of the fruit of Paul's preaching. I love them. Remember what they did when that eloquent young preacher Apollos turned up and was so effective in his preaching? The only problem was that Apollos had missed a significant part of the message. He knew some of the basic content and was a convincing herald of it, but he did not know of the power that came by the Holy Spirit. So, what did Priscilla

---

3. It is somewhat uncanny to me that you can even approach the fields of *ecclesiology* or *missiology* apart from this warfare worldview, so dominant a theme as it is in Scripture. Yet it is a very rare theme in theological schools or in standard writings on church and mission, alas!

and Aquila do? They took this preacher home for a meal and lovingly filled him in on the rest of the message. They mentored him into maturity, and so equipped that unique servant of Christ for a life of fruitfulness in the heralding of whole message. Good models!"

"Maybe we're back to our missional focus on church leadership?"

"You said it, not me!

"But, yes, that's a strategic mission objective, and it is not at all out of bounds for us. But it gets closer to home for you and me. We must do our homework well. We need to delve significantly into what Paul was talking about when he wrote to the Corinthian church: "For though we walk in the flesh, we are not waging war according to the flesh. For the weapons of our warfare are not of the flesh but have divine power to destroy strongholds" (2 Cor 10:3–4). It begins with our responses, our knowledge, our living out the divine nature given to us, love, grace—all with maturity and discernment and humility.

"We will certainly meet with lack of imagination, with non-comprehension, with cynicism . . . or maybe even with real hopeful inquiry! Whatever the responses, we need to remember that we are engaging the darkness and the prince of darkness *inside* the church, as well as in our own 24/7 lives.

"Some will take offense at this reality. Why? Simple: if one has never deliberately renounced the dominion of darkness, then one is still a part of it. We will be dealing existentially with the 'wood, hay, and stubble' in the foundations of a particular church community. Or, we will be confronting the reality of those who, as Jesus warned, will be resting in their orthodox profession, or on their remarkable good works, but not out of a response to Jesus himself.[4] Like, whenever, or wherever, persons (believers?) become somehow complicit with the agendas of the darkness, they become a contradiction to the true community of the new creation (the kingdom community).

"God's agenda is that the church be the dwelling place of God by the Holy Spirit, and so the veritable demonstration of the gospel of the kingdom. God's purpose is that we incarnate the divine nature of God to all whom we meet and influence, and that by the transformational work

---

4. Matt 7:21–23.

of the Spirit. We are called to be the children of the light, always, in the midst of the dominion of darkness.

"The possibility of the satanic ploy to insert inauthenticity into the church is tragically and dramatically illustrated in the early post-Pentecost church, when two of those early participants in that community engaged in a bit of self-aggrandizing deception. When the apostles confronted Ananias and his wife Sapphira, their question was: 'Why has Satan filled your heart to lie to the Holy Spirit?' The ultimate problem was that it was an intrusion of darkness into the community, and it had to be removed.

"Again, Alan, this is a critical dimension of creating true new creation community. Paul will include such a seemingly normal thing as anger as an entrance of darkness into a person's life: "Be angry and do not sin; do not let the sun go down on your anger, and give no opportunity to the devil" (Eph 4:26). These are words of instruction to the children of the light, and warnings about the intrusion of the darkness. In another incidence, Paul says that he is delivering two of the church folk to Satan so that they would learn not to blaspheme.[5] Does that mean that they were lost? Or condemned? That's not the issue. The issue is that within the community they were engaged in a behavioral pattern that was inimical to the children of the light, and the community of the light—they had become intrusion points of the darkness into the community, and as such had to be removed.

"The church community is always in process. There is always a degree of (what has been termed) 'messiness' in the creation of the church. But, remember, it is always formed by the grace and mercy of God. But its clear calling is a calling *out of the dominion of darkness* and *into the kingdom of God's dear Son.* That calling out of, and into, is always to be clear and up-front. It is always God's plan to conform his folk into the image of Jesus Christ.[6] Our salvation is *from* as well as *to.* It is a deliverance *from* bondage and captivity of heart and mind, and deliverance *into* God's intended freedom, hope, joy, and holistic newness.

"Satan is no dummy! To be naïve is to be vulnerable. In this warfare, skill and watchfulness are always required."

5. 1 Tim 1:20.

6. Rom 8:29.

The sun was getting low, and the evening customers were beginning to arrive at the Trackside. I could tell I was probably overloading Alan's systems (not to mention that he was overloading mine!). He needed time to digest all of the implications of what we had been talking about. He didn't answer for a few minutes. I had gotten used to his analytical mind over these past several years. After a while he responded.

"Sure, it's a beginning, but it raises more questions than we've got time to answer this afternoon. I know it's getting late, but for another time—all this being the case—who would you expect or anticipate could equip a church like North Park for such an understanding of this warfare? Who could introduce such a worldview into a community formed by something totally other than the gospel of the kingdom of God? Think of the turmoil it might cause in a comfortable congregation. Where would you begin?"

This (digested) conversation is by way of introduction. All that follows in this book flows out of these questions raised by my friend (continued in ensuing conversations). What follows will be the "homework" that I mentioned to Alan, which is a necessity for us if we are to be at all skillful in this warfare. It does, without a doubt, present a radical alternative to so much that has been accepted as normal ecclesiastical life for so long. But as the implications of this cynical post-Christian culture become more and more obvious and ominous, it is critical that we reclaim our biblical understanding of the kingdom community's disciplines, inner life, and formation.

It is critical that we reclaim the biblical warfare worldview that confronts the dominion of darkness. This requires that we confront the "wiles of the devil," which are calculated to emasculate the church, to neuter it as the missionary arm of the Holy Trinity, so that it is incapable of conquering Satan through the blood of the Lamb, through its life and testimony in the power of the Spirit.

2

Landscape: The Filtering Schemes of the Darkness

WHAT HAVE WE INHERITED?

THE DISTURBING QUESTION THAT was raised by Alan at our conversation at the Trackside Tavern, that of the presence of satanically provoked darkness inside of the Christian community—inside of *my own* Christian community—itself raises a whole plethora of related considerations. Right up front, we need to look at the vast diversity that exists within "the church, one, holy, catholic, and apostolic." That diversity is mind-boggling: venerable old church institutions, new church plants, house churches in all forms, large churches, small churches, healthy churches, struggling-to-survive churches . . . some fruitful, some, barren, some tribal, some orthodox, others doctrinally confused, many faithful, others compromised . . . and on and on.

The landscape of the church's incarnation is sobering. Look at it: complex, ambiguous, muddled, "wood and hay and stubble," "wheat and tares sown together" . . . stir in our risen Lord's irresistible intention to build his church, and it becomes almost overwhelming.

And, face it: this is not a subject, or possibility, that most church folk want to talk about. O, maybe they'll talk about it in the abstract, or theoretically, but certainly *not* that their own cherished Christian community should somehow be the context of, or unwittingly complicit in, any satanically provoked patterns, or paradigms, or subtle intrusions of his *relentless darkness*.

Such a suggested possibility will probably be met with raised eyebrows, incredulous that it should even be mentioned . . . or disdain . . . or maybe the response of the Gerasenes to Jesus: "What have we to do with you? Leave us alone!"[1]

---

1. See Mark 5:1–17.

Even gifted church leaders, theologians, and missiologists often tend to skirt the whole subject, or to speak only of *the forces of evil*. For instance, recently there have been several major international missionary conferences. In the reviews of two of them, the reviewers noted (with some amazement) that Satan either was not mentioned at all or that the subject of spiritual conflict was dealt with lightly and only in passing.[2] But, just to reiterate my point, such a skirting of the subject was not true of Jesus or the apostles. Jesus, to Jewish leaders who opposed his ministry: "You are of your father the devil . . ." (John 8:44); to Peter who sought to dissuade him from the cross: "Get thee behind me, Satan!" (Matt 16:23). Paul to the Ephesians concerning their deliverance: "you were dead in the trespasses and sins . . . following the prince of the power of the air, the spirit that is now at work in the sons of disobedience" (Eph 2:1–2); ". . . that you may be able to stand against the schemes of the devil . . . cosmic powers . . ." (Eph 6:11–12). Peter to the church: "Your adversary the devil prowls around like a roaring lion, seeking someone to devour" (1 Pet 5:8). And John to the church: "The reason the Son of God appeared was to destroy the works of the devil" (1 John 3:8). There is nothing fuzzy in the thinking of these about the very real adversary to the church's mission.

How, then, are we to be both charitable, and the same time brutally realistic about the church as it encounters corrosive powers of darkness that relentlessly work to diminish the light?

And where do we start? What is to be achieved in my writing on such a subject? How are Alan's questions to me to receive some kind of substantive response? How do we respond to the ever-apparent *relentless darkness* that is always seeking to inhabit Christ's church?

Well, I have this totally outrageous thought: that the whole purpose of my writing this is to somehow expose (and exorcize?) Satan's design to so possess the church with counterfeits . . . with *merely human*[3] religion . . . with a message of therapeutic deism, with angels of light and false prophets inside the community and accepted (2 Cor 11:13–15) . . . with

---

2. I am referring to reviews of the Edinburgh Conference and the Lausanne Conference at Capetown, both conducted in 2010. There was another major conference held in Tokyo, but I have not read a review of it.

3. The venerable King James translation uses the word *carnal* quite freely to translate several Greek words, while other translations translate the same as "merely human," and one Greek word indicates that it is seeking to convey that life and behavior that is done without the Holy Spirit—so "merely human" conveys my intent quite adequately.

frequent redefinitions of the message . . . with anything which would render the church distracted and powerless in the mission of God to which, and for which, it is called—which calling is (among other things) to be the "missionary arm of the Holy Trinity."[4]

Such would, indeed, seem to be outrageous were it not for the fact that in Paul's own letter to the church at Ephesus he eloquently heralds his passion for the glorious gospel of Christ, and how that the Ephesian believers were called out of the dominion of darkness, and equipped to live in the fullness of Christ . . . and how the community of the church is to be the very incarnation of the human community of God's new creation, supernaturally inhabited by the Holy Spirit.

But then (and we will come back to this letter in the next chapter) he concludes the letter by alerting them to the outrageous (have I over-used that word?) reality that this whole missional essence of their church community can come crashing down on their heads *if* they underestimate, or ignore, the pernicious schemes of the devil to render them passive about their calling. He then proceeds to spell out for them seven components of self-conscious new creation character (i.e., the "whole armor of God"), which they must diligently *put on* for their daily lives in that city.

Paul's portrayal of the God-given paradigm for the church has, in our day, been so truncated and reduced, and so often the church has too frequently (and quite happily) inhabited the darkness, and the darkness has inhabited the church . . . and *hardly anyone has noticed.*

And, if you were to ask: Why is this so? Or what lies behind the church's seeming incapacity to even imagine such a realm of darkness, and such a prince of darkness? . . . Then, you would inevitably have to conclude that the church has unwittingly accepted a reductionist, or truncated, version of the gospel of God and of the kingdom of God . . . that is without repentance, or any renunciation of the dominion of darkness, and that does not see itself as self-consciously countercultural. You would have to realize that much of the church lives with the illusion of a *neutral* cultural context, and that it certainly does not comprehend that the communities of God's new creation are always (to borrow from Lesslie Newbigin) *in missionary confrontation with the world.*

4. This wonderful picture of the missionary arm of the Holy Trinity I ascribe to one of the Latin American theologians. I was unable to find the source, but as I recall it was probably from Jose Miguel Bonino.

My purpose, then, is to seek to explore the satanic schemes that have debilitated the church. This must be done *before* the *weapons of our warfare* will make sense to us. This means, however, that if we are inclined, or determined—as much of the church seems to be—to preserve a comfortably subverted paradigm of what the church is to *be* and to *do* . . . then it will be next to impossible (with any integrity) to "build and to plant" (Jer 1:10) for an obedient future in the mission of God.

WHAT HAVE WE INHERITED? ANSWER: MULTIPLE FILTERS

So, on one hand we have the church as that awesome community that Jesus, this world's rightful Lord, is creating. It is a church against which he promises the *gates of hell* cannot prevail. We have the church as the "dwelling place of God by the Holy Spirit" (Eph 2:22). We have the church as the true "Mount Zion, the city of the Living God" (Heb 12:22–24). But this whole biblical portrayal is easily forgotten, diluted, or displaced as the church becomes captive to its institutional paradigm, and becomes, rather, the keeper of traditional, and merely human, religion.

Which brings us, on the other hand, to the very real and satanically energized *darkness* of this present age, which is, and always has been, the context into which the church has been called. This *darkness* is not out there somewhere, but is, rather, close at hand. It is immediate. It is *relentlessly present.* It is (usually) subtle and sophisticated. It manifests itself in the daily vicissitudes of my own heart and mind, and in our daily environment—not to mention that it is manifest in all too much of the life of our own particular local church communities (as the Scriptures attest).

Right up front, then, the satanically energized *drift* and *drag* (as my friend Alan termed that which he observed in his own North Park Church experience) are manifested, and we encounter them, in multiple filtering (or blinding) schemes, of which I shall name several. We inherit these, and we need to identify and define them. They are unquestionably part of the *relentless darkness* that is always at work to conform the church to itself. These filters have the potential of negating any other attempts we may make to talk about this subject of spiritual conflict or of the weapons of our warfare.

And, yes, these filters can rightfully be described as *satanic* schemes, or wiles.

Though all of this might sound unreal, outrageous, weird, or at least strange to our ears, it should *not*. There has always been an antipathy to the light within our fallen humanity. John put it quite plainly when he explained that "the light has come into the world and people loved the darkness rather than the light" (John 3:19). This affinity for the darkness, as we will learn later in Paul's writings, is the natural consequence of being captive to the prince of darkness (cf. Eph 2:1–2), the "prince of the power of the air." To say, then, Satan is not a benign myth, but rather is the pernicious enemy of all that is of God. But Satan is also remarkably relentless, clandestine, and clever in his works of darkness *inside of the* church.

For instance, we sing: ". . . the prince of darkness grim, we tremble not for him, his rage we can endure."[5] To be sure there have been, and are, those violent assaults against the Christian community by totalitarian powers, used by Satan to attempt to obliterate the church or take it captive. Such assaults could properly be described as Satan's *rage*, from the days of the Roman Empire right down to our own day in many parts of the earth. Such rage and persecution against God's faithful people has been, and is, a reality.

However, such rage is not Satan's only method of intimidation.

How is Satan's offense against the light expressed where I live and work? Rage and violence are not the only schemes in Satan's armory.

Look closer to home. Look at the church in North America in this twenty-first century culture, what with its consumerism, narcissism, demands for therapeutic resources, and its shallow lives . . . with it's proliferation of "God Bless America" bumper stickers . . . all of which find their way into the life of the church, and into the church's interpretation of the New Testament gospel.[6] In such a culture rage and wrath against the church would be too obvious, and the very thought of trembling at such would be laughable.

In such a cultural context, what about simply minimizing the urgency of the gospel as a clever scheme? Oh, maybe *zeal* and *urgency* would be appropriate for some (so-called) *full-time* Christian workers. But then, it might be a bit off-putting to our social friends, alas!

---

5. From Martin Luther's familiar hymn "A Mighty Fortress Is Our God."

6. It needs to be noted that in all too many churches the New Testament message is interpreted as a component of the dominant order of "patriotism."

Or, what about simply watering down, or soft-pedaling, not only the urgency of the gospel, but its content so that it becomes more conformed (comfortable) to what is acceptable, and thereby *morphs* into a religion that is genteel and inoffensive, i.e., simply redefine the glorious gospel of Christ into something non-confrontational, socially acceptable, and *merely human*—no necessary repentance and conversion, no renunciation of the darkness, no missionary confrontation with the world, no cross and no suffering, . . . and no expectation of any radical transformation of lives into the image of Christ?

Is such a non-offensive gospel, what with its familiar gospel words, but emptied of its transformational power, and made congenial to our culture . . . as effective as rage and wrath? The answer is: yes! It certainly accomplishes the same goal!

What we're talking about here is *spiritual warfare*. When we talk of spiritual warfare, however, we are not necessarily talking about some ominous conspiracy theories as proposed by some of the current crop of enthusiastic but questionably informed bestseller Christian writers. Nor are we talking about some pervasive suspicions that would give us a dismal, and somewhat paranoid, outlook on our lives as Christ's new creation people.

Quite the opposite: we are talking about the reality of a world with an alien occupation, a world that has now been decisively and redemptively invaded by its creator, its true Lord—a world that has received the thrilling announcement of God's irresistible design to deliver it from its captivity to an alien dominion of darkness, and to irresistibly usher in the kingdom of light: God's new creation in Christ.

This is all thrillingly focused and centered in the person of Jesus, the Son of God: the Word made flesh. Jesus has come to make all things new. Jesus has come to inaugurate his great *shalom* in and through his life, death, and resurrection. It is a message of high joy and hope and freedom. It is a message that God has reconciled the world unto himself through the cross of Jesus Christ—but . . . always aware of the darkness, and the dominion of darkness, and the prince of darkness out of whose domain we have been delivered.

It is because of this that we wholeheartedly sing: "Joy to the world, the Lord has come, let earth receive her King."

As an example of this, we will see in the next chapter that the apostle Paul, in his writing to the church, is always consumed (maybe overwhelmed) with awe at what God has revealed in Christ. It is that "mystery hidden for ages . . . but now revealed to his saints" (Col 1:26). But Paul does not deal in abstractions, or in disincarnated spirituality. Rather, he wants them (and us) to be fully informed of the existential contexts of our calling into Christ. Other New Testament writers will remind us that "the whole world lies in the power of the evil one" (1 John 5:19).

That being so, there is no place or time when that now *dethroned* and *disarmed* evil one is not seeking to influence, to hinder, to subvert or thwart God's people, and the church community, to keep it the from being what Jesus calls them to be and to do—from engaging in the mission of God.

Paul, also never fails to remind the church that it is supernaturally endowed for its task: "it is God who works in you, both to will and to work for his good pleasure" (Phil 2:13), which means that we live our lives as participants in Christ's victory, his triumph over Satan on the cross. In Christ we are a resurrection people, an Easter people. We are a people of hope, and purpose, and mission because of what Christ has done.

It is this dynamic engagement that we are praying about when we pray: "Thy will be done on earth as it is in heaven." We are praying for the demonstration, the practice, the expediting, the incarnation and radiant display of God's divine nature and of God's purpose—God's design in new creation . . . *right here* and *right now*, in this present world—this very world in which we are living. We are called by Christ to live out our new creation lives right here redemptively, subversively, hopefully, joyfully, and realistically.

We are praying as those living out God's life, living out of the Trinitarian embrace by the Holy Spirit. Our very human lives are to be incarnating God's new creation, demonstrating kingdom obedience. Our lives are always to stand in intentional missionary confrontation with all that is produced by that *alien will*, that *satanic will*, that world that "lies in the evil one"—that *relentless darkness*.

Got it?

Which, then, brings us to the first of the several filtering schemes that I mentioned above—schemes that are energized by: What? Who?

1. The Scheme of Non-Cognition: Incapacity to Even Imagine Such a Dominion of Darkness

First of all: there is the filter that is a pervasive *incapacity to imagine . . . or even to imagine how to imagine* (meta-cognition) such a dominion of darkness . . . much less to conceive that such a dominion would affect me, and us, in any way, or that "our own dear congregation" would in any way be the scene of such darkness. Raise the subject of this dimension of our Christian calling in all too many church communities, and with our friends who populate these communities . . . and the result is raised eyebrows along with incredulity that any thoughtful modern person could entertain such fantastic ideas. To borrow from J. K. Rowling's popular Harry Potter stories, it is like trying to convince a bunch of "muggles" that there is a world of wizards out there. It simply doesn't register with them as even a possibility.

For us to express a conviction (or for me to write) that there are real satanic forces, demons, and conspiracies of the darkness present seeking to subvert and emasculate the church of Jesus Christ (from the inside) in its God-given mission, in its thinking and behavior, and to truncate the gospel of the kingdom of God . . . is likely to be condescendingly consigned to some weird fringe elements within the church—or, more likely, received with contemptuous incredulity. In the thinking and imagination of a considerable majority of church folk, this is akin to science fiction, or to the realm of *transrealism*, and so to be consigned to a quaint mythology, or a premodern folklore of some sort.

Why is there no capacity to conceive of such a dominion of darkness? Why is there such blindness to the vast energy of evil that blights, defiles, and dehumanizes this present creation and the culture thereof? One wonders what inhibits folk from pondering the malevolence that masquerades under the guise of progress, or fiscal security, or defense of my right to ignore my neighbor, or bearing no responsibility for the stewardship of creation. Or, what explains the total lack of imagination that the church is to be anything other than the familiar institution of traditional religion with its ambience of spiritual comfort and security in a fast changing culture?

One witnesses this lack of cognition daily in the political, economic, cultural, and social dimensions of our lives—and, regretfully, all too much inside the church. This distressing absence of any capacity to even think or imagine such a dominion of darkness, then, *must* be exposed as a filter that we need to acknowledge, and a problem we will need to surface and engage. Be warned: such a reality will not be well received by all too many who profess to be Christian.

Such inability can accurately be designated as *blindness.* If you will remember from the previous chapter, and the conversation that Alan and I had at the Trackside Tavern about the *drag* and *drift* he observed inside North Park Church: "No one seems to notice!"

Ah, yes! We know from the New Testament writings that "the god of this world blinds the minds of unbelievers to keep them from seeing the light of the gospel of the glory of Christ" (2 Cor 4:4). Yes, and from such we can easily discern that *blinding* is one of Satan's tools. It follows then that if Satan can blind the mind of unbelievers, he can also persistently be at work deleting from the church's sense of calling any cognition that it is called to be a community of light in the midst of a dominion of darkness. This blinding and forgetfulness would be increasingly the case with second- and third-generation church folk. This would be inescapably true as the dynamic presence of the Spirit is diminished in the community called the church.

This dismissal of the *darkness* is so entrenched, at this point in the twenty-first century, that we not only have to reclaim a conviction that the church and its component members are called to be to be a dynamic missional community in a fallen world—that the church's calling and its intentional goal are to spread the liberating gospel of Jesus Christ through the agency of every baptized believer until it permeates every ethnic group in the world—but it demands of us, who would expose it, that we now must also *reimagine* a whole other concept of the church. We are forced to confess that the church itself might well be a mission field of significant proportions as it becomes indifferent to its missional essence.

We need to clearly articulate an *alternative ecclesiology*—and that not to mention the need to dramatically reconceive the liturgical and Eucharistic practices of the church so as to make them a dynamic component of that same radically alternative ecclesiology! We need an understanding of the church as the living and dynamic community of God's new and recreated humanity, which community itself incarnates God's incredible good news and God's divine nature, and thereby *puts the lie* to the satanic subversion.

At the same time we need to understand that the church is called to consciously engage the darkness, and the prince of darkness, and the culture of darkness—a community that renounces Satan and his domain of darkness as it expresses itself in every dimension of our lives, neighborhoods, workplaces, etc. The church is to be *salt and light* in the midst of darkness and corruption . . . all of which is close at hand. Jesus calls us to be the light of the world! This is the message that is replete in the New Testament from beginning to the end.

But such light is an offense to the darkness because it exposes and confronts it.

The context of our pilgrimage as the church of Jesus Christ is not in some neutral territory, but it is in the midst of cultural, social, cosmic setting in which that enemy of God, Satan, though now dethroned and disarmed on the cross,[7] still rages in all of his malicious, subtle, subverting, and destructive schemes against the church.

Part of our homework, then, is to discern how to be "sober and vigilant" (1 Pet 5:8) without being paranoid, joyless, and perennially captive to fear. Or, even more: How are we to include this in our joyous announcement of Jesus and the kingdom? Our deliverance is out of captivity to metaphysical, ethical, and epistemological darkness,[8] and into the glorious liberty of the children of God. This is our thrilling, liberating, transforming message.

Register, then, that this incapacity to even conceive of the *relentless darkness* is a filtering scheme.

And . . . *no one seems to notice!*

2. The Subjectivization, or Individualization, of the Gospel

The second filtering reality is related to the first. It is, namely, the *subjectivizing* or *individualizing* of our gospel, which eclipses or obscures the larger cosmic reality of our redemption. This is subtle and must be approached delicately because, on one hand, we do rightfully exalt the

---

7. Again, this is a whole critical understanding of the redemptive work of Christ that needs a study in itself, and is beyond the purpose of this book, though this book is built upon this understanding. Along with Gregory Boyd's magisterial two volumes on this subject, one might profit greatly from John Stott's *The Cross of Christ*, chapter 9. (Downer's Grove: InterVarsity, 2006).

8. *Metaphysics* is the study of our concept of being and reality, *ethics* has to do with the field of behavior, and *epistemology* has to do with our concept of knowledge.

joyous news of personal sins forgiven and the promise of new life by the Spirit . . . "ransomed, healed, restored, forgiven."

Yet, on the other hand, in so doing we can all too easily bring about a truncated version of the command to *repent* by narrowing it down to include only my own personal sin—and not having anything to do with my (our) complicity in a cosmic rebellion, and with the dominion of darkness, with Satan's animosity toward our God and his Christ—and toward God's whole creation.

Such a *subjectivization* fails to even ask: What energizes our brute self-interest (sin)? Or what am I really slave to?[9] Or, maybe even: What are the ultimate roots of the seven deadly sins (often mentioned in some church traditions)? This filter minimizes God's purpose for this very world in which we live, this creation, which "groans waiting for the redemption." Where does that energy—that proclivity toward all that which defiles, dehumanizes and destroys God's good purpose for his creation—come from?

To focus, then, *only* on my own personal sinfulness and brokenness (and make no mistake about it, this personal focus is absolutely essential) . . . is to miss the larger tragic context of the cosmic rebellion against the glory of the creator, against all that violates God's *shalom*. It is, in itself, a satanically inspired filter to blind us to power and dominion of the darkness, and to the prince of darkness . . . and to a necessary awareness that "the whole world lies in the power of the evil one" (1 John 5:19).

Put all of that down as one of the filtering schemes of the devil.

And . . . *no one seems to notice!*

3. "Christendom" Presuppositions and Ecclesiology

If we come to such a document as the Ephesian letter (as we will in the next chapter) with our ecclesiastical (church) presuppositions of *Christendom*[10] (which we have inherited at this point in the twenty-first century) in place, then we will thereby be assuming, presuppositionally,

---

9. A generation ago, Christopher Lasch wrote his milestone work, *The Culture of Narcissism* (New York: Norton, 1979), in which he described a culture obsessed with itself. It is an eloquent description of humankind's captivity to self-worship, with all of the frustrations and confusion that accompany that self-interested and therapeutic culture.

10. *Christendom* is a study in itself, and I can only refer my readers to my previous book, *Refounding the Church from the Underside* (Eugene, OR: Wipf & Stock, 2010), 26ff., or simply check the definition on Wikipedia.

the necessity of such questionable ecclesiastical accouterments such as, for instance: clergy, church buildings, elaborate liturgical rites,[11] and adequate (vast?) funding to maintain all of that—none of which are ever even suggested as any factor of Christ's, or in Paul's writings about the essentials of the church.

Paul has only a vision of a contagious missional community (a new creation community) of equipped disciples (i.e., disciples who are equipped to make disciples, who in turn make disciples, who in turn . . . etc.), ultimately determined to radiate the gospel of the kingdom of God to every ethnic group from here to the very ends of the earth. The church is never ever conceived as some kind of a *holding pen* for rescued and passive saints engaging in liturgical practices and "religious activities," while oblivious to those who live next door, whom Jesus came to seek and to save! Much less is the church conceived to be indifferent to its redemptive function in *this world*, what with all of the social, humanitarian, ecological, political, and environmental dimensions of this creation.

Is that an overstatement? I think not. Our very reading of the New Testament is critically distorted by such a Christendom filter.

If we are so *hiding out* inside of our church institutions that our neighbors (who are inhabiting the darkness) never see or know the light in and through us . . . then we are a contradiction! Which might even be to say that "going to church" may be the very most *un-Christian* thing we can do! (I could get in trouble for saying that!)

And . . . *no one seems to notice!*

But there's probably one more (of many?) filtering scheme we need to surface.

4. *The Displacement, or Demise, of Disciple Making as a Priority Discipline*

When the inescapable New Testament priority on Christ's command (or commission) to "make disciples" is either displaced, or forgotten, or diluted . . . the missional implications for the church are disastrous.

---

11. I will insist that church leadership ("clergy") and liturgical rites, for them to have any validity, must be fully informed by the gospel of the kingdom of God, and be so designed as to reinforce, illuminate, and equip God's people for their missionary calling in their 24/7 lives, and to renew regularly their vows of repentance and faith in Jesus Christ. I also think that this will necessitate a "reinvention" of such (leadership and liturgical rites), and this due to the subversions of Christendom, which have reduced these to institutional necessities, disconnected from the mission of God.

There is probably a no more effective filtering scheme than this one. It is complicit in the three aforementioned schemes. One could rightfully assert that it is because of this displacement that the darkness quietly takes the people of God, and the church of God, captive to its blindness.

No satanic scheme could be more effective.

If we follow the biblical thread here, we begin with Jesus' assertion at Caesarea Philippi that *he*, Jesus, would build his *ecclesia*, his church. That's all he says. He gives them, there, no blueprint of how he would do that.

So, what were the disciples to do? Or, what is their role in this all-encompassing *eschatological project* of building the church? Jesus certainly doesn't give them any "Ten Steps to Church Building." No! He will only say to them (later): "As the Father has sent me, even so do I send you" (John 20:21).

～ ～ ～

Stop for a minute and take note of a subtle but critical point here. Jesus did *not* say (in this declaration at Caesarea Philippi) that he himself was going to "make disciples." He certainly was obviously making disciples at that very time, and would ultimately commission them to do the same. Disciples are those individuals transformed by their encounter with Jesus and the gospel. Individual disciples were to incarnate the radically new patterns of thinking and living that came with God's kingdom. They were to be a countercultural humanity. Okay?

But here, at Caesarea Philippi, he declares that he is going to call out a *community* and transform it into a whole different *genre*: a re-created community that incarnates those same teachings in communal form. Such a community is to reflect the reconciled and redemptive relationships that are to exist in God's new creation. Those relationships, in turn, are modeled in the relationships that exist within the Trinitarian community.

In other words, the church would be the demonstration of human community as God designed it to be. What we will be learning in the New Testament documents is that this kingdom community is to be what God intends human community to look like. It is to be a very visible demonstration of an egalitarian community formed by the dynamic presence of God's Spirit, which will incarnate love, caring, sharing, justice, mercy, mutuality, joy, and self-giving, all out of reconciled and redemptive relationships.

The church Jesus will create is to be the visible human community as God intends it to be. It will not be a depersonalized society, but an intimate community where all have names and faces and stories—where all have gifts to share with the others. The church is designed to be the glory of God, the visible communal demonstration of the divine nature. Yes, it is to be such a demonstration to the watching world—to all who see and touch it.

The implications here are that not only are individuals messengers of the gospel of the kingdom of God, but the church is the messenger also. It is the "dwelling place of God by the Spirit" right in the midst of the realities of every day life—in the midst of the *stink and stuff* of this dominion of darkness.

Disciple making, then, is the formation of individuals to respond to Christ's teachings, but it is also a communal formation. It requires those individuals be equipped to live in the radical and subversive (I love those two adjectives—so appropriate) and countercultural community called: the church. The end result of disciple making is that Jesus is creating a new humanity that incarnates the reconciliation of heaven and earth by the cross both in individual persons and in such a new humanity.

Back, then, to our being a part of what the Father sent Jesus to be and to do.

What did the Father send Jesus to be and to do? (It's important to get this right, and to follow through the implications of this statement).

The Gospel writer Mark answers this question succinctly: "Jesus came into Galilee, proclaiming the gospel [i.e., the thrilling announcement] of God, and saying, 'The time is fulfilled, and the kingdom of God is at hand; repent and believe in the gospel'" (Mark 1:14–15). What in the world is he saying?

As it unfolds, Jesus is saying that it is *God's time* to come in person, and to inaugurate his new creation, his salvation, his ultimate end-time (or eschatological) purpose, God's great "search and rescue" mission— which mission is that of reconciling his whole creation to himself.

This creation's true Lord is now invading this same creation, which has for ages been in rebellion and has been captive to the dominion of darkness. All of this, Jesus will go on to affirm, is to be accomplished in and through himself, the rightful Lord of all. He will thereupon demonstrate his authority as this creation's true Lord by healing the sick, casting out demons (victims of the malice of the prince of darkness), and proclaiming the thrilling news of the kingdom of God.

In our first mentioned scheme (above) we raised the reality that folk do not have the capacity to even imagine the dominion of darkness. But just stop and think about what we have before us in the arrival of Jesus on the scene with such a message.

It is so outrageous, so humanly unlikely.

Here he is, an obscure itinerant peasant, heralding himself as the Lord of all. Here is this Palestinian unknown making such unbelievable statements as: "He who has seen me has seen the Father"—has seen God (John 14:9).

Any self-respecting skeptic would have to say: "Come on, gimme a break. Get real!"

Yet, throughout his several years of public ministry he unabashedly identifies all that he is, and is doing, as being from God. He verifies his authority with miracles, exorcisms, healings, and command over nature. But his ultimate message is _himself._ He is the one sent by the Father to accomplish cosmic redemption, to create all things new. Ultimately, he knows that it all will lead to shame, to a cross, to being "the Lamb slain from the foundation of the world," for the sins of the world.

All of this is so humanly unlikely . . . but all this will be vindicated by his resurrection (also incomprehensible by his followers).

So then, how does all of this relate to disciple making?

In answer: you keep following the thread of the New Testament accounts. It didn't take long before those hearing and witnessing what he was saying and doing, got curious and approached him and began asking questions. Jesus invited some of them to come and spend time with him.

This invitation is one critical _key to our understanding_ of disciple making: Jesus _spent significant personal time_ with those who were to be his disciples. He _processed_ his life and teachings to them, and with them, in intimate conversation, and all this in the midst of real life. Ultimately there were twelve persons who were invited by him to be his close, intimate travelling company of disciples over a period of a couple of years.

Call it, if you will, *immersion disciple making.* It was never done in the abstract, or in isolation from real life in the dominion of darkness, with all of its tragic aspects.

Again, there is a key to disciple making here: disciple making must include community formation, that is, a formation into communities in which the new creation is incarnated in flesh and blood. Such communal formation into true human communities is where the love, reconciliation, forgiveness, and the grace of God in Christ animate the relationships, and where disciples mutually (and inescapably?) grow into wholesome intimacy, into maturity and into obedience to Christ. These visible new creation (or kingdom) communities become essential components in the mission of God. In and through them Jesus builds his church.

There were evidently also many more beyond the twelve who believed what Jesus was saying and doing, and could be identified as followers, who listened and watched and at times were engaged in Jesus' ministry. This larger community is always just off of center stage in the New Testament accounts. One also dare not overlook that enormously effective and faithful company of women disciples who believed and who were there from beginning to the end. They were the first to witness the resurrection. They are always there and are always also just off center stage in the Gospel accounts!

Look carefully, now. The twelve disciples traveled with Jesus, and so they had intensive and intimate time with him. They heard him preach and teach in public. He taught them in private. He answered their questions. He sent them out on specific mission trips: "And proclaim as you go, saying, 'The kingdom of heaven is at hand.' Heal the sick, raise the dead, cleanse lepers, and cast out demons" (Matt 10:7–8). In short, they were to do exactly the same thing that Jesus was doing. They were to herald and demonstrate the inbreaking reign of the rightful Lord of all, Jesus. He sent them out. He called them back. He processed their experiences and answered their questions. He encouraged their obedience, but also rebuked their unbelief at times. He modeled before them what he was calling them to be and do.

He *immersed* them in his mission. No theoretical disciple making here. May I underscore this here? Fruitful disciple making is *disciple making by immersion.* One does not become formed as a disciple in a class safely inside the church house. That church house may be the site of a good staging area, in which you may be given instructions, edified, warned of dangers, teamed up with others . . . and encouraged. But one learns to be a disciple by being sent out into the realities and the conversations of 24/7 life, which often includes disappointment, rejection, suffering, and pain . . . as well as positive responses, fruitfulness, joy, and blessing.

Mind you, we must not forget that Jesus' preaching also always included the response that was necessary to what he was announcing: "The kingdom of God has drawn night. Repent and believe the good news." Men and women who heard him were invited to make a decision, to have a change of mind, that renounced a former way of life, thinking, and behavior—and that deliberately entered into a whole new one—a new life that was focused in Jesus himself.

The disciples were amazed at the response they received on their mission: "Even the demons are subject to us" (Luke 10:17). They were in the process of being made disciples. They were learning who Jesus was, what he came to be and to do, what power and authority over the forces of darkness he possessed. They learned by trial and error. He sent them out, and called them back. They were learning by *immersion*. They were often slow to learn, but . . . they were slowly being formed into agents of the mission of God.

Be aware, then, that when Jesus gave his great commission after his resurrection, what he instructed his followers to do was built upon their understanding of what he had done with them, and communicated to them: "All authority in heaven and on earth has been given to me. Go therefore and *make disciples* of all nations, *baptizing* them in the name of the Father and of the Son and of the Holy Spirit, *teaching them to observe all that I have commanded you.* And behold, I am with you, to the end of the age" (Matt 28:18–20, emphasis added).

You will see this disciple making design unfolding after Pentecost when the church was gathering in small configurations in homes, around meal tables, where they were immersed in the apostles' doctrine, in a kind of mutuality and formation into kingdom living that, in turn, created *organic growth.* You will see the church growing exponentially without institutional accouterments. You will see multitudes being baptized. Every believer was equipped (*discipled*) and engaged.

You will see it in Paul's word to the Ephesian believers, namely, that the ascended Lord gave those several equipping-for-mission gifts (apostles, prophets, evangelists, and pastor-teachers) so that every believer would grow into the fullness of the stature of Christ (Eph 4:10–16). You will see it in Paul's word to the Philippians: "What you have learned and received and heard and seen in me, do; and the God of peace will be with you" (Phil 4:9–10). You see it in Paul's passing along the disciple-making mandate to Timothy to commit the gospel to faithful men who will then be able to teach others also (2 Tim 2:2).

And so it goes. Disciple making was and is essential to the mission of God in and through the church.

What you have is a community that was vigorously reproducing so that the "word went everywhere," where the new believers were formed into new creation communities as part of the mission, and where multitudes were being added daily.

Disciple making sees every believer, and every Christian community, equipped for and engaged in Christ's mission. *Every believer* himself or herself in turn becomes a disciple maker. Every believer is a potential church planter. Every home is by virtue of its new creation inhabitants a place of hospitality, not to mention as the locus for a new church. Every believer is equipped in the formation for true Christian community with all of the mutual accountability and responsibility that goes along with that. Such formation of believers for all of this is the purpose of disciple making.

Now please note: *This command of Jesus to his infant church has never, ever, been rescinded.*

But . . . what if it somehow, through the *relentless darkness* . . . what if by some satanic scheme it has been forgotten, or diluted into something innocuous like recruiting new church members, or by marketing church membership? Or something inane, like what too often passes as: Christian education? When that happens the church loses it reproductive capacity in the mission of God? When that happens the church loses its vision for the passion of God for all people? What happens when the church becomes so depersonalized that it doesn't really incarnate God's design for truly reconciled and loving human community?

When that happens the mission of God is emasculated and rendered sterile.

When that basic requirement of New Testament for conformity to the image of God's Son (cf. Rom 8:28–29) is displaced, then the mission goes dormant and the *darkness* is not confronted. Church membership (a never-used designation in the New Testament) becomes more acceptably passive. Obedience to the teachings of Christ and maturity into fruitfulness cease to be the goals of our baptism.

The missional implications of this displacement are devastating. The clear "so send I you" mandate to every believer ceases to be a critical component of one's identification with the church. A *clergy class* is invented, which become custodial church professionals rather than engaged disciple makers. The clergy's role becomes to "keep them in the nest" and not to "teach them to fly!" Thus a particular community might well have only a one-generation lifespan, or (in missionary terms) might well itself become: an unreached people group.

No reproduction. No next generation.

This is a devastatingly effective filter perpetrated by the *relentless darkness*, alas!

And . . . nobody seems to notice.

∿ ∿ ∿

EXCURSUS: "THEY'VE NEVER KNOWN ANYTHING ELSE"

I need to stop here and be deliberately repetitive and redundant (admittedly).

I need to register again a personal hesitation. Writing on such a theme as I am, on the church and the *relentless darkness*, I have discovered in numerous conversations that there is a not-so-subtle problem that we need to engage as directly, as confrontationally, and as clearly as is possible—though it won't be simple.

The problem can be stated thus: Amongst a vast number of good church folk—sincere, believing, faithful participants in church institutions of all sorts—there exists no capacity at all to even comprehend or imagine what I am writing about . . . or to see that a great deal (if not most) of what goes on in their own particular churches communities has practically nothing at all to do with anything the New Testament documents teach about the role of the church in the gospel of the kingdom of God . . . and this is simply because *they have never known anything else!*

They want blessing on their church, but they can't, or don't, anticipate anything other than what they have seen and known and experienced!

So tragic. So sad.

This is true of a wide variety of church expressions, churches of every conceivable description and form. Still, please remember, that there are quite frequently, and probably somewhat out of sight, cohorts and conventicles of faithful believers inhabiting these forgetful church expressions, folk like the godly Simeon and Anna in Luke's nativity account, those who wait for the something more, for the "consolation of Israel," i.e., a day when the Lord visits his people. Yes, there are many such patient, praying saints . . . often frustrated and tempted to give up . . . but they don't.

I say this not as a critic, but as an observer and a fellow traveler, as one who has been long immersed in a variety of church expressions, and engaged in dialogue with a very large number of participants for a generation and more. Innocent sounding questions such as "What church do you belong to?" or "Where did you go to church?" or "Why don't you join our church?" can reveal this *total misunderstanding* of the church's necessary purpose and design in the redemptive plan of God.

So subtle is this erosion by the *darkness* that hardly anyone even remotely suspects such to be a very subtle and satanically provoked *subversion*. Our image of the church seldom includes substantive involvement in costly discipleship, or to obedience to the word and commandments of Jesus Christ, or of every believer's dynamic participation in the mission of God, or fruitful equipping to be children of light in our 24/7 lives. And because this is so, one can *join* a church and never sense any accountability for his/her incarnation of the divine image: the glory of God. One can *join* and never be formed into discipleship.

Does this inability to comprehend or imagine make this a "scheme of the devil?"

I'm willing to say that it is a *most effective* scheme of the devil.

Even my stating this incomprehension, or such an inability to even imagine anything other than what we have experienced . . . calls forth our prayers for the gift of imagination to be created in us by the Holy Spirit, in order that we may be able to *radically reimagine* the church—the thrill and dynamic and purpose and design of the church as "the dwelling place of God by the Holy Spirit," as the incarnation of God's new creation community, and as the missionary arm of the Holy Trinity.

So bear this in mind as we proceed and seek to provide some enlightenment and encouragement to God's faithful ones in this pilgrimage.

~ ~ ~

And now we're ready to move on to a case study of the church at Ephesus. Paul's letter to the church at Ephesus is a missionary manual to an infant church. It is to a church in a major city with a culture that was totally alien to what Jesus came to announce. This case study will put all of what has gone before in these first two chapters into an existential context, and give to us a sense of incarnational reality. I want us to take a missional walk through the letter to the church at Ephesus in the first century. So let us proceed to such a case study.

3

Case Study in Spiritual Warfare:
The Church at Ephesus

I HAD BEEN SENDING along all of these reflections and my ruminations about "The Filtering Schemes" (chapter 2) to Alan via email, just to keep him up to speed, and with where I was in seeking to answer the questions he had raised with me at our meeting at the Trackside Tavern. Several weeks later we met over coffee to pick up the conversation. After our sojourn together over these past several years, and "chewing on" the whole issue of the church—the "What is the church?" and the "Why is the church?"—I know him well. I didn't expect him to toss me any softballs this time.

I wasn't disappointed.

"Okay, Bob! Good stuff. So what do I do with it? It's still way out in the theological and cosmological ether as far as I'm concerned. Like: 'Earth to Bob Henderson: Hey! I'm down here in a twenty-first-century city, and in a real North Park Church.'

"Bob, I've got to confess that church is a total enigma to me . . . but then, it was you who encouraged me to get involved with it in the first place. And North Park Church is only one tiny factor in this complex city of Atlanta, which, in turn, is part of a cultural scene, and a global scene, that is crazy—nearly impossible to exegete.

"Add to that the suggestion in your last communication that you want to do a case study of the church at Ephesus. Come on! Ephesus was essentially a pre-Christian-era city (or, at the very least, early Christian era) from two thousand years ago. And Atlanta is, by any definition, a post-Christian-era culture. And then there is North Park Church, caught in that uncharted chaos between its Christendom founding and its bewildering post-Christian and post-Christendom present.

"I see those four filtering schemes you mentioned at work continually. I don't have any qualms about the reality of the darkness inhabiting the church. So where does that leave me? What do I do with it? How is a study of Ephesus going to help me here in Atlanta, in a church that has pretty much lost its sense of missional purpose—or even of any dynamic formation by New Testament Christianity? And sometimes I think that even Jesus might be a stranger to that scene . . . though nobody would ever, ever admit it . . . maybe no one even notices![1]

"Can you please, for my sake, come down to earth?"

"Actually, I am down to earth.

"Ephesus and Atlanta are cities with many striking similarities. Ephesus was the second largest city in the Roman Empire, an exciting city. It was a seaport city, which meant that it was also a commercial crossroads. It was multiethnic and multilingual. It had its civic religion focused on the goddess Diana, of the Ephesians, who was the pride of that city. Dominant among the influences and pressures of its civic life was the Roman Empire, in which the worship of Caesar was a *not-to-be-challenged* priority—required and expected. You could have all the religion you wanted to have, but Caesar was ultimately Lord.

"Stir in all of the daily realities of the populace. Prominent would have been the trade guilds, not unlike our labor unions. To be successful in any trade was to be part of a guild, otherwise you were ostracized. These guilds often included festivities and bacchanalia that were all so much a part of that pagan society. The demographic palette would include tradesmen, civil servants, religious persons involved in all of the pagan temples, landowners, journeymen of all sorts, inhabitants of the academy, slaves and free men, to mention a few. But mostly there was that vast host of ordinary, struggling-to-survive, marginal and threatened working folk. There was no dearth of religions and philosophies . . . and somewhere in all of that mix there was the synagogue, the colony of the Jewish dispersion.

---

1. In recent months I have been reading from both Søren Kierkegaard and Dietrich Bonhoeffer, and have been surprised at how they struggled with, and how clearly they both articulated, this same disconnect between the church and New Testament Christianity. So the battle is perennial.

"Apropos to our thesis, what you have in Ephesus is the context of the church's missionary mandate from the very beginning, namely, a people dwelling within the daily realities of the dominion of the kingdom of darkness—the dominion of *the god of this world*, who is Satan. Having said that, we also need to be reminded, again and again: '*For this purpose was the son of God manifest to destroy the works of the devil*' (1 John 3:8). The whole purpose of the church and its mission has always been, and is, to be an integral part of God's design to make all things new, i.e., to reconcile the world unto God through Jesus Christ. That mission begins with rescuing those very people from the dominion of the prince of darkness, which is accomplished through Christ and his gospel. Got it?

"So, Alan, just for our purposes here, we need to stop and think about this staggering question: How would you ever, *ever*, begin to obey Jesus' commission to 'go make disciples of every people group in the world' in such a very real city of, probably, about 250,000 persons in such a thoroughly pagan and untouched-by-the-gospel city as Ephesus? How would you infiltrate such an urban expression of the dominion of Satan, what with all of its self-sufficiency, civic pride, multiplicity of religions, and alien philosophies and lifestyles?

"Where in the world would you begin? Who would have ears to hear such an outrageous and unlikely (foolish?) message as that of some itinerant Jewish peasant who professed to be God, who was executed as a criminal by the Roman government, and then was ostensibly raised from the dead?

"You've got to admit that it is sort of a stretch."

"*You've got my full attention.*"

"And now for Atlanta.

"In many ways it is not all that different in looking at the city of Atlanta (or any city in North America, from San Anselmo to Provincetown) . . . except that our context of darkness is much more complex. The dominion of darkness in such a city is entrenched in a much more malignant and subtle fashion.

"It was this reality that missiologist Lesslie Newbigin discovered when he returned to England in retirement after a lifetime as a missionary in South India. He found that it was much more difficult to preach the gospel, and to get a hearing in post-Christian Birmingham,

England, than it had been for him in South India. In South India the Christian message was essentially new and fresh in virgin territory. It was a message about the life and hope and meaning, about the death and resurrection of Jesus along with his teachings. The culture of darkness was primarily formed by Hinduism, which dominated that culture. Newbigin was quite gifted in exegeting that Hindu culture, and speaking the gospel into it.

"What he found in England was that the British culture had heard the message of Jesus Christ. The populace knew the words, had lived with the church's rather dominant place in British history, accepted the church as a colorful and present, but essentially useless, irrelevant, archaic, and ignorable part of their present lives. For all practical purposes the UK had built up antibodies against the Christian faith. England had become a post-Christian mission field, he concluded.[2] And, tragically, the church had comfortably inhabited that post-Christian darkness and been unconsciously inhabited by that same darkness itself. The church enjoyed the *perks* of its status . . . and life went on in England pretty much oblivious to it."

"You're going to tell me that Atlanta is a mission field, and that . . . maybe worse, that the church itself may also be a mission field, right?"

"You said it, not me.

"But, yes. You could make that case.

"In a very real sense, Atlanta is on the opposite end of the missional spectrum from Ephesus. Ephesus was a pre-Christian urban setting, where the gospel of Jesus was obviously unknown, and not (initially) a factor at all in its civic life. Conversely, Atlanta is the quintessential post-Christian city. It has all of the monuments and remnants of a Christian presence, but basically the true culture of Atlanta is inured to the Christian message. It hardly registers on the screen of a large portion of the population. Atlanta can be totally dismissive of, and, frequently, just politely contemptuous of the Christian faith and church.

"Add to these realities the even more tragic fact that the existing churches, for the most part, have lost their missional DNA, have for all practical purposes forgotten their message, and so have become indif-

---

2. The writings of Lesslie Newbigin are some of the most seminal studies in existence on this whole subject; see *The Gospel in a Pluralist Society* (Grand Rapids: Eerdmans, 1989) and *Foolishness to the Greeks* (Grand Rapids: Eerdmans, 1986), among others.

ferent to the darkness that exists in their neighborhoods, among their friends, and in the totality of civic life. Most of the church folk will vigorously deny what I have just said, but our Bible Belt reputation has little substance. The light shines very dimly.

"This is what Lesslie Newbigin found in Birmingham, England, a generation or two ago, and it makes the mission quite difficult . . . unless one comes to understand the dynamics of the dominion of darkness, and the church's true God-given authority to exercise its effective weapons of warfare, which "have divine power to destroy strongholds" (2 Cor 10:4).

"All of those filtering schemes that I have shared with you (chapter 2) have been at work, even in this city of Atlanta. What you get too often is a truncated, or reductionist, or counterfeit version of New Testament Christianity that renders the Christian church, and the Christian faith, saltless salt . . . an easily ignored club for religious folk who like that sort of thing. To be sure, there are church buildings and church institution aplenty . . . but within them is, far too commonly, a vast ignorance of, as well as a disconnect from, New Testament Christianity: the mission of God in Christ.

"Much less is there much reality about the dynamic and transformative (even subversive) thinking and behavior of the kingdom of God. Folk have generally become immune, if not hostile, to it all. And where the church has displaced, diluted, or forgotten its true message and purpose, then it also reverts and becomes part of the darkness. 'If the light in you is darkness, how great is the darkness' (Matt 6:23b). *And nobody seems to notice . . .*

"What you get, then, is a false version of Christianity that is conformed to the culture of post-Christian darkness . . . rather than being a community radically transformed, so as to demonstrate God's (countercultural) new creation and, thereby, becoming a *transforming community* of the kingdom of God. Such a false version of the church can easily be (and is) ignored or dismissed by a large portion of the populace. Yet, it is this false version that has become the accepted version of far too many very respectable and popular church institutions.

"Atlanta is not a seaport such as Ephesus was, but in the twenty-first century it has the largest airport in the world, which makes it an international commercial center. It is multiethnic and multilingual as was Ephesus. It is the focus of huge economic and political forces, and of a vigorous civic religion (Bible-and-flag, "God Bless America" stuff).

It is the scene of a huge multiplicity of lifestyles and beliefs, of the social pathologies common to North America: consumerism, hedonism, narcissism, and the like—and perhaps the worship of *mammon* is the most dominant of all, in its focus on material prosperity. And it shares the pathology of most cities, what with the vast disparity between the wealthy and the impoverished among its citizens, with all of the social, economic, and justice issues that accompany such disparity.

"To be sure, Atlanta is also a setting of much that is commendable, by way of caring and community stewardship. But then, get real! Much of that good stuff is initiated by those who are indifferent to the Christian faith, or even hostile to its claims. The popular mind in a city like Atlanta, sadly, is too often the victim of, and reacts negatively to, the excesses and bizarre (or questionable) behavior of so many of those calling themselves Christian, along with church scandals, distortions, and conflicts ever present in the news."

"*So you telling me that the church is basically a non-factor in the forming of the city of Atlanta? That's pretty extreme isn't it?*"

"Yeah, I may be slightly overstating the case.

"We prophetic types tend to give ourselves to a bit of hyperbole, or exaggeration. Sometimes one has to overstate the case to get the attention of the somnolent. Or, maybe in the prophetic tradition, one has to '. . .pluck up and break down, to destroy and to overthrow,' before one can 'build and plant' (Jere 1:10). How does that sound?

"You yourself kept reminding me that as the darkness has inhabited the church, and the church has inhabited the darkness . . . 'nobody seems to notice.'

"You said that yourself!

"Of course, there are a whole lot of real disciples of Jesus inhabiting these same post-Christian church institutions, like exiles. But there isn't much evidence of dynamic organic growth and transformative influence on the larger scene, all that said.

"But back to your question about Atlanta being a mission field: You could make a pretty good case that, for all the proliferation of church entities around Atlanta, they really are having a minimal effect, and are hardly a formative factor in its civic life. The Barna Research Group found that there are something like twenty million folk out there in North America who call themselves 'born again believers' who find the church irrelevant to their lives, and have pretty much given up on it. And those who do participate do so because of habit, guilt, or friendships.[3]

"That's pretty devastating, but it conforms to what I have observed.

"A generation ago a friend of mine wrote a book about evangelizing 'neo-pagan' North America.[4] That's a pretty good description. About the same time, Mortimer Arias, an exiled Bolivian Methodist bishop, was writing and speaking about North America being a particularly difficult mission field, and that because people think they have accepted or rejected the gospel without really understanding it.[5] This post-Christian indifference and growing hostility to the gospel has been coming on for a long time, but not many noticed. We kept right on *playing church*, but by the patterns of a former time, a former culture.

"*Okay. You've made your point. Let's not get stuck there. What about Ephesians?*"

"Right. Just look at Paul, the apostolic church planter. In a very real sense, his letter to the Ephesians is an amazingly resourceful missionary manual for us. When you look into it, you see how profoundly he took the ominous reality of the spiritual warfare in which that infant church was engaged. It doesn't take much imagination to make the transfer from Ephesus to your own quest for faithfulness in the North Park Church, and in the post-Christian city of Atlanta."

EPHESIANS AS A MISSIONARY MANUAL
TO A YOUNG CHURCH

"In the nineteenth chapter of Acts, when Paul is on a journey from Corinth, he comes to Ephesus. The large and strategically placed city of Ephesus in Asia Minor was hard to avoid when travelling in that part of the world (sort of like avoiding Atlanta when travelling by air in the US).

---

3. That is the conclusion of the Barna Group of researchers.

4. Alfred Krass, *Evangelizing Neopagan North America* (Scottdale, PA: Herald, 1982).

5. I have this in an article about his address to the National Evangelism Symposium of the United Church of Christ. He went on: "The more I think of it, the more reinforced is my impression that this is one of the most serious obstacles for biblical evangelism in this country. How can you evangelize through millions of Christians who assume they have received the Gospel and that they are bearers of the Good News, but who are not at all excited about it?"

Knowing Paul's habits, he probably sought out the Jewish synagogue, but somehow he networked and discovered a dozen disciples, who were the products of the ministry of John the Baptist. John the Baptist was that anointed forerunner to Jesus who declared Jesus as: the Lamb of God. Those dozen disciples, however, were unaware of the actual ministry of Jesus to whom John pointed. That would have meant that they were incomplete believers, in that all they knew was John's baptism into repentance as a preparatory discipline foreseeing the coming of the long-awaited Messiah.

"Now take note of this: in a city of a quarter million inhabitants Paul found twelve disciples of John. So what was the plan? The plan was that Paul got himself together with them and filled them in on the rest of the story, the story about the one to whom John pointed: Jesus. The twelve believed what Paul relayed to them about the message about Jesus. Then they were baptized, and they 'began speaking in tongues and prophesying' (ah, those supernatural phenomena so strange to our 'Christendom ears,' but not to New Testament Christianity).

"The record says that Paul then went to the synagogue and for three months spoke boldly about Jesus and the kingdom of God. Please note the subject of his message. The message Paul taught there bore fruit. But shortly it got tense in the synagogue because of opposition to the message, so Paul and the believers went to a rented hall, and for two more years, daily, he taught them the word of Christ. He also reports that he taught them house to house. He performed miracles, healings, exorcisms, and those visible signs of the powers of the age to come.[6]

"Bottom line: Paul effectively planted a contagious new church in Ephesus, and the result was that (because Ephesus was a commercial city) 'all the residents of Asia heard the word of the Lord' (Acts 19:10).

"Question: From whom did all the residents of Asia hear the word of the Lord? I would propose that it must have been from those whom Paul had discipled in Ephesus, who took the message with them as they traveled. Who else could it have been?

"Then, along the way, this new community of the kingdom of God became a threat to the commercial interests of the city of Ephesus and caused a riot. But note this: the church had the full attention of the city,

6. Cf. Heb 6:5, as a reference to the divine powers that evidently were very much a part of that early Christian community, and which seem so strange to so much of the church today.

nevertheless. Note, too, that the heralding of the gospel of the kingdom of God is often disruptive and divisive as it exposes the darkness. At the same time it is redemptive and reconciling.

"The plan was that Paul made disciples and immersed them in the teachings of Jesus, and modeled before them the power of the gospel, so that they in turn could make disciples, and know the power of the gospel. He created a contagious community, one that would grow organically and so permeate Ephesus. No passive, dependent membership there!

"Rather, they were disciples who were themselves disciple makers, and ultimately, also, potential missionary church planters. Every believer brought with him his contacts with family members, neighbors, working associates, and friends from a variety of contexts—all potential disciples.

"There is not a shred of evidence that he felt constrained to ordain any *clergy* to be in charge. As a matter of fact, clergy is never a category anywhere in Paul's thinking or writings. As a practical matter, he most probably assigned some of the more mature and wise to be elders in order to give the community some oversight . . . but this was a *people movement*, pure and simple.

"That was and *is*: the plan.

"And then he left and moved on to Macedonia. However, he left behind a church, a vital, contagious church in that vast city. He had equipped *all* of the believers to walk as children of the light.

"A colony of the light was created in the culture of darkness.

"Then, at a later date, he would write the letter in which we want to *marinate* here in our conversation. Ephesians is more of a missionary manual in letter form to this young church (knowing that it would be circulated to the other Christian communities nearby in Asia Minor) than is generally recognized."

WE NEED TO UNPACK PAUL'S OWN CREDENTIALS

I ultimately want to get to the heart of Paul's teaching about our warfare with the powers of darkness, and with the weapons of our warfare. He does this by spelling some of them out in the last chapter of letter to the Ephesians. He does this under the metaphorical figure of the *whole armor of God.* He will exhort those believing folk of the necessity to diligently *put on* such armor if they are to survive at the end of the day.

But before we go there, we need to understand what were the influences that formed Paul himself. We need some biographical insights that will help us understand his authority to say these things.

First, personality-wise: Paul was obviously an achiever—the kind that did not "suffer fools gladly." He was the intense kind of a guy who would be impatient with any compromise with those were less zealous than he. He had been on the fast track to an impressive role in the Jewish leadership by attempting to stamp out this new sect of the followers of Jesus. He was an accomplished student of one of the giants among the Jewish teachers of that period: Gamaliel. That would mean that he would have had an exceptional knowledge of the Scriptures: the Law and the Prophets. He was also a *purist,* and thereby was also a member of the Pharisee party of the Jewish community.

That would also mean that the whole Jesus phenomenon was an offense to him (in his pre-conversion days), and motivated him to excessive efforts to purge it from the scene by persecution and jailing. In short, Saul of Tarsus (Paul) was the classic type-A personality.

But, then, *secondly,* he would later come to realize that, in his pre-conversion days, he had been part of Israel's blindness, and of its violent hardness toward God's messengers. He would later write: "the god of this world has blinded the minds of the unbelievers, to keep them from seeing the light of the gospel of the glory of Christ" (2 Cor 4:4). He would come to know that there is a spiritual blindness as well as a moral and an intellectual blindness. He also came to know that the source of that blindness and darkness is not at all some impersonal influence, but ultimately the one who has always sought to usurp God's glory, namely, Satan. Paul would come to be acutely aware that the existential setting of his life and mission were not in neutral territory.

This brings us, then, to the critical *third* thing we need to understand about Paul: his conversion from enemy to faithful disciple of Jesus.

What happened to him was the last thing he ever expected to happen: he was profoundly (even traumatically) converted from his darkness to the light by meeting the ascended Lord Jesus one on one, face to face, and inescapably. On one of his journeys to make life miserable for the followers of Christ, he was literally *blown away* by a brilliant heavenly light, so that he fell to the ground in confusion and dismay. Talk about a conversion! Then he heard a gentle question: "Saul, Saul, why are you persecuting me?" His answer: "Who are you, Lord?" (I love to let my imagination run free on that encounter).

There was Jesus, the great rescuer of the captives of Satan (the god of this world), who with consummate gentleness confronted such a belligerent troublemaker, and answered him: "I am Jesus, whom you are persecuting. But rise and enter the city, and you will be told what to do" (Acts 9:3–6). Right up front, this fascinating, stubborn, brilliant zealot is humbled and brought inescapably to repentance and to faith in Jesus.

And, so, *fourthly*, this brings us to the missionary commission given to him by the glorified Jesus. This commission is at the heart of our whole discussion here. Paul would later relate the rest of his conversion encounter with Jesus:

> But rise and stand upon your feet, for I have appeared to you for this purpose, to appoint you as a servant and witness to the things in which you have seen me and to those in which I will appear to you, delivering you from your people [the Jews] and from the Gentiles—to whom I am sending you to open their eyes, so that they may turn from the power of Satan to God, that they may receive forgiveness of sins and a place among those who are sanctified by faith in me. (Acts 26:16–18)

Note carefully here that the commission given to Saul (Paul) includes deliverance from the power of Satan. The promises of forgiveness, reconciliation, new life, adoption into God's family, and transformation into the image of Christ all are part of the thrilling news . . . but there is a bondage that first must be encountered. That piece of the church's mandate gets left out of far too much the current understanding of the mission of God.

The original twelve disciples, who had been called by Jesus, and who had lived with him for a couple of years learning, being sent on missions, being refined and rebuked until they had a working grasp of what he was sending them to do as his disciples, were told (after his resurrection) to "go make disciples."

But Paul was a special case.

He would describe himself as "an apostle born out of due time" (1 Cor 15:8), who was called and discipled by Jesus in ways that we can only begin to fathom by some extrapolation from other New Testament documents. Immediately after his conversion, he was taken to the house of one Judas, in Damascus, and for three days (at least) was blind and fasted.

What would we give to know what went through Paul's heart and mind during those days?

What went on inside of Saul (Paul) was obviously both traumatic and enormously liberating, not to mention that it had to be totally enlightening. A disciple named Ananias was sent to minister to Paul and to restore his sight. Paul then was immediately filled with the Holy Spirit. He was then baptized into the name of Jesus.

He would, subsequently, spend time with the disciples in Damascus. Don't you know that there were some fascinating discussions, question-and-answer sessions, and experiences that would constitute him a disciple? Whatever took place in those days immediately after his conversion, it produced an immediate response, and he began to proclaim Jesus in the synagogue, and to the amaze (understatement) those former victims of his malice who heard him. He was, then, taken under the wing of dear Barnabas (I love Barnabas), that encouraging and self-effacing disciple who will appear time and again fulfilling his name (which means something like *son of consolation*).

Barnabas took Paul to Jerusalem and vouched for him and introduced him to the apostles. Amidst the company of the eyewitnesses of Jesus, Paul was being formed into a disciple who understood clearly the teachings of Jesus, and how Jesus was the fulfillment of God's great *eschatological design* to make all things new. He would see clearly how the sacred writings of Judaism all pointed to Jesus, and how the plan of God hidden for the ages was now revealed in Jesus. And, evidently, later there are veiled references to the fact that he spent some time in Arabia alone with the Spirit of God—with the ascended and glorified Lord. That might be what is behind another account of his in which he relates an enigmatic experience of being lost in the Spirit in a mystical encounter in which much was revealed to him—those two events conceivably refer to the same episode.[7]

What had been produced by all these events (ultimately by Jesus himself) was the formation of Paul, the disciple, the apostle, and the missionary church planter . . . who would, in turn, introduce the Christian

7. Cf. Gal 1:11–24; 2 Cor 12:1–5.

faith into the Gentile world. What had been, in his former blindness, an intense animosity toward Jesus and his followers, became now a total passion *for* Jesus, and for all that which Jesus came to teach and to do.

Paul's whole story plays in here as we continue with our discussion about the *relentless darkness*. It also serves to give us clues about interpreting (among other things) his metaphor of the whole armor of God, which will, in turn, illumine something of the nature of those weapons of our warfare that are not of the flesh but have divine power to destroy strongholds (2 Cor 10:4). And . . . it will spell out the understanding that Alan, and all of us, require of our calling to Christ and the implications of such a calling.

Let Alan, and all of his counterparts of the world, be warned: What I have just written is not at all safe!

There is a direct link from Jesus' word to his disciples: "As the Father has sent me, even so am I sending you" (John 20:21) . . . right through the apostle Paul, down to the twenty-first century, to you and me. It was this same Paul, who had met the ascended and glorified Lord Jesus, who had been powerfully converted to that divine-human Person, who had been commissioned by him, and sent out . . . who would then write to those Ephesian followers: "Therefore be imitators of God, as beloved children" (Eph 5:1).

So, what does that look like?

Again, he wrote: "Be imitators of *me*, as I am of Christ" (1 Cor 11:1). Or, even more incredibly (to our sense of false humility): "What you have learned and received and heard and seen in *me*—practice these things, and the God of peace will be with you" (Phil 4:9).

Whose responsibility was the ongoing mission to the city of Ephesus? Whose responsibility is the ongoing mission to the city of Atlanta? If the essence of being a disciple of Jesus Christ is being conformed to his image (Rom 8:29); if it is being sent into the world as Jesus was sent into the world (John 20:21); if it is being an imitator of God as dear children (Eph 5:1); if it is being an imitator of Paul as he was of Christ (1 Cor 11:1) . . . then whose responsibility?

Or, if Alan's North Park Church has become more and more conformed to the religious darkness, and so becomes a field of mission itself . . . then whose responsibility?

The account of Paul's two years in Ephesus relates how all the residents of Asia heard the word of the Lord, both Jews and Greeks. Again, I ask the question: Heard it from whom? How did that happen? Or, it also relates that "the word of the Lord continued to increase and prevail mightily" (Acts 19:20). By whose agency did that radiation of the message take place? Certainly not by the faithfulness of just one person! No, we're talking about some kind of a *people movement* for which all were equipped, and in which all were involved.

(Note again: There is never, anywhere, any mention of church professionals or of clergy in this letter, and its description of the life of the church. That is worthy of our notice.)

All of which makes this letter of Paul's, his missionary manual to that church, the more critical for our own understanding of the missional purpose of the church. It is essential for us because it enables us to understand how the church is to conceive of itself in that context of the dominion of darkness, which held the city of Ephesus captive . . . and which holds Atlanta captive also.

EPHESIANS BY THE BACK DOOR

I ask my readers to grant me some hermeneutical, or interpretive, liberty in dealing with this passage. My purpose it to reflect on it in the light of Paul's other writings as well as out of my own focus as a one who defines myself as: a *missional ecclesiologist*. Others have done superb exegetical expositions, some as academicians, some as pastors and missionaries, and I greatly indebted to them for their works.[8]

I am choosing to come into Ephesians by the back door of chapter 6, in which Paul concludes his letter with a passage that has the potential of shedding much light on what goes earlier in this epistle. In Ephesians (as I have said above) I see as something of a very practical manual whose purpose it is to instruct the Ephesian believers in their missionary task.

I, personally, am intrigued by the fact that Paul concludes this remarkable letter with a warning about the hazards of their calling to

---

8. I have profited by the commentaries of Peter T. O'Brian (most helpful), Gordon Fee, John Stott, Frank Thielman, and Markus Barth.

Christ, and how he explains to them the urgency and necessity of their putting on "the whole armor of God," both individually and corporately. He chooses to use that metaphor of armor since every person in that society would have been familiar, as most of the occupying soldiers of the Roman Empire wore such armor. He names seven pieces of this whole armor of God: 1) the belt of truth, 2) the breastplate of righteousness, 3) the shoes of the readiness given by the gospel of peace, 4) the shield of faith, 5) the helmet of salvation, 6) the sword of the Spirit, and, finally, 7) prayer in the Spirit.

To be sure, Paul has a proclivity for using aphorisms, or the clustering of descriptive concepts, in his teachings. Take for instance, his assumption of our predestined calling, as believers, to be conformed to the image of Christ (God) in Romans 8:29, and his later explanations of what such an image involves: true righteousness and holiness (Eph 4:24), and knowledge (Col 3:10). Or, think of his soliloquy on love in 1 Corinthians 13, which he closes with a threesome of Christian virtues: faith, hope, and love. Such images and understandings feed right into what is included in this metaphor of the whole armor of God.

In the earlier sections of this letter/missionary manual Paul communicates his total awe at that the One whom he had met so unexpectedly on the Damascus road. Paul is overwhelmed by his love for Christ, and so waxes eloquent over the sheer magnitude of what has God has done in his Son. Then he reminds the Ephesians believers of their own experience of being delivered out of their captivity to the darkness by this same Christ—and rescued for a purpose.

What follows are some wonderful and essential teachings about the nature of the gifts of the Spirit given to the church to equip it for its task. Then, Paul follows that with a most significant explanation of the relationships of love that are to exist among them and within the community called the church. It is this community that Christ is creating to demonstrate redemptive relationships that is to be a visible demonstration to the world outside. Their life together in this community, which we call the *church*, is to be that veritable demonstration, within the recreated human community, of the relationships that eternally exist among the three persons of the Trinity. It is only by such a breathtaking concept that what he spells out in chapters 4–6 makes sense.

But then . . . in what almost seems a *non sequitur*, Paul segues right into this sobering *reality check* regarding the impending and ominous danger that they face:

> Finally, be strong in the Lord and in the strength of his might. Put on the whole armor of God, that you may be able to stand against the schemes of the devil. For we do not wrestle against flesh and blood, but against the rulers, against the authorities, against the cosmic powers over this present darkness, against the spiritual forces of evil in heavenly places.
>
> Therefore take up the whole armor of God, that you may be able to withstand in the evil day, and having done all, to stand firm. Stand therefore, having fastened on the belt of truth, and having put on the breastplate of righteousness, and, as shoes for your feet, having put on the readiness given by the gospel of peace. In all circumstances take up the shield of faith, with which you can extinguish all the flaming darts of the evil one; and take the helmet of salvation, and the sword of the Spirit, which is the word of God, praying at all times in the Spirit, with all prayer and supplication. To this end keep alert with all perseverance, making supplication for all the saints, and also for me . . ." (Eph 6:10–19a)

First, is this passage a *non sequitur*? And, secondly, look at all the questions it raises, such as:

1. Exactly what is it that we are to stand against? What does that look like? Where are these ominous forces located?

2. What are all of those pieces of armor to look like on me?

3. "Evil in heavenly places?" What's that all about?

4. Spell out "this present darkness" for me, will you?

5. What does this have to do with what Paul has been saying up to this point?

All those questions are just a prelude to our thinking here.

Remember that, just previous to this passage (acknowledging that our translation's chapter-and-verse divisions often complicate things), chapters 4 and 5, and the first nine verses of chapter 6, deal with the redemptive and refreshing new creation relationships within the community. Again, one is somewhat overwhelmed by the very thought that our relationships with the Christian community are intended to be a visible mirror, before the watching world, of the relationships that exist within the Trinitarian community. By the Spirit of God, we are actually embraced within the Trinitarian community: "Yet she on earth hath union with God the three in one, and mystic sweet communion with those who rest is won . . ."[9]

Then, almost abruptly, comes this passage alerting the church to an ever-present darkness, and the ominous and perilous *schemes of the devil.*

Or is it abrupt? Is it actually, rather, Paul's ultimate purpose in the very writing of this particular letter to begin with?

The question of Paul's motive in writing this letter is, of course, impossible for us to know—except that we *can* extrapolate that Paul, as a missionary, and who also is keenly focused on the missionary purpose of the church, knows quite well all of the subtle seductions that could derail the missionary purpose for which it was founded (or called). Yes, these schemes could effectively cause such a community to wander off into conformity to the culture of darkness again, and be diminished in its new creation (kingdom of God) essence. So this exhortation would be critical to the very missionary survival, and fruitfulness, of the Ephesian church (or to Alan's North Park Church, or any St. John's-on-the-Boulevard Church of our experience).

It is not at all difficult to imagine Paul thinking and praying about this community out of his fatherly love for the real persons whom he knew there. After all, he had spent so much more time there than in his other missionary locations. It is not at all inconceivable that arriving at this very point in his letter was his whole primary purpose—his Spirit-given concern for the hazards that the darkness of Ephesus and Asia Minor (or Atlanta?) posed for the church. It's like he was saying:

> Brothers and sisters, the point I'm getting at in all that I have written in the first part of this letter is only introductory to my concern here. Unseen and clandestine forces could well be your undoing if you are not alert to the relentless darkness, and the prince thereof. Your calling is to be the veritable incarnation of the image of God, the divine nature, in your life together. It is, therefore, critical that you remember that you're facing forces of the dominion of darkness that are not crude or obvious, but subtle and seductive . . . so much so that unless you are sober and vigilant, they will render

---

9. From the familiar hymn by S. J. Stone, "The Church's One Foundation" (1866).

you fruitless, and sterile in your mission . . . and nobody will notice! Recognize that the schemes may well take on *spiritual* and *religious* expressions, so that you will not be expecting them, and so they will be able to eviscerate your redemptive presence. The darkness will come through the very cultural air you breathe. It will come in your relationships, it will come in unexpected places, and it will be ever present—anything to prevent you from being the glory of God that you are called to be.

. . . Something like that.

For our purposes here, consider this letter to be a *missionary guide* (have I said that often enough?). Shortly we will look back over the first five chapters of Ephesians, and at the portrait Paul paints for the purpose of the church's calling in the eternal and eschatological design of God in Christ. We will see how he reminds them of the redemptive relationships, and the *gifting* of the church, so that the community and its constituent members will be equipped for participation in this mission.

Think, then, of all that precedes this "whole armor" passage as something of a *prolegomenon* (an explanatory introduction) to their calling to be the community that incarnates the divine nature right in the midst of that strategic *civitas*, that commercial center called Ephesus, that aggressive culture of darkness—then translate that into whatever your own *civitas*, or scene of your own incarnation, might be.

THE ARMOR OF LIGHT

What Paul knows is that all the forces of hell are bent on keeping the Ephesian believers from being that very incarnation of the community of light, of the kingdom of God, of God's new creation. I love the description of the church by some of our Latin American colleagues as the missionary arm of the Holy Trinity.[10] Paul knows that they aren't going to make it unless they are adequately and maturely equipped. (It is no less so in Atlanta, lest you forget the immediate challenges that face each of us in the twenty-first century.)

How, then, to communicate to these Ephesian followers of Christ the specifics, the practicalities, of how they needed to be equipped for

10. In particular, by José Miguez Bonino, *Faces of Latin American Protestantism* (Grand Rapids: Eerdmans, 1997), 141.

their confrontation with this present darkness? He is indicating that for them (and us) to fail to come to grips with our need of the armor of God will be disastrous. This is to say that if we fail to put on this armor we will not still be standing at the end of this evil day. But that raises yet another question: What is the evil day? Or where do we encounter the evil day?

And, comes the answer: the evil day is here and now.

The evil day is this present moment and this very place. It is not, ordinarily, some dramatic or esoteric spiritual battlefield, such as was Luther's nailing of his *Ninety-Five Theses* to the cathedral door at Wittenberg, or Christians choosing to be thrown to the lions rather than deny Christ in the early generations of the church's history—though it might well come to that for some. Rather, it is probably more like the reflection of Ransom about his somewhat hidden role in the ultimate design of Maleldil (the god figure), in C. S. Lewis's *Perelandra*. He muses to himself: "This chapter, this page, this very sentence, in the cosmic story was utterly and eternally itself; no other passage that had occurred or would ever occur could be substituted for it."[11]

Our calling is to be authentic, discerning, steadfast, and faithful demonstrations of God's new creation humanity right in the midst of the *daily stuff* of home, neighborhood, workplace, schools, office, shop . . . whatever, and wherever, our lot falls. It most likely will never be in some dramatic military-type engagement, such as in the hymn: "The Son of God goes forth to war . . . who follows in his train?" No, our probable scene of encountering the darkness will much more likely be in the ordinary, unsuspected, and accepted circumstances dwelling seductively both inside the *religious Christianity*[12] of the church and in our daily marketplace. (It may well appear in some well-touted spiritual program!)

Our calling to be the children of the light is our daily mission.

It may also involve engaging the darkness right in the midst of the church, but it will always depend upon our putting on the daily dress of the divine nature given to us, and self-consciously seeking to be the glory of God wherever that may take us. It is a calling to excellence in whatever our hand finds to do. It is (to use James Davison Hunter's

---

11. C. S. Lewis, *Perelandra* (New York: Macmillan, 1944), 146.

12. This description of a culturally and politically accommodated version of the faith and the church was used by Dietrich Bonhoeffer to describe what he was encountering in the German church during the Nazi regime in Germany.

term) a calling to *faithful presence* as God's kingdom people, and thus becoming a culture transforming force.[13] It is (to use Stanley Hauerwas's suggestion) to seek to be *significant* in the sense of lives of "quiet serenity, capable of attending with love to the everyday without need to be recognized as 'making a difference.'"[14]

We are to stand in the armor of light wherever we are, and all the time. It is when we least expect the *relentless darkness* that we are in the most danger! So, back to Paul's teaching on the daily dress of every follower of Jesus Christ, which will enable him or her *to stand* in whatever circumstance, routine, or challenge each day brings in each believer's life, inside of the church and out. This is not the armor provided for some *extraordinary* Christian workers—the Christian counterpart, say, of the Navy Seals—but rather, that of every ordinary believer. It is that necessary dress that creates us as authentic new creation persons and communities, and as such, the children of the light.

It is as such that we give the lie to the prince of darkness and his dominion. It is in faithfully wearing this dress that we overcome the devil. It is wearing this that displays in our lives the divine nature, and thus our faithful presence as kingdom folk.

From his own Hebrew roots, Paul, no doubt, calls up Isaiah's metaphor: "[The Lord] . . . put on righteousness as a breastplate, and a helmet of salvation on his head; he put on garments of vengeance for clothing, and wrapped himself in zeal as a cloak" (Isa 59:17). At the same time, he would be quite confident that with the omnipresence of Roman soldiers in Ephesus, this same metaphor would be effective with the Ephesians. So, using that metaphor he spells out the essentials of their own visible daily dress, which would be necessary for their (and our) faithful missionary confrontation in their assigned place of kingdom presence— their calling to be "salt and light" in the midst of all the "unspiritual" and gritty realities of their lives in that city.

Paul, elsewhere, has a proclivity of choosing to use the image of clothing to represent the visible and demonstrable kingdom incarna-

13. James Davison Hunter, "Toward a New City Commons: Reflections on a Theology of Faithful Presence," essay III in *To Change the World* (New York: Oxford University Press, 2010).

14. Stanley Hauerwas, *Hannah's Child* (Grand Rapids: Eerdmans, 2010), 95–96.

tion, which Christ's followers are to regularly put on. Notable is his word to the church in Rome: "The night is far gone; the day is at hand. So then let us cast off the works of darkness and put on the armor of light. . . . But put on the Lord Jesus Christ, and make no provision for the flesh, to gratify its desires" (Rom 13:12, 14).

To the church at Galatia he would write: "For as many of you as were baptized into Christ have put on Christ" (Gal 3:27).

Or, in the Ephesian letter: ". . . put off your old self, which belongs to your former manner of life and is corrupt through deceitful desires, and be renewed in the spirit of your minds, and put on the new self, created in the likeness of God in true righteousness and holiness" (Eph 4:22b–24).

And to the church at Colossae he would write: "Put on then, as God's chosen ones, holy and beloved, compassion, kindness, humility, meekness, and patience, bearing with one another, and, if one has a complaint against another, forgiving each other, as the Lord has forgiven you. . . . And above all these put on love, which binds everything together in perfect harmony" (Col 3:12–14).

Such apostolic instruction to put on a whole and radically new way of life that demonstrates the very divine nature, the glory of God . . . is, by its very essence, *countercultural* . . . or, as has been said by some: such lives stand "in missionary confrontation with the world."[15] Such passages give us strong clues about how we are to understand this "whole armor" passage in Ephesians 6, how such armor enables us to stand, what it is that we are standing against, and how we engage in such a confrontation. It is the existential reality of this warfare here and now that I want to bring within our reach.

At the same time, it seems to have been more than a little urgent for the apostle to say it to the Ephesian followers of Christ. For us, it is equally urgent to hear it today, and wherever we live.

First of all, as I have noted above, this is a *metaphor*. It is a teaching tool. It is a practical aid, or a checklist, that is simple and graphic and easily called to mind.[16] Then, remember that these pieces are all symbi-

---

15. Lesslie Newbigin, among others, employs this figure of a redemptive confrontation.

16. Many Christians are familiar with St. Patrick's "Breastplate," celebrated in song and in spiritual formation literature. For Patrick it was important each day, as he laced up his tunic, to make each course a reminder of a specific essential for his Christian mission: the triune God, God the creator, Christ's birth, death and resurrection, etc. He reminded himself each day with this simple discipline.

otic, i.e., they inform and interpret each other. They relate to each other and are interconnected. Consider also that there is nothing new here. It is worth remembering that in chapter 4 of this same letter Paul gave us a fascinating and much-overlooked clue to the place and express purpose of the *gifts* given to the church by the risen Lord Jesus: ". . . to equip the saints for the work of ministry, for the building up of the body of Christ" (4:12).

If one stops and reflects on that earlier passage, one will note that Paul commented there that the ascended Lord gave gifts to the church to "equip the saints" and to grow them up into mature, functioning, fruitful participants in the ongoing ministry of the mission of God in the world. But that raises another question: What, we might well ask, would be necessary to constitute, or create, *mature saints*? What would such a mature follower look like? This is not at all a theoretical question. Paul writes this letter "to the *saints* who are in Ephesus" (1:1). He never foresees any follower of Jesus as being somehow a passive consumer of *church stuff*.

Which could raise another question for us: In chapter two, he tells the Ephesian believers that God's grace has saved them through their faith, and so created in Christ "for good works" (2:8–10). So what would those "good works" look like in our flesh and blood lives here and now? I am proposing that the metaphor of the whole armor gives us a rich clue into the answer to such a question.

This present (chapter 6) teaching, then, about the whole armor gives us strong clues as to the answer to all of these questions. It spells out a simple catalog of kingdom character qualities, qualities that will enable us to stand in the evil day. This is a good starting point. We will find, in various writings of Paul, that he will add more specifics about this necessary equipment.

Paul will also, elsewhere, set himself up as a model of what he is teaching: "What you have learned and received and heard and seen in me—practice these things, and the God of peace will be with you" (Phil 4:9). This is critical. The *equippers* are also to be models of what they are given to provide for the church. What we learn and receive and hear are not to be abstract theories, but are to be modeled in the practitioners or . . . *equippers*. The disciples of Jesus need to have models, and they need to be models themselves of what Jesus called them to be and to do.[17]

---

17. As I write this, one of the remarkable Christian teachers of the twentieth century has died: John R. W. Stott. Stott was not only a gifted expositor of Scripture, but was a

We need to remember, also, that Jesus himself was continually reminding his followers that it was those who *had his word and kept it* who were his true disciples . . . and that, in the end, it all depended on knowing him (Matt 7:21–27). Those who missed this critical principle, Jesus stated, were like those who built their house upon the sand. Conversely, the house built upon the rock consists in one's knowledge of Christ's teachings, obedience to them, and all this in response to one's faith in, and love for, Christ. Our teaching here in Ephesians 6 has a similar ring to it.

So, let's begin.

COSMIC POWERS, SPIRITUAL FORCES OF DARKNESS, SCHEMES . . . AND ALL OF THAT

For the sake of emphasis, allow me to include a refresher question here (mainly because this subject is so tragically missing in most discussions about our calling): What's this ominous prediction about spiritual forces of evil, and such, all about? What is Paul thinking as he introduces this final word to the Ephesian believers with such an urgent warning?

It really should not surprise us. Remember that in Jesus' introduction of the whole subject of the church that he would build (Matt 16:18–19) . . . he did so in the context of "the gates of hell," which would oppose such a building, but would not ultimately be able to prevail against it.

That *heads-up* by Jesus is inextricably connected to this very point that Paul is trying to seal in the minds and hearts of this missionary community—and by extension, to our minds in our own North Park (or St. John's-on-the-Boulevard, or Shalom Community, or the church at Tom and Betsy's house, or whatever our particular Christian community is called). Satan's ultimate *scheme* is to render the church impotent as a dynamic factor in the mission of God, which mission is to declare the gospel of the kingdom throughout this whole world.

This ever-present reality of the *relentless darkness* makes most critical, for us, what he is presenting to them. These new believers must be alert, and must be equipped to recognize the satanic subversions, i.e., "the schemes of the devil." Frankly, the church has definitely *not* been

---

beautiful model of Christian wisdom, humility, gentleness, love—not to mention his keen intellect. One could get close to John Stott. He was personable. His love for Jesus Christ was contagious. Yet his quiet demeanor and the twinkle in his eye were disarming. He was to many of us the epitome of Philippians 4:9.

all too swift in this department for most of its career. When Satan drops the iron fist on the church, such as happened with the Roman Empire in the early centuries, or with the "Cultural Revolution" in China, or other oppressive regimes in our own present moment—then the church wakes up and recognizes the satanic opposition for what it is.

But . . . when Satan comes clandestinely and seductively *inside* the church as an "angel of light," and takes his place among the respected participants and traditions, then the church all to often succumbs to the drift away from its mission, and gladly engages in religious activities that distract it, and have no relationship to its primary purpose. It is that seduction away from the church's missionary *raison d'être* that we must address here.

And again, it is no less a confrontation when the *relentless darkness* so interprets to us the cultural setting in which we live that some counterfeit good, some political agenda, some social movement that is inimical to God's glory and purpose for his people, conforms even God's people to "this world" (it is to such conformity that Paul speaks in Romans 12:1–2).

First: The Belt of Truth

"Stand therefore, having fastened on the belt of truth . . ."

In New Testament Christianity, Jesus is the Truth. Jesus is the glory of God in flesh and blood. Jesus is the focus of the mission of God, and it is as such *Incarnate Truth* that all else is interpreted and understood. The priority of the Christian's armor is: Jesus, the Truth.

There is no way that this belt of truth is anything other than the requirement that the Christian warrior (i.e., every follower of Jesus) be keenly focused on, and informed by, the centrality of Jesus Christ: his teachings, his life, his death and resurrection, his ascension, and the certainty of his ultimate return—all that is contained in the four Gospels.

There is no way that this can be any abstract philosophical concept of truth.

Consider who is writing this, after all. We're talking about the same Paul who says elsewhere: "But put on the Lord Jesus" (Rom 13:14); "For I decided to know nothing among you except Jesus Christ and him crucified" (1 Cor 2:2); "But far be it from me to boast except in the cross of our Lord Jesus Christ, by which the world has been crucified unto me, and I unto the world" (Gal 6:14); and ". . . my little children, for whom I am in anguish again in the anguish of childbirth until Christ be formed in you" (Gal 4:16).

Lest there be any doubt that the belt of truth refers to Jesus Christ, ponder especially his awesome description of Christ in Colossians 1:15–20:

> He is the image of the invisible God, the firstborn of all creation. For by him all things were created, in heaven and on earth, visible and invisible whether thrones or dominions or rulers or authorities—all things were created through him and for him. And he is before all things, and in him all things hold together. And he is the head of the body, the church. He is the beginning, the firstborn from the dead, *that in everything he might be preeminent.* For in him all the fullness of God was pleased to dwell, and through him to reconcile to himself all things, whether on earth or in heaven, making peace by the blood of his cross.

And as if that were not sufficient, then look at Jesus' own self-definition: "I, even I, am the way and the truth, and the life" (John 14:6, author's translation). In another discourse he identifies himself as the truth when he tells his disciples: "If you abide in my word, you are truly my disciples, and you will know the truth, and the truth will set you free. . . . So if the Son sets you free, you will be free indeed" (John 8:31b–32, 36). The truth will set you free . . . and the Son is that truth.

Our daily dress as Christ's followers, both individually and as a community, begins with our formation in Christ, with the truth—the knowledge of who Christ is, the knowledge of his life and death and resurrection, and our faithful obedience to his teachings about that kingdom of God—that kingdom which he came to inaugurate.

A first scheme of the devil is now, and always has been, to ever so slightly take the church's focus off of Jesus, to deny his uniqueness, or to somehow obfuscate the biblical understanding of his incarnation. How easily the church becomes preoccupied with *religion*, or with its own institutional life, that it unwittingly neglects its whole reason for existence.[18]

---

18. Case in point is the church at Laodicea (Rev 3:14ff.), which had left Christ outside the door. The whole section of letters to the seven churches concludes with this exhortation: "He who has ears to hear, let him hear what the Spirit says to the churches" (3:22). It is obviously quite easy to become deaf to the Spirit.

The drift that Alan questioned me about at the Trackside Tavern, not uncommonly, begins with the drift away from the centrality of the Truth: Jesus Christ. Jesus is the light that the darkness cannot abide.

"Stand therefore, having fastened on the belt of truth."

The Breastplate of Righteousness

In the marketplace of daily life, and in the context of the dominion of darkness, the children of light are to be visible by their works. This piece of the armor has to do with our *character*, or our *praxis*, as the bearers of the divine nature: God's righteousness. Those fellow sojourners who are our neighbors and friends and associates can't see what we believe or think . . . but they are keen observers of who we are, of how we relate, respond, and live out our life in Christ in the daily routines and stresses of life.

Jesus, early on in his career, spelled out kingdom *character* and *praxis* in his Sermon on the Mount (Matthew 5–7) and his Sermon on the Plain (Luke 6). He concludes the first part of the Sermon on the Mount by saying: "You are the light of the world. A city set upon a hill cannot be hidden . . . let your light shine before others, so that they may see your good works and give glory to your Father who is in heaven" (Matt 5:14–16).

For our purposes here, let me say that I am convinced that living out the Sermon on the Mount is essentially synonymous with "putting on the breastplate of righteousness."

The figure of a breastplate of righteousness is out of Isaiah, where the Lord "put on righteousness as a breastplate" (59:17). Righteousness is also descriptive of the divine nature that has been given to us. There are early references about God's intent to create his chosen ones as those who "keep the way of the Lord by doing righteousness and justice" (Gen 18:19). Paul wrote to the Christians in Rome that, before they turned to Christ, they were slaves to sin and death, but by their obedience to Christ they have become "slaves of righteousness" (Rom 6:15–18). And the (often controversial) letter of James extols the place of that kingdom behavior, of the works of righteousness that makes our faith visible to the watching world.

The children of darkness . . . those sojourners whom someone described as "spiritually confused god-seekers," are totally unimpressed by religion, and by religious talk, but they cannot deny, or gainsay, the life that incarnates the image of Christ. Hence, I deliberately want to underscore the essential nature of this piece of the armor. It has nothing to do with "going to church," and everything to do with the mission of God in the world.

For Shoes: The Readiness of the Gospel of Peace

Oh, yes! Never forget that Paul is a missionary church planter.

When those to whom he writes have fastened on their belt of truth, and put on the breastplate of righteousness . . . then they put on their feet their readiness to be part of the mission of turning men and women from darkness to the light, and from the dominion of Satan (darkness) to the dominion of God's dear Son. In so doing, they forsake any passivity about the darkness and the dwellers in the darkness around them. They are imbued with "the gospel of peace." They become the embodiment (individually and communally) of the Jesus who came to "seek and to save those who are lost," to be the "light of the world" in whatever circumstances they find themselves. They put on the shoes of "the readiness given by the gospel of peace" (Eph 6:15).

Again, this figure comes from Isaiah's prophecy: "How beautiful upon the mountains are the feet of him who brings good news, who publishes peace, who brings good news of happiness, who publishes salvation . . ." (Isa 52:7). Paul will pick up this figure again in his letter to the Christians in Rome: ". . . 'everyone who calls upon the name of the Lord will be saved.' But how are they to call upon him in whom they have not believed? And how are they to believe in him of whom they have never heard? And how are they to hear without someone preaching? And how are they to preach unless they are sent? As it is written, 'How beautiful are the feet of those who preach the good news!'" (Rom 10:13–15).

The bottom line here is that this gospel of peace needs feet, i.e., it needs messengers. And Paul is saying that an essential part of every believer's daily dress (or armor) is that his or her feet are available for the task of being messengers[19] of this gospel of peace.

---

19. Don't get put off by the word "preach" in these texts. This is a matter of communication by whatever means. It can be heralding something publicly in the town square, or the quiet conversation over coffee, or almost any conceivable method of telling the other(s) of God's peace. Maybe even email or a blog should be included in this information age.

Christ's true followers have their Father's DNA in them: "As the Father has sent me, even so do I send you" (John 20:21). This is true both individually and communally.

It is worth pausing to look at this designation of the gospel as the "gospel of peace." Other scriptures remind us that Jesus made "peace by the blood of his cross" (Col 1:20); "blessed are the peacemakers" (Matt 5:9); "For [Jesus] is our peace" (Eph 2:14); "And [Jesus] came and preached peace" (Eph 2:17) . . . among others. This description is so beautiful, and so poignant as we confront a culture of discontent, and lives in turmoil. It is fascinating to consider that it is also one of the weapons of our warfare, by which we aggressively destroy the strongholds of darkness in the lives of real people whom we know.

And *readiness* instructs us that we are to be expectant in the ordinary and extraordinary of each day's experiences. Surprises. Interruptions. Whatever our lot, we are ready. Paul, in another letter, says something of the same thing as he explains that Christ has reconciled us to God, and then given to us the ministry of reconciliation . . . entrusting to us the message of reconciliation. We are, in Christ, reconciled to God, but then we are reconciled to each other, and that message of reconciliation becomes our ministry as Christ's ambassadors (2 Cor 5:18–21).

The Ephesians passage before us says that it is everyone's mission. When Paul (as we wrote above) found the dozen believers in Ephesus, it was not long before all Asia Minor heard the word of the Lord. This could only have happened if this infant colony of the gospel was faithful in this ministry. And we also need to be reminded that the context is not always congenial—more likely hostile or dismissive. It reminds us that our context is the dominion of darkness, and that we are agents of the light.

Two unusual illustrations may be useful here. In the outbreak of the gospel that took place in the early 1970s called "the Jesus Revolution," there was one ministry in that awakening that called itself: the Christian World Liberation Front. The leader, Dr. Jack Sparks, was a former university professor who saw the darkness in the lives of that counterculture among the restless and rebellious younger generation. He, with a small band of other Christians, moved into the heart of the counterculture scene in Berkeley, California.

I had spent a couple of weeks with that movement learning their methods and observing their lives. It was something so amazing that I had never witnessed before. When I asked Jack Sparks how he explained the fruitfulness of it, and the obvious working of the Spirit of God to open eyes and hearts to the gospel, his gave an answer worth repeating here: "I believe that God delights to do his saving work where the darkness is the greatest!" And so I watched God at work in that scene, and the gospel of peace brought peace to a host of those who had been captive to the darkness.

The second illustration is from recent missionary reports. There has been a team of Mennonite missioners who have been seeking dialogue with militant Islamists, and have been very fruitful in doing so. Their approach is right in the front door of asking for conversations. They simply tell their Islamic conversation partners that Jesus came preaching peace, and forgiveness of enemies, and reconciliation. They also remind these folk that the Quran also speaks of peace, so that there should be some common ground to meet and remove hostilities. Amazingly, such an approach has born fruit. How do you gainsay love for enemies and forgiveness, and a message of peace?

This piece of the armor is also informed by, and informs, "the sword of the Spirit," which is the speaking of the word of God, to which we will come shortly.

The Christian warrior (every believer) moves toward those sojourners who are still outside in the darkness. They do not create ghettos of believers fortifying themselves against the risks of the mission inside their church clubhouses . . . but, rather, are eager to be light, to be messengers of the gospel of peace.[20] In Atlanta, as was undoubtedly true in Ephesus, there are all the ethnicities, the minorities, the literate and illiterate, the social classes, the lifestyles, the multiplicity of world religions, the sexual orientations, along with whatever the current dominant social order might involve.

---

20. A lesson may be learned here from the experience of the church in China. The gospel grew "out of control" when the government expropriated their church buildings, and outlawed the Christian church. So the church went into homes and "underground" and continued to grow very rapidly. When some were imprisoned, they no longer had to be secretive, and so made concentration camps a place of proclamation of the gospel of peace, and it kept growing. In the midst, the fires of persecution kept the church close to its New Testament roots.

It is in this context that we are called to put on the whole armor of God. Actually, for us, this is more than thrilling . . . it is a missionary challenge and opportunity that no other has ever had, or ever faced: that of bringing the light and Life into the crumbling remnants of the Christendom darkness, into the post-Christian context that has been put off by so much that has called itself: Christian.

Thus far . . . this all sounds good in *theory*, in the abstract. It sounds quite plausible while sitting in the ambience of our community's worship gatherings singing: "Onward Christian soldiers, marching as to war . . ."[21] or "Who is on the Lord's side? Who will face the foe . . . ?"[22] or "Behold! The Christian warrior stands . . ."[23] . . . but then comes the reality of our daily missionary confrontation with the *darkness* in the context our 24/7 daily incarnations, and we are likely to think back to those hymns and say: "What was that all about?"

For most of us, the confrontation will not be all that dramatic or consequential as it was, say, for one such as Dietrich Bonhoeffer as he sought to stand in the face of the wickedness of the Nazi attempts to co-opt the church, and to redefine the Christian faith. Or, perhaps like the late U.S. Senator Mark Hatfield, whose Christian convictions opposing U.S. militarism put him into conflict with his own Republican colleagues, and in opposition to the engagement of the United States in the Vietnam War. No, rather, for most of us it will be more subtle and less obvious, but equally as effective for rendering us "saltless salt."

Before we go on, it is worth remembering that the "schemes of the devil" will never cease to seek (quite skillfully) to minimize, or trivialize, or forget, or theologically redefine one or all of these pieces of the armor into something that is not that much of a threat to Satan's dominion of darkness. Church history is replete with incidents of such vulnerability, which has periodically rendered the church sterile in the mission of God.

Be alert!

But now, on to *the shield of faith* . . .

---

21. "Onward Christian Soldiers," by Sabine Baring-Gould (1864).

22. "Who Is on the Lord's Side," by Frances Ridley Havergal (1877).

23. "Behold the Christian Warrior Stands," by James Montgomery (c. 1850).

In All Circumstances: Take Up the Shield of Faith

God's "saints" may be ever so faithful in girding on truth, in wearing the breastplate of righteousness, and committed to wearing the shoes of readiness in our obedience to the mission of God . . . but there will inevitably come those insinuations of the darkness, questioning all that we are, all that we believe about Jesus, all we are doing, and by every other devious means, in order to intimidate or frighten us away from the mission given us by our Lord Jesus Christ. One has only to read the church's history, or the biographies of God's faithful people, to see that such doubts nearly always appear to challenge and erode that same faithfulness.

"Who are you to think you can do this?"
"What will people think?"
"Don't rock the boat."
"How can you believe such a weird thing?"
"You will upset your neighbors."

Or, our own "in all circumstances" may involve those compromising assaults such as temptations to ungodly behavior or to doubt (and self-doubt), despair, or hopelessness. They may involve external assaults, persecution, imprisonment, or threat of death. They may also insert false teachings. And not a few believers have been destroyed by moral, ethical, or sexual assaults. The list is endless. Satan knows a person's weak spots, and he knows a particular Christianity community's places of vulnerability. One only has to read the letters to the seven churches in Asia Minor (Revelation 2–3) to see graphic examples of this.

It is the awareness of this clash of kingdoms that would provoke Paul, then, to use the metaphor of the Roman soldier's shield, and its purpose against terrifying weaponry. The shield mentioned here was a whole-body shield. It was something like four feet tall and two feet wide, made of a couple of layers of wood and covered with leather. You could hide behind it. This wasn't the little round shield, which was useful in a different kind of conflict. The reason? Fiery darts. In warfare, armies used darts, or arrows, or javelin-like weapons that were dipped in pitch and ignited, then hurled at the enemy to inflict both fear and painful damage. The tall shield was an effective defense against such.

The imagery of God being our shield goes back to the beginning of Scripture. God told Abraham: "I am your shield; your reward . . ." (Gen 15:1). The psalmist will say: "The Lord is my strength and my shield"

(Ps 28:7). Here, Paul is teaching us that *faith* is what this shield is all about. That raises its own question: How to define *faith* in this image? Paul has spoken of faith numerous times in this letter already.[24] His own understanding of the rich substance of this faith is perhaps described in his prayer for them earlier (Eph 3:16–19). It speaks of the believers laying hold of God's resources and power given in Christ, appropriating the promises of God.

The New Testament conception of faith always has within it the components of *repentance, knowledge, trust* (or *confidence* in Jesus and his word), *the promises of God,* and *obedient response*—which includes a strong *moral-volitional* element. Jesus came preaching "repentance and faith" (cf. Mark 1:15). There is always the reality that we, by an act of will, must turn *from* our affinity, or bondage, to the rebellion and the dominion of darkness . . . and deliberately embrace Jesus as the true Lord of all.

Paul has already reminded the Ephesians (in chapter 2) that they were once dead in their sins, and following the course of this world and its prince of darkness . . . but that God in his mercy has delivered them, that they are saved by grace through faith, and are now his workmanship created in Christ Jesus for good works. Such a passage gives us the flavor of the reality of combined repentance and faith, and the resultant good works. They are rescued out of the dominion of darkness and translated into the dominion of God's dear Son, into God's new creation in Christ. By the grace of God they are God's new creation (kingdom of God) folk. Such confidence informs us as to the necessity of the shield of faith in the warfare.

There is also Jesus' word that those who are really his not only confess him and embrace him, but also *do* his works, or keep his commandments (Matt 7:21–27).

We have seen this rich understanding already in the belt of truth, the breastplate of righteousness, and the shoes of the readiness of the gospel of peace. It is our embrace of both the promises and the commands of Jesus as well as our continual renunciation of the dominion of darkness, no matter the consequences. We will see it again when we look at the helmet of salvation, and that will have to do about our minds being formed by the plan hidden from the ages, but now revealed in Jesus.

What it is all about is *Jesus.*

---

24. Eph 1:13, 15, 19; 2:8; 3:12, 17; 4:5,13.

Our *faith* is in who Jesus is, in what he has done, in what he has taught, and in what he calls us to be and to do . . . that he is God made flesh and blood, come to reconcile the world unto God by his blood—the central reality of time and eternity. It is a confidence in what are called "the unsearchable riches of Christ" by Paul earlier in this letter (3:8). This is our faith. This is what makes the shield of faith such a crucial piece of God's armor given to us.

Its absence makes us totally vulnerable. "The forces of the evil one are incredibly powerful, and left to our own devices we would certainly fail."[25]

Such faith is, and has always been, such a vital part of the life of faith among God's people. Think back to the prophet Habakkuk: "Though the fig tree should not blossom, nor fruit be on the vines, the produce of the olive fail and the fields yield no food, the flock be cut off from the fold and there be no herd in the stalls, yet will I rejoice in the Lord; I will take joy in the God of my salvation. God, the Lord, is my strength; he makes my feet like the deer's; he makes me tread on high places" (Hab 3:17–19). That is to say, when all of the physical evidences are missing, yet there is a confidence in God and his promises. This is faith.

This passage before us also has within it something of the necessity of Jesus' own teaching about the cost of discipleship in Luke 14:25–33: "So, therefore, any of you who does not renounce all that he has cannot be my disciple" (v. 33). It is, perhaps, most eloquently spelled out in Paul's testimony to Timothy about the reasons that he is able to endure such sufferings for the gospel (2 Tim 1:8–14), which includes this affirmation: ". . . for I know whom I have believed, and I am convinced that he is able to guard until that Day what has been entrusted to me" (v. 12).

In a later century, the Heidelberg confessors (1562) would eloquently answer the question "What is your only comfort, in life and in death?" with the stirring answer:

> That I belong—body and soul, in life and in death—not to myself but to my faithful Savior, Jesus Christ, who at the cost of his own blood has fully paid for all my sins and has completely freed me from the dominion of the devil; that he protects me so well that without the will of my Father in heaven not a hair can fall from my head; indeed, that everything must fit his purpose for my sal-

---

25. Peter T. O'Brien, *The Letter to the Ephesians* (Grand Rapids: Eerdmans, 1999), 480.

vation. Therefore by his Holy Spirit, he also assures me of eternal life, and makes me wholeheartedly willing and ready from now on to live for him.[26]

Let me say it once more: Whenever we set ourselves to put on Christ, and our readiness to be engaged in the mission of God, in the gospel of the kingdom of God . . . count on it: some kind of counter-suggestion or attack will come . . . some gossip, some insinuations, some taunts within our subconscious, some self-doubt, some hint of negative consequences. In such we are encouraged by our New Testament faith to put on the whole armor, to lay hold of Christ's promises, to renounce the dominion of Satan, to bind the strong man by the power of the greater (Luke 11:22), for such is the shield of faith: our "ultimate defense against the devil's strategies."[27]

Yes, our missional incarnation is humanly impossible, but we dare not succumb to the suggestions to compromise, to leave out the sharp edges, to forsake the field, or: to leave well enough alone.

In John's Revelation, there is the account of God's saints conquering the beast (Satan): "And they have conquered him by the blood of the Lamb and by the word of their testimony, for they loved not their lives unto death" (12:11).

No matter the consequences, we are called to walk as children of the light, and so to dispel the *darkness*, and in this walk we daily, of necessity, must "take up the shield of faith."

All of this presupposes, also, that our minds are being renewed into the image of the creator, in knowledge—minds formed by the word of Christ, minds renewed by the Spirit. Such a presupposition reminds us again of the inter-animation of all of these pieces of the armor on the others. There is a proclivity of the church to allow one or another of these pieces of the armor to be trivialized, or forgotten, or replaced . . . so subtly . . . *that no one seems to notice.*

When this does, in fact, take place, it is so tragic because it gives the *darkness* another entrée into the individual believer, or into the com-

---

26. Question #1 from the Heidelberg Catechism.

27. Frank Thielman, *Ephesians* (Grand Rapids: Baker Academic, 2010), 427.

munity, which significantly hinders their ability to "stand against the schemes of the devil."

So now we turn to *the helmet of salvation.*

"Take the Helmet of Salvation"

Once again, Paul reaches back to this figure of armor from the prophet Isaiah: "The LORD saw it, and it displeased him that there was no justice. . . . He put . . . a helmet of salvation on his head" (59:15, 17).

Again, I want to ask my readers to allow me some interpretative liberty here, because it is far too easy to nod our assent to this exhortation, but to miss how crucial it is if we are to stand against the very real schemes of the darkness that perennially assault the believer and the Christian community. I want to look at the helmet from the perspective of our practical understanding, and our daily discipline of putting on the whole armor as it has to do with our mental and intellectual vulnerability. Such an interpretation of this metaphor may need a dose of healthy imagination.

First of all, *salvation* is a huge word. It is on one hand a very versatile word. It can refer to my own personal saving encounter with Jesus Christ. But it also has all kinds of breathtaking cosmological, salvific, and eschatological dimensions that encompass God's eternal purpose to reconcile the world unto himself, and to create all things new in Christ Jesus.

Paul has already spoken of that "mystery of his will, according to his purpose, which he set forth in Christ as a plan for the fullness of time, to unite all things in heaven and things on earth" (Eph 1:9–10); and "what is the plan of the mystery hidden for ages in God who created all things" (3:9). Add to those descriptions (which suspend the horizons of ordinary thinking) his prayer that the Ephesian followers of Christ "may have strength to comprehend with all the saints what is the breadth and length and height and depth, and to know the love of Christ which surpasses knowledge, that you may be filled with all the fullness of God" (3:18–19).

Stop and contemplate that. What has been revealed in the coming of Jesus is the revelation of what this whole creation is all about: *the mystery hidden for the ages, now made known through Jesus Christ.*

Hold that for the moment and look at the figure of the helmet. The helmet goes on the believer's *head.* What needs divine protection is the believer's head, which is where his or her *mind* is located. This should ring a familiar bell to those familiar with New Testament teachings. Paul's letter to the Christians in Rome contains the familiar passage: "Do not be conformed to this world, but be transformed by the renewing of your mind, that by testing you may discern what is the will of God" (Rom 12:2). The renewed mind is a critical component in our engagement with this present age, the dominion of darkness.

That may sound simple enough, but don't be taken in too easily by the subversions of the darkness. Yes, to "take the helmet of salvation" is to equip your mind with the knowledge of God's salvation—but please note what we have been trying to assert from the beginning of this conversation: God's great salvation in Jesus Christ is *radically countercultural*. To have one's mind formed by such kingdom teachings as the Sermon on the Mount is not tame religion. It does not promise "safety, certainty and enjoyment."[28] Rather, it puts us in missionary confrontation with most, if not all, dominant cultures within which we live (even within all too many church communities).

If the breastplate of righteousness is understood as the behavior, or the *praxis*, of the kingdom of God (of new creation)—perhaps better stated as our *living Christianly*—then the helmet of salvation might well be defined as *thinking Christianly*. It is the mind formed by the gospel of the kingdom of God, formed by the knowledge of Scripture, or: the mind of Christ.[29]

But that sounds too simple.

The thinking so formed is not genteel religious meditation, but rather a radically, and transformationally, new understanding of God's design for his creation in and through Jesus Christ. It informs our conception of the mission of God.[30]

The Christian mind (the helmet of salvation) discerns, by the Spirit, the thought patterns of the darkness, the omnipresent *zeitgeists* that assault every generation, the "other gospels" that offer themselves to us perennially, the ever-so-slight aberrations of the truth given us in Christ that in time lead us off into some truncated or trivialized or distorted

---

28. This was the title of a very widely used gospel tract a generation ago.

29. 1 Cor 2:16.

30. Theologian Stanley Hauerwas (someplace) describes the result of such kingdom thinking as: "Making the world the world." I like that. It enables us to be agents of God's new creation in Christ.

version of New Testament Christianity. This becomes a critical and daily discipline for every believer. The Christian mind, the helmet of salvation, is not the preserve of some elite class of intellectuals, or theologians, or the church's "ordained" pastors. Rather, it is a practical and necessary part of the armor of every saint, no matter how modest or simple his or her gifts in the community might be.

One can be grateful for skillful teachers and theologians, but if New Testament Christianity, the living and thinking of the kingdom of God, are reserved only for the academy, or for church professionals . . . then they contradict their very reason for being. The purpose of such gifts is so that *all* of God's people may be equipped for their work of ministry, and may grow into maturity—may grow up into Christ (Eph 4:12–16). This also is a primary function of the Christ's commission to "make disciples . . . teaching them to observe all that I have commanded you"(Matt 28:19–20).

As the prince of darkness is able to diminish this discipline of *thinking Christianly*, then the whole of the mission of God is diminished.

An example of this is my own particular tradition within the body of Christ. The Presbyterian church is a venerable old Reformation tradition, which was founded on solid biblical and theological foundations several centuries ago. It has produced impressive confessional statements, and had an impressive history in the larger church. But over the generations the tradition drifted from its roots. Its self-consciousness of its biblical and theological and missional treasures was displaced by institutional hubris and a comfortable place in the society. Result? It began to diminish in influence, and worship, and growth, and mission.

Twenty or more years ago, a denominational poll was taken to assess the health of the denomination, and discerned that the Presbyterian Church (USA) was essentially a denomination of biblically and theologically illiterate laity! It had ceased to equip it constituent members to *think Christianly* . . . and no one seemed to notice, or be particularly disturbed. And the Presbyterian church is far from alone in this drift, alas![31]

31. During my own pastoral sojourn in the city of New Orleans, I was in proximity, and marginally involved, with the charismatic movement within the Roman Catholic community there. What was interesting was that when these traditional Roman

≈ ≈ ≈

"Take the helmet of salvation!"

In his second epistle, Peter begins with a word of promise, which says that grace and peace are to be multiplied to us "in the knowledge of God and of Jesus our Lord." He follows that with the assurance that God's divine power has granted to us all things that pertain to life and godliness "through the knowledge of him who called us to his own glory and excellence" (2 Pet 1:2–3). And then he closes this same epistle with the exhortation to us to "grow in the grace and knowledge of our Lord and Savior Jesus Christ" (3:18).

Yes, and in Paul's fascinating teachings about the practical results of God's calling of us, we learn that the (predestined) purpose is first of all that we be conformed to the image of his Son (Rom 8:29). He fleshes that out in another passage by teaching us that that image of the God in us includes "true righteousness and holiness" (Eph 4:24). But then, apropos to our discussion here about the helmet of salvation, he teaches that this new self is "being renewed in *knowledge* after the image of its creator" (Col 3:10).

And, dear reader, connect the dots: this helmet of salvation, this mind "renewed in knowledge after the image of its creator" . . . informs all of the other components of the whole armor of God, and equips us for our daily participation in the *mission of God* in the particular marketplace in which each one of us lives and operates.

Why does this focus on *knowledge,* on the use of the renewed mind in the service of God, seems strange to so much of the grassroots of our current Christian scene? Chalk it up to the effectiveness of the schemes of the devil: to minds still conformed to, or captive to the thinking of, this age . . . rather than to that of the age to come, which Christ has inaugurated.

"If then the light in you is darkness, how great is the darkness"
(Matt 6:23).
"Take the helmet of salvation!"

Catholic folk were "baptized with the Holy Spirit" they almost immediately realized how ill equipped their priests had allowed them to be in the knowledge of Scripture. There was a huge resurgence of Bible study and a hungering to understand the word of God within that vigorous charismatic awakening.

The Sword of the Spirit

In the same sentence as that above, we are also told to *receive*, or *take*, not only the shield of faith, but also the sword of the Spirit, which is the spoken or proclaimed word (*rhēma*) of God. This innocent appearing exhortation is fraught with all kinds of implications that are thrilling and demanding . . . and crucial for the fulfillment of the mission of God.

Note, first of all, this whole passage is not spoken to some select group of teachers or church leaders, but it is given to every disciple of Jesus Christ, since every one of such believers is engaged daily (like it or not) with the culture and schemes of darkness, and this darkness exists both outside and inside of the church. Paul will reiterate this in his letter to the Christians at Colossae, when he tells the believers there: "Let the word of Christ dwell in [among] you richly, teaching and admonishing one another in all wisdom, singing psalms and hymns and spiritual songs" (Col 3:16).

This is all to say that the biblical literacy of the individual believer, as well as of the Christian community, is not somebody else's responsibility, but it is everybody's responsibility. All of us, therefore, must heed this word to receive "the sword of the Spirit, which is the [spoken] word of God" (Eph 6:17).

Secondly, we need to notice that Paul does not use the more familiar Greek word *logos* here (which refers to content), but rather he uses the Greek word *rhēma*, which refers to the word spoken or proclaimed. This is to say that in keeping with the whole armor, this is our offensive weapon. It is the proclaimed, or preached, or talked about, or communicated word of God.

Third, what is to be noticed is that it is the *Spirit's* sword! It is not an unempowered word that we employ, with only our limited human resources. No, it is divinely animated. This comes out quite clearly in other scriptural references that we need to keep front and center:

> For the word of God is living and active, sharper than any two-edged sword, piercing to the division of soul and of spirit, of joints and marrow, and discerning the thoughts and intentions of the heart. (Heb 4:12)

> All Scripture is breathed out by God and profitable for teaching, for reproof, for correction, and for training in righteousness that the [messenger] of God be competent, equipped for every good work." (2 Tim 3:16–17)

We are told (imperative) to take, or receive, this terrible, this awesome weapon, namely, the *Spirit's sword*. It is not to be tamed or trivialized. The word of God and the Scriptures are identified with each other in New Testament teachings. And since the New Testament teaches that *all* of Christ's followers are to be his messengers, we thereby see that, as such, we are all to be competent and equipped for every good work by Holy Scriptures.

This word is alive and anointed by the Spirit. Our role is to be so formed by these New Testament teachings (and all of Scripture) that they become inescapable in all of our conversation. Some have the opportunity to speak or preach it publically. But all have opportunity to speak it in personal conversation, and especially when we are asked to "make a defense," so that when anyone asks us, we can give an answer "for the hope that is in [us]" and "do it with gentleness and respect" (1 Pet 3:15). As we are formed and thrilled by this word, we will become contagious with it and seek occasions to communicate it (wisely).

It is interesting to note, in Acts 19, that soon after Paul introduced the disciples in Ephesus to the good news of Jesus, the word went everywhere and all Asia Minor heard this word. However that took place, the believers in Ephesus took the Spirit's sword and put on the shoes of the readiness of the gospel of peace . . . and it produced a missionary movement that radiated across Asia Minor.

Every believer was equipped with this understanding of the word of Christ. In the early post-Pentecost church in Jerusalem, we read the record of the believers meeting together publicly, and in homes: "And they devoted themselves to the apostles' teachings and fellowship, to the breaking of bread and the prayers" (Acts 2:42). Those thousands of believers were equipped in the word of the apostles, i.e., the word of God.

It is worthy of our notice, also, that earlier in the Ephesian epistle Paul tells us that the risen Lord gave the church four gifts for the equipping of God's people for their work of ministry, and one of those gifts iss the *teaching shepherd* (or pastor-teacher). Such equipping informs all of the other pieces of the armor, but is given as a sword so that all might be equipped to engage the realities of each day's encounter with the darkness, and with those friends and neighbors still captive to its power. Scripture has its own power to accomplish its purpose.

But, for the record, the prince of darkness will use every attempt to domesticate or obscure this all-powerful weapon. One of Satan's (his infernal majesty's) primary schemes is to assault the veracity of the biblical accounts with very sophisticated scholarship, or cynical put-downs, or outrageous distortions. But the word of God will not be bound.

The venerable old Westminster Confession begins with a chapter on Holy Scripture, in which it affirms that:

> All things in Scripture are not alike plain in themselves, nor alike clear unto all; yet those things which are necessary to be known, believed, and observed, for salvation, are so clearly propounded and opened in some place of Scripture or another, that not only the learned, but the unlearned, in a due use of the ordinary means, may attain unto a sufficient understanding of them.[32]

Jesus was very plain-spoken when he reminded his listeners that it was those who *did* his word, or continued in his word, that were his true disciples. In the long history of the church, time and again, when the church is taken captive to the darkness, there will emerge a person, or a group of persons, who rediscover the word of God in Holy Scriptures, and determine to obey the Spirit and so to refound the church, engage in mission, take bold stands against principalities and powers, invite their neighbors for coffee and share with them the gospel of peace . . . and in this present day it continues to be so, frequently in the most difficult contexts.

It is fascinating to read the records of the faithful church's engagement in the mission of God in the book of Acts (and afterward), which demonstrates that the word of God grows, multiplies, spreads, increases, and bears fruit in unimaginable ways and places.

Prayer in the Spirit

". . . praying at all times in the Spirit,
with all prayer and supplication." (Eph 6:18)

For many New Testament expositors, this imperative to be praying in the Spirit is not considered as one of the weapons. But such interpretation misses the absolute necessity of prayer in the warfare. The sheer hu-

---

32. The Westminster Confession of Faith, chapter 1, proposition 7. The WCF is a seventeenth-century confession by a body of Christians out of the Reformed tradition, for the purpose of giving a unified understanding of the Christian faith for the church community within Great Britain. It stands as one of the great confessions of Protestant church history.

man impossibility of the task given to the church by Jesus Christ . . . that of making disciples of every people group on earth, of turning men and women from darkness to light, and from the power of Satan to God . . . demands that we be empowered by God, by the Spirit, and in continual communication with the triune God through prayer in the Spirit. It has to do with Jesus' own statement to his disciples that "apart me you can do nothing" (John 15:5), after which he promises to come to them by the Spirit and empower them for the mission.

The warfare in which we are engaged daily is not a merely human enterprise. The very fact that Paul initiates this section with the warning that we are not dealing with flesh and blood, but with principalities and powers, should wake us up to our need of the powers of the age to come, i.e., the power of the Holy Spirit. Prayer is at the very heart of our access to the realm of the Spirit. It should be of no surprise to us that as the church moved from Jerusalem to Rome (in the Acts history of the early church) that the people of God are always praying! They don't engage in liturgically perfect worship services. No! They pray. They really pray. They lay hold God in prayer for each day's vicissitudes and dangers as they obey the mandate to be Christ's witnesses.

It is only by the Spirit that eyes can be opened, ears made to hear, hearts made sensitive to God. It is only by the Spirit that the gifts of the Spirit emerge in the community to equip it for the practical realities of its life as the body of Christ, as the community of the kingdom of God on earth.

Prayer in the Spirit is a critical necessity as it animates and empowers the other six components of the whole armor of God given to the church.

SUMMARY

We have, now, walked through these seven components of the whole armor of God. They compose "the armor of light" (Rom 13:12). It is as we believers faithfully put on *every* piece of this armor that we demonstrate our calling to be the sons and daughters of the light, and that, as such children of the light, we dispel the darkness. Jesus was the light of men, the light that shines in the darkness, and the darkness cannot overcome that incarnation of the light. Jesus calls all of his followers to be the "light of the world" by their daily and diligent *putting on* of those components, which we see in this metaphor of the whole armor.

The seven pieces are inter-animating, symbiotic, complementary, and interpretative of each other, and each is critical to the whole. Satan's schemes are to relegate one or more of these into some diluted or dis-placed or forgotten role—some minimalized and non-critical place in the panoply. This leaves the believer, the warrior, vulnerable at that point, and it is as such that darkness effectively begins to inhabit the believer and the community. It is when the church becomes casual about the whole armor that the salt becomes more and more saltless.

These seven pieces of the armor God gives us provide us with a marvelous and effective daily checklist that enables us to be the faithful presence of God's kingdom people as light in the darkness, whatever our context or circumstance. It is by such faithfulness in putting on the whole armor that we are, thereby, able to stand against the wiles and erosions of the prince of darkness.

4

Feedback: Ephesus Revisited

THE WHOLE ARMOR OF God is not an *elective* for us, but rather it is an urgent, even critical absolute *if* we are to survive, to stand, to prevail against the schemes of the devil in the "evil day" (here and now) both individually and communally—and not someplace else or at some other time but right here and right now, in the immediate context of my life, or our lives.

The point being that, whenever I, or the community, become casual about any of these pieces of the armor, or water them down . . . caution lights should go on, and alarm bells should sound. The more these are forgotten, displaced, or diluted, in our immediate consciousness, then to that same extent the light dims and the relentless darkness prevails in our lives individually and communally.

The motivating and evangelizing center of our lives should be our passion and thrill at our calling to be the living breathing incarnation of what these seven *whole armor* components demonstrate, namely, lives that are focused on, and flowing out of, our love for and obedience to Jesus Christ—who he is, what he has done, what he taught. But there must also be a quest for maturity in our understanding of the weapons of our warfare!

Alan and I had reconnected some weeks later. He wasted no time:

"Okay. So I quite agree with all the good stuff you've been forwarding to me. But what do I do with all of it? What does it have to do with my involvement with North Park, where most of these components are (to be charitable) somewhat watered down, or given short shrift, or hardly even

acknowledged (if at all) by a significantly sizeable portion of the North Park folk whom I know?"

"Good question. Here are some more for you: When is a church a *church*? When is a church leader a true leader? When is a church member a disciple? How do you discern these essential components? What does one do in response? Is the church ever perfect? And on and on . . .

"At the end of the day, we have to be intentionally discerning. We have to make choices. We have to be critical (in the best sense of the word). For far too long it has been deemed inappropriate, or impolite (or just plain wrong?) to critique the church, or its professional leadership, negatively. Because this myth has been swallowed, God's people have just 'hunkered down' and gone along with stuff that not only doesn't make much sense, but seems inimical to God's purpose for the church in the first place, and to the faithful appropriation of the whole armor of God."[1]

"So the relentless darkness prevails, inning after inning . . . is that what you're saying?
"I'm still fuzzy on where all this goes. Help me."

～ ～ ～

"Alan, let me shift gears. You have often spoken to me about a gang of your friends who call yourselves "the church around the table," because you get together informally and periodically to encourage one other in your lives as disciples. Right?"

"Yeah. Great bunch. We have something of an agreement to be responsible for each other, and to hold each other accountable—very informal, but very real. We have great discussions about Scripture passages, about what we're reading, about our workaday world—along with some rollicking humor, and good beer. Why?"

"Have you ever discussed these conversations that you and I have been having with them?"

"No. Why?"

1. A piece of this is the *clergy domination* of the church, which needs to be brought into the daylight as significant in the drift factor.

"I have a proposal. I would love for you to forward to them this whole discussion that you and I have been having, and especially the stuff I have written on the whole armor. Process it together with them. Chase all the rabbits you want. Revisit the whole Ephesian church episode, and whatever this provokes by way of discussion and questions. Then feed it back to me. Take your time. But I'm not sure I want to proceed until I know how to put handles on this to make it practical and encouraging for you and your friends.

"I wouldn't want to blog it into cyberspace if I had no idea how your gang (and the generational culture they are part of) is hearing it, and what questions it raises with them . . . and where they would like to see it go.

"Tell me about these folk. How do they relate to the church, to what we're working on here?"

"You'd love them.

"They are participants in several church expressions, though they all have some roots in North Park Church. They mostly don't feel confined to it as the sole focus of their Christian relationships. But that's where we all met. A few have become parts of a couple of new church plants, but all have the same questions about, and affection for, North Park that I do. A couple of them are real church vagabonds, still looking but not finding a community that they can relate to.

"The questions actually spill over into the challenges faced by the new church plants that some are part of. We've had more than a few really good discussions over recent months on our appraisal of the whole 'church thing' as it relates to our own mutual role in the design of God.

"But, hey, I think your suggestion is fantastic!

"My gang will love the challenge. Stand by."

That brief conversation with Alan was the genesis of what follows. I value it more than I can say, because Alan and his friends are a fresh new generation who have the capacity to imagine, and reimagine, what the older generations (mine and their parents) are too cluttered with (or captive to)—past understandings and paradigms and definitions of the church, and the mission of God—to even imagine anything different.

What I found out was that Alan's friends have an uncanny capacity to discern the church's treasures from the past, and yet still know how to retrieve those treasures from out of the rubble of the Christendom church's institutions that have too often buried those treasures, even as they have also forgotten their own missional essence and calling.

It was many weeks later that Alan checked in and said he was ready to give me a progress report. He even sounded excited. Evidently his friends had not only spent time together working on this, but had kept emails and tweets busy sharing information, sources, and progress.

So, he and I landed one Saturday morning in Joe's Coffee Shop for him to report. Joe's is a fun place—funky, friendly, with laptops everywhere and great coffee. He brought along with him Lucy, another from his "church around the table" bunch, to monitor Alan, and to make sure he was reporting accurately. She was a look-you-in-the-eye young marketing professional in a large corporation. Lucy was in her late twenties, and the wife of a high school advanced studies teacher (who is also in their community). Just to alert my readers: Lucy's focus is primarily on the human equation of the scene of church and the relentless darkness— the real people who are unwittingly victims of the schemes of the devil.

This all became something like a two-hour conversation (with several refills and a couple of bagels). What follows is essentially from Alan and Lucy. I will only try to report the essence as faithfully as I can. I tried to keep my mouth shut and listen (no small accomplishment for me).

ALAN AND LUCY'S REPORT AND REFLECTIONS

LUCY: *"Bob, I'm glad to finally meet the guy behind all stuff we have been processing. Wow! Have you ever dropped a mindbender on us? We're totally, I mean totally, hooked. It is more than a little scary for us to think of the implications of this darkness theme in Scripture—but it is somewhat inescapable, isn't it? At least for me, it is the first time I have ever had to consider the context of my Christian life, and that of the church, not as some neutral, rational, and 'spiritual' scene . . . but rather as a deliberate counterculture operating in the midst of the dominion of Satan. Explains a lot . . . and doesn't get much press!*

"There are ten or twelve of us in our 'church around the table' bunch. No sleepy minds involved. We were all quite taken, from the outset, with this whole darkness-vis-à-vis-light cosmic conflict. It unveils a dimension of our Christian calling about which we, for the most part, were all quite unaware—but it is so obviously there, especially in Ephesians 2 and 6.

"How could we have missed it?

"Plus, it has given us something of a thrilling and frightening and challenging new sense of our own calling to be contagiously and creatively demonstrators of the light, able to discern the schemes of the darkness in the realities of our own here and now incarnation—how to understand the daily discipline of putting on the whole armor . . . and without being paranoid.

"Face it: we all want our lives, and the church, to be light to our everyday friends, to our neighbors, to those of our own generation, to our working colleagues. But our contemporaries haven't got any patience with the religious stuff that doesn't relate to anything, or with those churches that are nothing more than religious clubs, or that are nothing less than confederations of religious strangers. If the church is really to be the communal dimension of the gospel (as you've proposed to us), then we all agreed that we want to be agents in imagining and creating it to be just that—not somewhere else, but right where we are . . . like North Park for instance.

"Yeah, and we also came to the conclusion that this is not as simple as it sounds.

"It could get really troublesome and complex, couldn't it? But then again, we're not in this on our own. Thankfully we do have promises from God."

ALAN: *"What we did, for starts, Bob, was to go back to the whole Ephesus scene that you spelled out in the recent stuff you sent. We revisited that Acts 19 account where Paul found those dozen disciples of John the Baptist. We are assuming that he found them in the synagogue at Ephesus, since that seems to be the venue where Paul always plugged in first in strange cities.*

"That synagogue figures significantly, by the way, in what we concluded about our connection through North Park Church. Stand by!

"Paul spontaneously filled those disciples in on the rest of the story, and about John pointing to Jesus as Messiah. (Paul was never casual, or

passive, about occasions to tell folk about Jesus, have you noticed?) Those twelve got the message and believed. They were baptized. They immediately became contagious sons (and daughters?) of the light—speaking in tongues, prophesying, and demonstrating other confirming signs of the Spirit's presence in them. They became the initial community of light, the initial church, in Ephesus.

"What follows, again, is instructive.

"Paul entered the synagogue and for three months and boldly argued, reasoned and persuaded the folk there about Jesus and about the kingdom of God. The rabbinic tradition made such reasoning not at all strange. It even encouraged questioning concerning the Torah and its teachings, and Paul was magnificently trained to use those sacred writings to point to Jesus.

"Ultimately the darkness of unbelief prevailed and Paul was stubbornly resisted by the synagogue folk. That being so, he and those who had believed resorted to a rented hall, and there, daily, for two years continued with his teaching and disciple making.

"Result? (This blew our minds): 'All of the residents of Asia heard the word of the Lord, both Jews and Gentiles' (Acts 19:10).

"What that obviously implies here, for our purposes, is that it means every baptized person became a missioner. Got it? The missional DNA was implanted in that infant Ephesian church, and so it was subsequently implanted in all who believed. All were equipped as kingdom of God persons. All became living human incarnations of the light. All incarnated God's new creation in Christ. All renounced the dominion of darkness and of Satan. No obstacle seems to have been able to quench their excitement and their joy at such a calling.

"Of course, what follows was (to understate it) some turmoil and civic unrest, namely, because of how radically this all challenged the dominant social order of the civitas! Result? Paul was forced to leave town after a 'dust-up.' But . . . he left behind a vital witness to the light in the midst of the Ephesian darkness.

"Then at some later time (Acts 20) Paul stopped by the port city of Miletus and called the elders from that Ephesian church to meet him there. In the record of his career with them, he revealingly notes how, for those years, through all the conspiracies of some Jews and other consequent dangers, he had met with the believers publicly and from house to house, equipping them with 'the whole counsel of God' (20:27)—and by

the way, that 'whole counsel' piece deserves our attention too, doesn't it? He reminded those elders that such was now their own ongoing steward-ship, namely, that of equipping every believer in the whole counsel of God.

"There were to be no passive, defenseless, uninvolved participants in the family of God.

"But, our gang also decided that this equipping would have to have in-cluded some very specific teaching on the warfare with the dominion of darkness, and at least some introduction to the weapons that God has provided for us in this relentless conflict."

LUCY: "You won't believe that we spent a whole evening wondering, among ourselves, whether Paul's affinity for the synagogues, and his love for Israel, were in some ways a counterpart to our affinity for North Park Church—along with our involvement now with several others—and our sense of Christ's true purpose for his church.

"That possibility all began to surface when someone in our group raised this very question as we looked at some of Paul's reflections in Romans (9–11), especially his words of sorrow and love as he looked at his own kinsmen, the Jews: 'to them belong the adoption, the glory, the covenants, the giving of the law, the worship, and the promises. To them belong the patriarchs, and from their race, according to the flesh, is the Christ who is God over all, blessed forever. Amen' (9:4–5).

"There is that whole host of Christendom churches, along with North Park, who would somehow fit under such a description—so much rich heritage, yet blindness and forgetfulness, and detachment from their true calling, and self-conscious purpose to be communities of God's new creation in Christ.

"Our conclusion was that you don't just stomp the dust off of your feet and abandon such, even though, like Paul, you can be realistic about the blindness and darkness that inhabits such bodies. When Paul became persona non grata in the synagogue, he rented the Hall of Tyrannus in Ephesus, and continued his public teaching from there . . . though he still was a Jew and still had a passion for Israel, and the synagogues, to em-brace Jesus as 'God over all, blessed forever.'

"What we came up with were several paradigms for ourselves: 1) the church as a synagogue, or assembly, that should, in fact, recognize the all-consuming place of Christ and his kingdom in the design of God; 2) the *alternative assembly such as illustrated in the Hall of Tyrannus (a rented meeting place for teaching and equipping); and 3) the more intimate and pervasive church meetings from house to house. This latter has roots all the way back to the post-Pentecost pattern, when you had thousands of new disciples in a hostile environment meeting together in homes to share their lives, to be accountable, to break bread (Eucharist?), and to learn the apostolic teachings.*[2]

"*It doesn't take too much imagination to realize that Paul's focus on the believers' ministries to one another could, realistically, only be carried out in such house-to-house gatherings, where such intimacy was possible, since in such a small community all were known to each other, and somehow accountable to each other in their quest to live out their kingdom lives.*

"*Out of this pattern each church planted other churches, and so heralded the gospel of peace across the length and breadth of the Roman world.*

"*My own personal and continual issue (along with our table bunch) has been: What do you do with all of the great 'religious' folk in a scene such as North Park, who have never known anything else, and so assume that what they are experiencing is what the church is all about, namely, participating in the religious activities of the church, since no one seems to have told them anything else—and certainly never told about anything so majestic as their calling to be agents of making known 'the mystery hidden for ages and generations, but now revealed, the mystery of Christ in you the hope of glory' (Col 1:25–27)?*

"*It brought us back to Alan's lament to you that 'no one seems to notice' that so much of church stuff seems to have nothing to do with the missionary nature of the church, nor with the gospel of the kingdom of God. These dear folk assume that 'going to church' and engaging in the 're- ligious Christianity'*[3] *in that particular location is what it is all about. So, with Paul, I (and we) have great sorrow and unceasing anguish of heart for our much-appreciated friends in that setting of religious darkness.*

---

2. Acts 2:46–47.

3. Again, this designation of what is expressed in so many forgetful churches is by Dietrich Bonhoeffer in his appraisal of what was taking place in the churches he ob- served both in Germany and in his experience in New York in the 1930s. Such religious Christianity uses the terminology of the Christian faith, but misses the transforma- tional reality of the New Testament gospel.

"All of which, again, brings us back to the relentless darkness that would foist such a clever counterfeit and seduce folk into accepting it as the real thing. The church becomes a confederacy of religious people who have no self-awareness of what Jesus intends for them, and very little true commonality or mutual accountability . . . other than a weekly church service in which they can be the passive consumers.

"That just doesn't do it!

"But what do I, what do we, do? So much of the church that we have experienced is still in the darkness, and, weird as it may sound, is itself therefore, in the true sense, a mission field.

"We were continually wrestling with the issue of how we can be effective and contagious children of the light in the 'synagogue,' while at the same time being equipped to be children of the light, 24/7, in our neighborhoods and workplaces—when the 'synagogue' is neither a place of teaching nor equipping for mission. How are we to understand (or keep focused) that we, and the church, and all of God's people are always in missionary confrontation with the dominion of darkness . . . inside the church and outside?

"How's that for a bundle of good issues? Am I reporting accurately, Alan?"

GENERATIONAL DRIFT

ALAN: *"Lucy, you are remarkable, and spot on."* But as we grappled with these questions, we spent a whole other evening wondering what the lifespan of a congregation really is. That question was provoked by the reference to the church at Ephesus in Revelation 2—only one generation after its apostolic founding. By the time the Spirit of the Lord addressed that church (late in the first century we assume), the church at Ephesus had a lot of good stuff going still. They had preserved a healthy degree of orthodoxy as to the apostolic message. They had been able to maintain some purity within the fellowship, and to engage in hard work with good results. But then they are soundly rebuked for having forsaken 'the love which you had at first' (Rev 2:4).

"This one sneaks up on you, but upon reflection is it obvious why the Risen Lord issues such a warning. In the Ephesian epistle, Paul opens with breathtaking statements of adoration around the awesomeness of what God has done in Christ, and how the mystery of his will, the whole mean-

ing of creation, has been revealed through what Jesus did through his life, teachings, death, and resurrection. He then reminds them of their own deliverance, by grace, out of captivity to the god of this world. He gives them direction that such calling is into a whole new humanity that is the dwelling place of God by the Spirit.

"What follows are those several chapters in which he spells out how that new community is equipped, and what its redemptive relationships look like. It is a community that expresses the reconciling love of God in the relationships of its members to one another. The very flavor of the New Testament church is to be that of faith, of hope, and especially of love. Elsewhere, Paul says that it is love that binds it all together in perfect harmony (Col 3:14). This is such a critical part of the church's calling—so much so that even though it may be doing so many commendable things, it succumbs to the darkness when it loses its rich flavor of love for one another, which love is to be visible to the watching world.

"To our own culture of inclusiveness this rebuke, at first blush, seems pretty picayune. But the Risen Lord doesn't think it is a minor chink in their armor. After all, it is by their love for God and each other that Christ's disciples are to be known to all the people with whom they come into contact. Those still in the darkness can see love demonstrated. They cannot see orthodoxy, or hard work, or patient endurance within the new creation community, and among its participants. But they can see the true love of the believers. The church as a community of the light of the gospel demonstrates its radical difference by the praxis of love in its inner relationships, as well as in its encounters with those outside, even love for enemies.

"The letter says that this is such a serious breach of calling that the church at Ephesus stands in danger of having its 'lamp removed,' i.e., ceasing to be an agent of the light of the gospel. The relentless darkness had so soon caused a partial blindness and deafness to come upon them, so they are told that whoever has ears to hear needs to listen to 'what the Spirit is saying to the churches' (Rev 3:2).

"Our bunch saw this warning in Revelation as another manifestation of the insertion of the darkness into the Christian community, so subtle and gradual that no one seemed to notice, what with their zeal for so many other commendable activities.

"If Satan can simply depersonalize the church so as to lose its primary component of love, then what a coup for the dominion of darkness!

What a huge piece of the church's visible witness to the watching world is darkened!

"We also spent time comparing North Park with new church plants. North Park is many generations old in age, but a few in our table bunch are part of new church plants, and we were all wondering about the lifespan of congregations, and how we could have ears to hear what the Spirit is saying to us, and where the blind and deaf vulnerabilities show up in these communities. History rather reinforces the reality that forgetfulness sets in quite quickly. Essential truths get watered down. Religion takes New Testament Christianity captive.

"Christianity taken captive by religion . . . how do you like that idea?

"The armor of God is relegated to the trophy case . . . and the darkness prevails . . . even though the church institution may be thriving.

"What we see, in all of this, is how easily the more essential components of the whole armor recede into unimportance, and how, when this happens, the church becomes less the church. The church increasingly diminishes as the dwelling place of God by the Spirit, and as the missionary arm of the Holy Trinity. Rather, it becomes more (as we have said before) of a confederacy of religious strangers.

"Is that too severe a judgment?

"In some ways we got sort of bogged down at this point. We had this mix of the synagogue metaphor, which we had cooked up, and then we had our engagement with North Park Church. We saw spiritual deafness and blindness as, early on, reinhabiting the church. All of these realities were before us. We know that discernment is necessary, and that choices must be made. We know that it is not all black and white, that it is (as you have often reminded us) complex and ambiguous. We know that the darkness is relentless. Wow!"

LUCY: "One thing our gang wants us to process with you, Bob, is: How do we go about discerning between the form of the church and (how to say it?) the church's new creation dynamics?

"You've taught us, and we have noted that Paul and the other New Testament writers give us no pattern for the form of the church. We see that early church inventing itself as it goes along. But where does that leave us? The Ephesian letter highlights important pieces . . . and opens up *the whole of that 'beyond asking or imagining' potential that Paul mentions (Eph 3:20). Does that free us to creatively imagine a church expression that we haven't seen or experienced yet?*

"Actually, it is something of a glaring issue. We did what you asked us to do, and walked backwards through Ephesians, beginning with his sobering warning about the assaults of the darkness and about the whole armor. What is obvious is Paul's passion for the message of the gospel focused in Christ, and about the integrity and equipping of the Christian church for its mission. That's all marvelously obvious in those six chapters.

"What is not there at all is any vague reference to the form of the church. The reference in Acts 20 about 'public and from house to house' is about as specific as it gets. But it is quite the contrary in so much of our experience, especially with North Park and its counterparts. What we now experience is a focus on the form of the church: its institutional buildings, staff, budget, tradition, activities, permanence, pulpit, services—but little about what Paul seems so focused on.

"We called Paul's emphasis: New Creation Dynamics. Included under that rubric would be the message ('the whole counsel of God'), the relationships, the empowering, the mission, the authenticity of kingdom community . . . all as demonstrations of the light and salt of kingdom living. Then we saw the absolute necessity of the gifts of the Spirit given to the church in order to equip all of God's folk for engagement in ministry and mission.

"It's like two different worlds, isn't it? Our sense in seeing all of this is that it is an incredibly effective redefinition by the darkness, which redefinition, in turn, makes the whole church into a comfortable religious expression of the dominion of darkness—which looks so good to so many, but misses the point of Christ's calling."

This is all something of a digest as I remember (and recorded) it from that Saturday morning. We had been at Joe's Coffee for a couple of hours, actually, and all had other engagement to go to, and so we signed off agreeing to continue the conversation as soon as convenient, so that I could keep up with their reflections on our *relentless darkness* focus. Alan had one parting piece of the report to hang on me as we got up to leave:

ALAN: *"Bob, our table bunch is really captivated by the potential and implications of all of this. Thanks for including us in your own thinking. What we have reported here is only the tip of the iceberg of our discussions over these weeks. You cannot imagine all the 'rabbits' we chased in the course of our long conversations. But here's a piece of it that you may be responsible for provoking, but which is so crazy and outrageous that I hesitate to even say it, but we think you will understand:*

"We aren't willing to sit around waiting for someone else to come up with some course of action for us. We'd like to see ourselves in a threefold ministry, with our table bunch being a support group for us, and an accountability group—like maybe a house church of sorts. We see ourselves as: a) ecclesiastical archaeologists, discovering the treasures from the church's long traditions that we need to appropriate and emulate for our building up; b) a faithful presence of kingdom people, sons and daughters of the light, in our 24/7 lives, and in the midst of the real people whom that involves; and c) imaginative and creative architects of the church for the next generation.

"But we are not willing to be passive. After all, this is, according to the New Testament, our true calling. We want the 'shoes of the readiness of the gospel of peace' to be on our feet so that we are engaged in the mission of God in the brief lives God gives us. Okay?

"Stand by."

With that we finished out coffee and took our leave, with mutual agreement that we had just begun this journey.

5

When Darkness Inhabits the Church . . .

L ET'S GO BACK TO our original question: "When darkness inhabits the church . . . and the church inhabits the darkness . . . what then?" Or maybe to Alan's question to me about how to explain the church's drift away from its self-conscious understanding of its own essence, purpose, and mission . . . like: Where does the drag come from? Which, in turn, leads us again to Paul's warning concerning the schemes of the devil . . . which, in turn, raises its own questions:

Where does the devil come into this thing?

Who, in fact, is the devil?

Where in the world does the devil come from?

What does the devil have to do (if anything) with North Park Church and its counterparts?

Here is this enigmatic figure, who is so present in the biblical narrative from one end to the other, and yet . . . on the church scene today the devil seems almost like Voldemort in the Harry Potter stories: "the one who must not be named." Those who should be the teachers of the word of Christ seems to intentionally avoid significant engagement with, or even mention of, the subject, lest they seem somehow archaic, or non-scholarly, or somehow suspect if they should confess belief in such a personal devil.

And yet, there this devil[1] is from the beginning of our biblical narrative with an alternative agenda, like it or not. Without our honest engagement with the reality of the devil, so much goes unexplained in our faith journey (or, in the colloquial, *doesn't make a lick of sense*).

In order to get at this, I ask my reader's indulgence if I am deliberately redundant (a bad habit of mine), and especially because our under-

1. Διάβολοσ in Greek, meaning something like "slanderer," "treacherous one," or "traitor."

standing is so clouded on this subject. I actually want to do two runs at the same story, in order to get an answer from two different dimensions necessary for our generation to adequately embrace the critical nature of what Paul describes as "the whole armor of God."

FIRST RUN: A SUBTLE, CRAFTY, DECEIVING ADVERSARY

Our biblical documents open with a couple of chapters (chapter divisions being an innovation of translators to give us landmarks along the way) of marvelously illuminating, colorful folk history,[2] which introduces all that follows. This understanding is critical to answering Alan's question.

It all begins with the basic reality: God.

God is creator, artist, and architect. God is a God of order and beauty and infinite goodness. God is a personal God who reveals himself and who talks . . . "In the beginning, God . . ." From this primary understanding flows a remarkable story that explains to us our world, our social-cultural context, our humanity, and . . . the reality of an alien presence to which we give the designation of *evil*.

I repeat: the two initial chapters speak of God as the architect and creator of a *good* and harmonious cosmic scene, which very creation displayed God's own divine nature. He created all of the components: day and night, land and sea, seedtime and harvest, birds that fly, fish that swim, all manner of creatures to populate the earth. And then God created *humankind* in God's own image and likeness. Having created each beautiful part of this earth in order to display his own divine nature, he declared them all *good*. God is the God who is there, and whose infinite goodness unfolds more and more right down to the last page of the Bible.

Chapter 2 of the Genesis account describes a state of total (awesome?) good that we humans have never known since that primordial setting: absolute *shalom* (harmony, peace, wholeness). Such wonder becomes the more amazing when we see that the created man and woman also actually commune with . . . they walk in the garden with . . . they are

---

2. I call this "folk history" because it is the story of beginnings passed down in oral tradition for untold time, told in broad strokes, and yet it conveys the necessary truths of the beginnings of our cosmos and of our human history in story form. Some call it "myth" in the classical sense of that word. Whatever you call it, it introduces all that follows, and in a very real sense none of the rest of the Bible makes much sense without this account.

in the embrace of God their creator. They are naked and without shame. They are also innocent. They have never known anything other.

But then, there abruptly enters the scene a tragic note of dissonance.

Enter the suggestion that perhaps God has a less than honorable agenda in the one prohibition that he had given his creatures, namely, that they refrain from eating of the tree of the knowledge of good and evil. To my readers: please don't rush through this. To unpack the implications of this has all kinds of implications about the *metaphysical*, *epistemological*, and *ethical* dimensions[3] of our life and human history, not to mention our own quest to somehow understand the warnings of the apostle Paul to the Ephesian Christians.

There comes to these two naïve and untested and innocent humans this suggestion of some questionability about God, and requires of them that they make a choice.

They have a choice?

Here, I want to slow down and do a bit of interpretation. The text (Genesis 3:1) describes the questioning as coming from a serpent figure, who was: *more subtle*, more *crafty*, than any other beast of the field that the Lord had made. So, please note: the serpent is a creature. He was not at all suspect by those two inhabitants of the garden. He was just another of the creatures in that primordial scene. This indicates that the serpent (only much later named as Satan, or the devil) was not some grotesque, or radical, or obvious, or in-your-face confrontational accuser of God the creator . . . not at all.

Put your imagination to work and you can probably hear the serpent suggesting that maybe they should ask why God might have commanded them not to eat of the tree in the midst of the garden—questioning what God's motive might be in denying them this experience. Eve enters into a dialogue with the serpent, and states that God has said that they would die if they eat of it. That was true. But the serpent then puts his own spin on that prohibition: "Maybe it's not as bad as God makes it sound. Like: God may be overstating it a bit—maybe even being a bit deceptive in order to deprive you a real wonderful experience."

What, in fact, the serpent is doing is questioning God's goodness, God's integrity, God's purpose in the prohibition, and even questioning the completeness of their present paradise . . . as though there were

---

3. In philosophy these refer to: *meaning, knowledge,* and *behavior.*

something even more desirable, more ultimate. The serpent doesn't come outright and call God deceptive, but the implication is there.

Or again: "Hey, it may not be all that bad. Maybe there's something else. I wonder why God doesn't want you to eat of that tree. Maybe God knows that if you eat it you'll know something he doesn't want you to know because then you'll be on the same footing as he is. Get it? You'll be like God. Cool, huh?

"But I doubt you'll really 'die,' whatever that means. But, on the plus side, you may become more in charge of your own life and destiny. How about that?"

"More crafty" or "more subtle" are indicative of the very nature of this *accuser* who inhabits the biblical story, and whose agenda is always an agenda alien to God's agenda, and who always seeks to subvert God's glory and purpose (even after he will have been disarmed and dethroned by the Son of God at the cross).[4]

The result of this encounter was that a huge, even cosmic, tragedy took place. God's design was profaned and God's creation violated, and those first parents learned what it is like to have to seek life on their own. They never denied God's existence. But they had made a choice to try to live their lives somewhat autonomously, or by their own wits and with their own resources—an attempt to live life in which God, and the design of God, and the glory of God were no longer their primary frame of reference.

I need to make an inadequate attempt to demythologize, or maybe paraphrase, or reinterpret, what theologians and the church have cast in ominous definition as: the *fall* into sin.

I want to attempt to state it so that it is no less tragic in results, but maybe in less stark and more understandable terms for our contemporary, and biblically uninformed, generation. The choice made by Adam and Eve resulted in a total reorientation of life, in which they chose to seek autonomy rather than to put faith and trust in the one who created them. They found themselves laboring to live with their merely human resources, in an *anthropocentric* existence, where God became more of a peripheral and utilitarian God, i.e., a God-out-there-somewhere, who

---

4. The many names given to this rebel creature in Scripture make clear that he has no creative power, only distorting, destructive, and deceptive power.

might respond if and when they called upon him in time of need, but who is certainly not the dynamic *raison d'être* of all things.[5]

Satan does not deny God, please note. Satan actually believes in God more than so much of humanity . . . but Satan continually fashions counterfeits of God, or caricatures of God, in order to subvert God's purpose in glory. Satan obscures what it is that makes "the whole creation groan" (Rom 8:22), and his own behind-the-scenes complicity in this distortion of God's creative design.

Now, note: this brings us right back to how this threatens the church at Ephesus. Satan will continually use all of his wiles, schemes, subtlety, and craftiness as the church's adversary in order to reinterpret even the church as a merely human (but *religious*) entity . . . or what some currently are designating as *religious Christianity*.[6] In such a merely human version of the church, what you produce are *churchified* participants, who are quite content to be passive recipients of church services, while at the same time satisfying themselves with being spiritual—and, in a sense, they are innocent, having never known anything else—and so remaining essentially part of the dominion of darkness.

As Alan has suggested, such a church becomes itself a mission field.

Herein lies the beginning of an answer to Alan's insistent question about *drift* and *drag*, and its source.

SECOND RUN: SATAN'S HOSTILITY TOWARD THE CHURCH

With that kind of background before us, it becomes insistent to us that Paul's alert to the Ephesian church, and his metaphor of the sheer necessity of the whole armor, is not at all an innovation on his part, but rather reflects a pattern that my Alan and his bunch of ecclesiastical *archaeologists* and *architects* will surely discover as they unearth the history of God's people right back to its primordial roots.

5. Millennia later would come the classic definition of *secularism* by one George Jacob Holyoake, which stated something like: "The doctrine that morality should be based on regard to the well-being of mankind in the present life to the exclusion of all considerations drawn from belief in God or a future state" (as I remember it).

6. This is primarily Dietrich Bonhoeffer's definition of what he found in the German church.

The clash of darkness and light is there in the biblical story almost from the beginning. I say "almost from the beginning" because just as Paul begins the Ephesian letter being personally overwhelmed by his awe and adoration of Jesus—whom he had encountered and whom he knew to be the very key, the answer to the "mystery" of this whole cosmos and of the human community—so also the biblical record begins with the affirmation that there is one transcendent creator and personality, who is humanly incomprehensible, and whom we call *God*. It is this person-God who creates it all and declares it to be really *good*. This opening affirmation is essentially a statement of worship.

And, what is the more marvelous, this God, from the very beginning, desires to be known and loved, and so reveals himself to his creation. The Scriptures begin with awe and with worship.

"In the beginning, God . . ."

This establishes our major presupposition for all that follows: the whole creation and the human community are created to be the radiant display of the divine nature and design. God's creation was the scene of harmony (*shalom*), of true meaning, of love and mutual acceptance, of life and hope, of creativity and beauty, and a whole ethos that was in the embrace of the triune God. So Paul will later speak of God's new creation design in Christ as a reality that surpasses knowledge, or is humanly unimaginable, and he speaks of God who is able to do abundantly more than we can ask or think (Eph 3:18–20).[7]

The Scriptures refer to that original scene as: the Garden of Eden, and as *paradise*.

Exactly!

This historical find is important for our quest here, in answer to the questions raised by Alan, in that it gives us clues about the purpose of God's creation, and now it tells us something of the essence and purpose of God's new creation human community, called the *church*.

What transpired in that Garden of Eden scene is written for us in language and images variously called (as we noted above) "folk history" or, sometimes, "myth," in form. But by whatever literary genre it is called, it points us humans to the historical reality of that real moment, which explains so much of the God of glory, the Creator God. The crown of that creation is humankind, and that first human community. "It is not good for man that he should be alone," God said (Gen 2:18). Those per-

7. Cf. Col 1:15–20 and the vision of the "Peaceable Kingdom" in Isaiah 11.

sons were so created in the image and likeness of God in order that they could display that divine nature, and walk in intimacy with their Creator God in that garden, and so realize the full meaning of their humanity.

A part of that humanity, in the image and likeness of God, was the capacity to make free choices. That gift was given so that they could freely choose to respond to God, otherwise they would have been automatons. But such a gift carried with it the inherent potential for choosing *not* to choose to live within the divine purpose. Theirs was an innocent, and at the same time untested, freedom.

It is at this point in the biblical story that we are introduced to the mysterious, clandestine, and destructive personality about whom Paul, millennia later, would warn the Ephesian Christians, using the appellation: the devil. Only, in the garden scene this devil comes in the figure of a serpent . . . that talks!

A LIAR AND THE FATHER OF LIES

This should raise the question in any thinking person: Where in the world did this creature come from? And how do you explain such? The thoughtful answers to such questions need to be carefully addressed, but are beyond the primary purpose of our journey here.[8] However, a basic and broad-stroked answer is that what is implicit, from one end of Scripture to the other, is the reality of a whole other created order of angelic beings—supernatural in powers, but created. One gathers that the angelic beings were to be something of an order of guardians and stewards of the created order, and messengers on behalf of their Creator God.

What is also implicit (often between the lines) is that there occurred a rebellion fomented by one of the angels, by the name of Satan, who in turn recruited others of the angelic order to join with him in this rebellion against God, and so to create a seditious warfare against their very creator, and thereby seeking to usurp God's place of preeminence.[9] Jesus will ultimately speak of the destruction of "the devil and his angels" (Matt 25:41). Then, in turn, we find this rebel angel appearing to those two initial human occupants of God's paradise in order to seduce them away from God.

---

8. Again, I heartily commend the magisterial work by Gregory Boyd, *Satan and the Problem of Evil* (Downers Grove, IL: InterVarsity, 2001).

9. This rebellion is hinted at in Isa 14:12–15.

What is explicit in the Genesis account is that this serpent-devil was fully aware of their ability to freely choose, or not to choose, to walk within the created order. He is deceptive to a fault.

God had, indeed, and in love, forbidden Adam and Eve *not* to eat of the tree of the knowledge of good and evil. This enigmatic prohibition is fraught with implications, but acknowledges that there was, and is, the potential for an alternative attempt to live life apart from God, which ultimately leaves one with too many unanswered questions about the mystery of our humanity, and which will only, finally, produce death. It is a life cut off from its roots, and is an attept to live life without dynamic relationship to the God who creates, and in whose purpose is: true meaning, destiny, and hope.

The serpent is not at all seeking the welfare, or blessedness, of those human creatures. He is, rather, proposing to them a lie, a lie both about God and about the potential of the act of rebellion he is inciting. It sounds so familiar. We hear it all the time, right down to this moment: "You can live life more fully by calling your own shots. God doesn't want you to know this. Assert your right of autonomy, and you will be like god. Don't let God deny you what is your potential." The implication of such insinuations is that God isn't really good, that God is somehow deceptive and oppressive.

Sound familiar? The apostle John will one day call Satan "a liar and the father of lies" (John 8:44).

Note that Satan doesn't deny that God is a reality. He is only proposing that humans live their lives on their own terms, and so relegate God to the margins of existence—you know, maybe to call on him if you get into jam, or something, but not as the one to whom your heart is captive in love.

The serpent figure did not tell them the rest of the story. He certainly did not tell them of the consequences of severing their beautiful and unhindered and free communion with God, with all of its blessings. Those first parents were too untested, and too naïve, to realize that out of such communion with God came all true meaning and hope and peace. It was out of that relationship that there came true life, and the veritable display of the divine nature in their human lives . . . all of this to be lost if they chose to disobey God and launch out on their own, and futilely attempt to be their own gods.

Result? They listened to the pernicious serpent in their naiveté . . . and their lights went out. Darkness intruded into God's creation. A rebellion occurred. Death became an ominous reality. The payoff of their decision was that they cut themselves off from the giver of life and blessing, and so received the wages of their act: death. *Shalom* was replaced by radical estrangement and alienation, not only with God, but also with each other, and with nature. The darkness, with all of its false gospels of autonomy, its confusion about life's meaning, its destructive relationships, its fear of death . . . became the ethos of this *dominion of darkness,* energized by the prince of darkness: one Satan.

Leaping ahead, for a moment, you will remember that Paul was commissioned to go and turn men and women from darkness to light and from the power of Satan to God (Acts 26:18). He will describe those inhabiting that dominion of darkness as both blind and captive to the devil. Just don't lose that thread as we pursue our understanding of how and why the church drifts.

In the Genesis account God pronounces some curses on Satan and on the ground, and foretells of the new and painful labor-filled life that these rebellious humans must now endure. There is no question that God is angry. Who wouldn't be angry to see such a creation violated so despicably by a rebel angel in his malice toward God? God is angry, but also heartbroken that the crown of his creation has become party to such a violation.

But, in a sense (if I may be indulged some paraphrase), it is something like God saying to Adam and Eve: "Okay guys, you've made your choice. Lot's of luck! In my garden you could live harmoniously and eat of the fruit of the trees of the garden. It has all been totally perfect. That was all part of the blessedness that flows from my love. No more. Now that you want to be your own gods, you're on your own to try. You'll have to labor, and because of your rebellion the whole creation will suffer and groan. You want to determine your own destiny? Fine. Have at it. You want to pursue your own happiness? Best wishes. But you have no idea what you have unleashed here."

But note here a couple of things: God doesn't love them any less, and God isn't taken by surprise by all of this. He tells them, both the man and the woman, as well as Satan, that there will come the "seed of a woman" who shall inflict a mortal wound on Satan's head.

God, right away, inserts this note of hope.

But between here and there is a long history of humankind struggling with the consequences of this aberration, which took place at the beginning—and all of the devastation, and alienation, that have been the fruits of it.

And, please take note: what is essential for us to recognize, in this present quest, is that the darkness has a continual and pathological energizer, right down to the present, in the prince of darkness.

Attempting to be as God is not all it's cracked up to be! Yet such resulting attempts to live independently of God the creator is perennial in this age of darkness. Alan's bunch of archaeologists-architects will discover that this very perennial attempt to live by our merely human resources is quite evident even in the church today, i.e., in our distressing proclivity to create religious institutions that call themselves Christian but in reality are so formed that they do not need to depend really upon God in any dynamic sense.

Take note of the *relentless darkness* that began in the garden and continues to exercise its malice and rebellion right down to the present... and even present inside of so much of what goes under the designation of: the *church*.

At the same time, this awful tragedy has left a huge vacant spot in the human heart. Even though those persons sought autonomy, humankind ultimately knows that there are powers at work that are far beyond their human resources. On one hand, the ancients fashioned for themselves all kinds of gods, representing the things they couldn't control. Moderns do the same with their *designer gods*, i.e., gods whom we put together to fulfill our quests for "spirituality." Yet, in its rebellion, humankind will also exalt its own autonomy, as over against God, by fabricating grotesque caricatures of the God who reveals himself in Jesus and in the Holy Scriptures.

Apropos to Alan's questions about the church, note that *religious Christianity* is well populated with those whose faith is in a God "who is there when I need him," i.e., a utilitarian God who comes to our aid on call, alas. In much of the Christendom church, the church phenomena at which we are looking in these discussions, God is relegated to a ceremonial place on the margins of our lives. Such religious secularism begins early. Even when God had revealed himself so dramatically to those children of Israel at Mt. Sinai, and had given them the tabernacle as a tent of meeting where God's glory dwelt . . . it soon became only a symbol, as did the later temple in Jerusalem. Somehow it seemed important for their security, but had little dynamic influence with their calling to be a kingdom of priests, and certainly not with the dynamics of daily life for most, and for many centuries.

Why?

Answer: Because the darkness has always been relentless. In one way or another the darkness will continually attempt to relegate God to the margins.

It is here in our pursuit of some understanding of how all of this relates to the church with which we are familiar—North Park and its myriad counterparts—that we need to invoke again the word of the apostle John: "The reason the Son of God appeared was to destroy the works of the devil" (1 John 3:8). And again: "Since therefore the children share in flesh and blood, he [Jesus] himself likewise partook of the same things, that through death he might destroy the one who has the power of death, that is the devil" (Heb 2:14).

Such passages are critical if we are to understand the non-neutrality of our own ecclesiastical and cultural context, and the presence of a relentless darkness, and thus the urgent and critical importance of Paul's word to the Ephesian Christians about the necessity of the whole armor of God.

So, with that rambling (maybe even tedious to my impatient readers) introduction to the reality of the dominion of darkness and the prince of darkness, we can begin to connect the dots to the other end of the biblical story. An early stopping place would be with the encounter of a God-fearing Middle Eastern sheik by the name of Abram with two (angelic?) messengers of God, who announced to him that, because of his faith, through his progeny all the earth would be blessed. He would be a blessing and in him all the nations of the earth would be blessed (Gen 12:1–3).

Is that an enigmatic and outrageous promise, given the circumstances? Answer: humanly, yes! But the divine plan unfolds significantly from this point.

God has a plan to bless the whole earth. This note of God's saving design is another clue to the *mystery* of which Paul speaks in his letter to the church at Ephesus.

At the other end of the biblical story (in broad strokes) comes God himself in the person of Jesus, the anointed Son—as we noted above—to destroy the works of the devil, and to destroy him who has the power of death, namely, the devil.

So what is before us in this subject (which Alan proposed to me at the Trackside Tavern) is not at all a minor theme in the story. This being so, one wonders: Why does it get so little attention in the church, and in the understanding of the church about its purpose and mission?

Jesus came to announce and to inaugurate a "new heaven and a new earth in which righteousness dwells" (2 Pet 3:13) . . . and to finally destroy the great deceiver in the lake of fire. It was by his cross that Jesus, in principle, ultimately destroyed Satan's power.

So it is now that we need to retrieve for ourselves the persuasion that it is the church's mission to be the agent of heralding the joyous news of God's great salvation, his great deliverance from the power of the darkness. It is against Christ's church, *when it is true to its calling*, that Satan and the (defensive) gates of hell have no power. The church, with her Risen Lord, is God's missionary agent to push back the dominion of darkness. The church is to be the community of light, so that no matter how hostile and vindictive the darkness may be, it cannot quench that true light.

This is why the cross stands as the Great Event of human history, and at the very center of the church's worship.

What lies between the first pages of the biblical story and the end is a record of cosmic warfare that has so many ramifications: a continual clash of darkness and light, between blessing and cursing, between God's design in glory for this created order and the forces of chaos continually provoked by the prince of darkness, between God and Satan. Again, Paul describes this as "the mystery hidden for ages and generations, but now revealed to his saints" (Col 1:26).

So, if my readers are tracking with me, this clash brings us right down to Alan's observation of the *drift* and *drag* that is continually at work to diminish the church as a community of the light, i.e., "the schemes of the devil."

THE COSMIC WARFARE:
ENTERS THE DOMINION OF DARKNESS

There it is! There has entered into God's creation an alien will, a rebellion in heaven, and a human community seduced into that rebellion . . . with unimaginably tragic results.

Yes! There enters into the cosmic scene the prince of darkness, whose purpose it is to usurp the Creator God's glory, but whose only powers are negative. He can deceive, malign, counterfeit, murder, afflict, blind, possess, and accuse—but Satan has no creative powers, and no power to bless. Thus, we are introduced to the entrance of the dominion of darkness controlled by the devil and his angels.

This sounds so unlikely, so weird, or even insane to our modern ears[10] . . . and yet there it is confronting us from one end of the Holy Scriptures to the other.

Is the world, the cosmos, any less God's? Is it any less created to be the expression of his divine nature, and the object of his infinite love?

Not at all. *Not at all!*

Yet, what unfolds is the presence of this prince of darkness blinding the minds of the human community, and taking them captive to his dominion. It is with the cosmic reality before us that Paul's commission, given him by the Risen Lord, is: "to open their eyes, so that they may turn from darkness to light and from the power of Satan to God, that they may receive forgiveness of sins and a place among those who are sanctified by faith in me" (Acts 26:17–18).

It is this reality that gives us the urgency to keep clearly in mind the apostle John's explication of the ever-present reality of this cosmic warfare that is focused on the advent of the "seed of a woman," when

---

10. Again, it is so fascinating to look at the enormous popularity of the J. D. Rowling's Harry Potter stories, with a similar supernatural and evil figure in Voldemort, who also has a similar negative agenda, and to wonder at the resistance to the biblical story and the presence of Satan!

he states: "The reason Son of God appeared was to destroy the works of the devil" (1 John 3:8). We've looked at this passage several times in this journey, but it is an all-interpretive fact that keeps getting obscured in all too much of the contemporary church.

But also, apropos to the quest of Alan (and his "bunch"), is the telling statement in the Ephesian epistle:

> "To me, though I am the very least of all the saints, this grace was given, to preach to the Gentiles the unsearchable riches of Christ, and to bring to light for everyone what is the plan of the mystery hidden for ages in God who created all things, so that *through the church the manifold wisdom of God might now be made known to the rulers and authorities in heavenly places.* This was according to the eternal purpose that he realized in Christ Jesus our Lord, in whom we have boldness and access with confidence through faith in him." (3:8–12, emphasis added)

Yes . . . note that "the mystery hidden" that Paul is declaring has now become revealed in the advent of Jesus Christ (the "seed of the woman"), and that it is in that advent that our history is interpreted, and finds meaning, not to mention what it explains about our human lives and their meaning, hope, and peace in God's reconciling love (cf. Eph 1:3–10). Or (to put it in the colloquialism of my part of the country), without this understanding of Christ and the warfare: "Nothing makes a lick o' sense!"

This same passage is also a critical clue as to why Satan will undoubtedly and relentlessly focus his malice, and his schemes, to see to it that the church is diverted from its calling and purpose. It is precisely why Paul concludes his letter to the Ephesians with the teaching about the schemes of the devil, and the urgency of the discipline of putting on the whole armor.

The perpetrator of the rebellion, whose claims to world dominion must be exposed for what they are, and whose major weapon, death, must be destroyed by the destruction of the one who has that power (cf. Heb 2:14–15). Yes, from the tragedy of that initial intrusion of the darkness in Genesis 3, Satan and his darkness defile God's creation. Satan is variously called "the god of this world" (2 Cor 4:4) and "the prince of this world" (John 14:30), not to mention that John will state: "the whole world lies in the power of the evil one" (1 John 5:19).

AN ERA OF PREPARATION FOR THE UNFOLDING
OF GOD'S PLAN FOR THE AGES

What unfolds, then, after the tragedy of Genesis 3, and in the ensuing era, is a time of preparation (which we designate as the Old Testament era), in which humankind experiences the continual corrosive power of darkness, and into which God continues to show his continual caring and preserving love for his creation by sending the rain upon the just and the unjust (Matt 5:45) . . . and in which "the heavens declare the glory of God, and the sky above proclaims his handiwork" (Ps 19:1). God periodically breaks in and reveals his glory to individuals, such as the prophet Isaiah or his gathered people at the foot of Mount Sinai. A pattern emerges, especially in the account of Isaiah, that we will need to remember as we proceed with this quest. When God reveals his glory, it is always in order that he may call his people to repentance and faith, and then to obedience and to his mission to bless the nations.

These revelatory moments always begin with adoration—by being overwhelmed by the sheer glory of the one who reveals himself. This results in those who are beholding this glory being reduced to contrition, repentance, and confession of unworthiness. God responds with grace, forgiveness, and cleansing. God will then give a call to obedience and to a task, and when the worshipper responds, God gives instructions for the mission. It is from this pattern that the classic Christian liturgies are designed. It will also be informative as we look at the components of the whole armor of God.

God reveals, again and again, that he wants to be known, loved, and obeyed because we love God. God reminds us again and again that he desires to bless us. Yet . . . again and again, after brief episodes of response to God, the drift into the darkness comes unremittingly, so that even those who pertain to be God's people become comfortable with, and conformed to, the dominion of darkness.

It becomes obvious that human religion, formed by merely human conceptions and resources, will not suffice to ultimately transform, given the blindness and the captivity of minds and wills to the darkness that is the natural state of the human community. Paul gives a telling comment on this blindness and captivity in seeking to explain the resistance of his own Jewish kinsmen. "To them," he explains, "belong the adoption, the glory, the covenants, the giving of the law, the worship, and the promises" (Rom 9:4). In another letter he spells out that what is needed is not religion, or religious rites, but rather a whole new creation: "For neither circumcision counts for anything, nor un-circumcision, but a new creation" (Gal 6:16).

The mystery of which Paul speaks in the Ephesian letter, then, is that all of that which had transpired in the past was necessary by way of preparation to make ready for the great cosmic encounter in which God himself would invade his own rebel creation in human form, in flesh and blood, and do battle with the prince of darkness from the very beginning of God's human incarnation in Jesus as the Word made flesh.

THE PLAN UNFOLDS: ENTER THE HIDDEN REVEALER

What is so incredibly wonderful about the entrance of God into human history is that it is so totally off the chart in its unlikeliness.

Paul will understate it when he teaches that Jesus Christ, "though he was in the form of God, did not count equality with God a thing to be grasped, but made himself nothing, taking the form of a servant, being born in the likeness of men. And being found in human form, he humbled himself by becoming obedient to the point of death, even death on a cross" (Phil 2:5–8).

This being so, it was not lost on the prince of darkness. On one hand is the marvelous Christmas account of Mary, the virgin mother who in her "Magnificat" senses the cosmic significance of the one she carries in her womb. The humble circumstances of the birth of Jesus are well known. But, evidently, this was not lost on the prince of darkness. What is not often even acknowledged in the Christmas celebration is Herod's satanically inspired attempt to destroy this Christ child by having all the boys under two years of age killed in what is called "the Massacre of the Innocents."

Nor was Satan unaware of the implications of the Son of God arriving on the human scene—though Satan did not in any way comprehend "the mystery" of the cross. Immediately after Jesus' baptism by John, and the descent of the dove and the proclamation that "This is my beloved Son, with whom I am well pleased," . . . Jesus was actually led *by the Spirit* into the wilderness to be tempted by the devil in a one-on-one confrontation (Matt 3:17—4:1).

Oh, but this is a most critical and much neglected or misunderstood encounter. Satan is essentially seeking to divert Jesus from whatever mission he is on, and to recruit Jesus to be part of his own dominion. To this end Satan seeks to tempt Jesus, first, to use his divine power to turn stones into bread—maybe to provide food for the masses and so attain economic power (an interpretation). Jesus rebuts this with his affirmation that one lives by the word of God.

Then Satan tempts Jesus to attain to himself popular power by jumping off of the temple and letting the angels bear him up, and actually quotes from Psalm 91 (note: Satan knows some Scripture!). Jesus responds that one does not attempt to tempt the Lord your God. Finally, Satan pulls his trump card and offers Jesus the kingdoms of the world if Jesus will simply bow down and worship him. This is very revealing, because Satan actually did have world power to give. Jesus retorts that one worships and serves only God the Lord.

What is significant here is that Satan knows enough to know that Jesus is somehow the one who has come to destroy his own diabolical power, though he seems not to know exactly how that is to transpire. But Jesus knows his own mission, and that he has come from the Father to be the firstborn of a new creation. The first Adam succumbed to Satan's temptation, but this second Adam does not. Rather, he forthrightly rejects Satan's temptations and remains the spotless Lamb, the second Adam, and the one who shall inaugurate God's new creation. Satan evidently knows that something huge is afoot and so is seeking to divert Jesus. Satan loses that battle.

DESTROYING SATAN'S WORK

Jesus thereupon begins destroying Satan's afflictions on the human community by proclaiming the joyous news of the kingdom of God,[11] casting out demons from those possessed, healing the sick, and offering good news to the poor, to the imprisoned, to the blind and oppressed. In all of his ministry Jesus is beginning the work of destroying the blight, the blindness, and the imprisonment of the human community by the prince of darkness.

Then, as his ministry of preaching, healing, and casting out evil spirits unfolds, Jesus sends out seventy-two of his disciples to do the same thing. When they surprise even themselves by the fruitfulness of this ministry, they return and exude to Jesus: "Lord, even the demons are

---

11. It is worth reiterating that the designation "the gospel of the kingdom of God" is the primary term given to Jesus' gospel in the New Testament documents.

subject to us in your name. And Jesus said to them, 'I saw Satan fall like lightening from heaven'" (Luke 10:17–18).

All of this is to clarify our understanding that the encounter of Jesus, the Light, with Satan, the prince of darkness, is no minor theme in the Gospel accounts. But, perhaps, it should become most obvious when Jesus inquires of his disciples, finally, who the populace is saying that he is . . . like: "What is the talk on the streets? What are folk saying about me? Who do they think I am?" The disciples answer that the common opinions are that he is Elijah, or Jeremiah, or maybe John the Baptist. Then he puts it to them: "But who do you say that I am?" And when Peter responds that Jesus is "the Christ," Jesus commends him as having responded by the Spirit of the Father, not by any merely human insight.

At this point, however, comes the word of Jesus that informs the mission of the church:

> And I tell you that you are Peter, and on this rock I will build my church, *and the gates of hell shall not prevail against it.* I will give you the keys of the kingdom of heaven, and whatever you bind on earth shall be bound in heaven, and whatever you loose on earth shall be loosed in heaven." (Matt 16:18–19)

When the church is truly the church, please note, it cannot be ultimately defeated in its calling to push back the powers of darkness, i.e., the gates of hell. The church becomes, in its very being: the missionary arm of the Holy Trinity, and as such is a ministry of deliverance from all the malicious effects of Satan's blight. (Where and why, dear reader, have we lost this?)

What Satan did not comprehend was the *cross*.[12]

Satan was not privy to "the mystery hidden for ages." When Satan saw the effectiveness of Jesus in bringing deliverance and healing to Satan's victims, and when Satan could not dissuade Jesus in the wilderness, then the next step would be to murder Jesus. And it is in this murderous design that the Gospel will record that Satan filled the heart of Judas to betray Jesus to the Jews.

What Satan did not know was that in so doing he was, in principle, destroying himself, as we have pointed out above. The record of guilt against us was cancelled, nailed to the cross. Trespasses and sins were

---

12. 1 Cor 2:8: "But we impart a secret and hidden wisdom of God, which God decreed before the ages for our glory." None of the rulers of this age understood this, for if they had, they would not have crucified the Lord of glory."

forgiven thereby. And since Jesus took the condemnation of death upon himself and then rose triumphant over death, Jesus destroyed Satan's power of death.[13] Reconciliation between heaven and earth took place on the cross. "For our sake he [God] made him [Christ] to be sin, so that in him we might become the righteousness of God" (2 Cor 5:21).

Immeasurable grace and peace unfolded on the cross.

By Christ's cross, and by his resurrection, Jesus inaugurated the kingdom of God, the new creation . . . and yes: the cross inaugurates the Age to Come. That event stands at the center of time and eternity.

And that is the message that the now dethroned and disarmed powers of darkness will try in every way to obscure. This cross is at the heart of the church: the community of the light. And please note: in John's Revelation it is stated that God's people have conquered Satan ". . . by the blood of the Lamb [Christ's death on the cross], and by the word of their testimony, for they loved not their lives even unto death" (Rev 12:11).

Yes, and remember: it is through the church that the manifold wisdom is manifest to the rulers and authorities *in heavenly places* (Eph 3:10).

This being so, it should not surprise us that the church itself will become the primary target of Satan's schemes and devices to render it inept in its true calling. The *drift* and *drag*, so-called by Alan, should not be a surprise. And it was to such a potential for the emasculation of the church that Paul would conclude his remarkable letter to the Ephesian believers with his sobering word about the utter necessity of putting on the whole armor of God if they were to survive.

Yes, and it should also be no surprise to us that in myriad familiar expressions of religious Christianity, such at Alan's North Park Church and its counterparts, with their comfortable gatherings for worship, what with vested clergy, musical ministry, and all of the expected ecclesiastical accouterments in place . . . that so many of the passive worshipers do not notice that the transforming gospel of the kingdom is often so obfuscated, if indeed present at all. The choir sings well, but the words they are singing are hardly comprehended. Hymns are sung automati-

---

13. There is no more graphic and colorful explanation of this than that which C. S. Lewis includes in his Chronicles of Narnia, when the white witch slays the redeemer lion, Aslan, not realizing that this is all a part of the "deeper magic" that ultimately determines history.

cally. Sermons, though well presented, are too often just a smorgasbord of moralistic, or spiritual pep talks unrelated to the awesomeness of the mystery now unveiled in Christ, which Paul extols.

This being so . . . no one seems to notice . . . because this is what has come to be expected, and this is all that they have ever known. The church as the community of the new creation that is to make known "the manifold wisdom of God" is not at all the self-understanding of such communities. This being so, they dwell comfortably within the darkness, albeit a religious and spiritual darkness. Alas!

And, again . . . this being so, it should not surprise us that within a generation of its founding the church at Ephesus is rebuked by the risen Lord for not only having somehow forgotten a major piece of their armor, namely, love . . . but also having diminished or lost even their ability to hear what the Spirit of was saying to them (Rev 2:1–7).

It happens. It should be instructive to us that in the other letters given to the church in Asia Minor (in that same passage), all with some apostolic roots, something essential to their armor was being neglected, forgotten, or displaced —with the exception of the two churches that were suffering persecution (persecution has a way of refocusing a church on its calling).

Alan's lament about the *drift* and *drag* that he observes has a source, and that source's name is: the prince of darkness . . . whose malice is subtle, clever, and relentless . . . assaulting particular churches where they are most vulnerable and least expectant.

So we need to return, now, to Paul's letter and how it embodies in its content the seven components he addresses in his metaphor of the necessity of the whole armor of God. With that return, we need to keep before us the goal of our whole quest, started at Trackside Tavern, with the question: How does the church maintain its integrity as a community of the light, or how do Christ's disciples maintain their wholesome and effective role as the *faithful presence* of the light in the existential realties of daily life (including participation within the church community)?

6

Back to the Ephesian Letter and the Armor

APPROACHING PAUL'S REMARKABLE LETTER to the Ephesians once again, allow me to insert several preliminary points that I think we need to underscore:

1. The warfare theme is inescapable and replete in all of Paul's teachings (cf. 2 Cor 10: 3–4; Rom 13:12; 16:20; Col 2:15, etc.). In our modern, or postmodern, era one of Satan's affective schemes is simply persuading the church that he (Satan) does not even exist![1] The malignant reality of Satan will not be the main theme of Paul's in this communication to the church at Ephesus . . . but he does, with obvious intent, conclude the letter with a sober warning that Satan's schemes are an ever-present reality that jeopardizes their very ability to be what God has called them to be and to do, hence, to understand this is critical to their very existence.

2. Another scheme of the devil that is so very effective in our present cultural setting is: that folk rather mindlessly assume that what we currently experience as *church* . . . is just the way that the church *is*, and that we should charitably accept it. We assume that it's probably not going to change, so why fight it? There is a contentment with this church-as-it-is, even though it may have nothing to do with what God's intent for the church is to be in his eternal (eschatological) purpose—there is little sense that the church is to be the demonstration of true human community (or new creation community) as God actually created it to be, intends it to be, and is now recreating it to be through Jesus Christ. There seems to be little thought that it is to be the missionary arm of the Holy Trinity

---

1. C. S. Lewis's unique book *Screwtape Letters*, written more than half a century ago, deals with this obscuring reality quite brilliantly.

(among other things), and hardly any sense that it is in actuality the very Body of Christ before the watching world. Rather, there is a contentedness with accepting the church as it is, and without any hope that we are to be part of that Spirit-created community[2] that is actually to make known to the principalities and power the manifold wisdom of God (Eph 3:10–11).

3. Another thing that is quite clear in Paul's teaching here, and in his approach to the reality of this cosmic warfare . . . is that the first and essential priority in engaging in such warfare is that one must be unequivocally, and foremost, a *worshiper* of God our Father and the Lord Jesus Christ. In this letter, Paul beautifully illustrates this by his own contagious adoration. Essentially the whole first chapter is his own being overwhelmed with the unsearchable riches of what God has done in Christ. It should teach us that before one is able to be a warrior, one must be a worshiper. This, I think, informs something of the content of the first-mentioned piece of armor: the belt of truth (not to mention the helmet of salvation). This is eloquently displayed in the very design of this letter of Paul's.

4. Paul, it would appear, is not primarily conceiving of warfare in some dramatic, or grandiose, terms such as the noise of human warfare—"For not with swords loud clashing, Nor roll of stirring drums"[3]—but rather he sees this warfare as the believer's daily and ordinary encounter within his or her daily context, and in the missionary confrontation of his or her engagement with this present darkness, what with its familiar routines, persons, neighborhoods, challenges, conflicts, and responsibilities—whoever we are and wherever we are. It is in our calling to be a *faithful presence*[4] as a child of the light, and as the church community demonstrat-

---

2. In a former book of mine, I described the church as "enchanted community," and I stand by that description, even though some folk balked at it. But my contention is that if the church is, as Paul describes it, "the dwelling place of God by the Spirit," then it surely fits the classical definition of *enchanted*. See Henderson, *Enchanted Community: Journey into the Mystery of the Church* (Eugene, OR: Wipf and Stock, 2006).

3. From the hymn "Lead On, O King Eternal," by E. Shurtleff (1888).

4. Again, this wonderful description of the believer's calling is borrowed from James Davison Hunter's seminal work *To Change the World: The Irony, Tragedy, and Possibility of Christianity in the Late Modern World* (New York : Oxford University Press, 2010).

ing the reconciled and reconciling relationships as the communal expression of that light. The warfare, for us, is in our incarnation of the light—and our incarnation as the light means we are always to be pushing back the relentless darkness, whether in the home, the neighborhood, the workplace, the civil society[5] . . . and, yes, inside the church as it drifts back into conformity to the darkness.

5.   Yes, and one more point of awareness, one more scheme, that may be a bit more difficult to articulate: All too much, in our post-Christian culture, we are captive to the image of the church as a *place* . . . we "go to church," or we say that something happens "at church," or maybe: "our church has been on this corner for generations." This is so common that most can't conceive of the church other than as some kind of a sacralized place where we "attend church," and where certain "church activities" take place. But before we approach the letter to the Ephesians we need to be alerted that: place, or institutional form, are not a part of Paul's understanding, or explication, of the church before us here in this letter. Rather, Paul's vision is of a veritable, and visible, Spirit-created, *new humanity*, created to be the demonstration of the communal formation of the kingdom of God. It can gather anywhere: in a living room, on the seashore, in the park, in a ballroom, in a prison, around a table at the neighborhood pub—in the most unlikely places. It is the versatile and mobile and flexible (and perhaps temporary?) recreation of the human community as God intends it to be. As such it is a critical and contagious component of our glorious gospel of Christ. Its unmistakable sense of identity is that it is the community in which all are self-consciously aware that they have been rescued out of the dominion of darkness, and translated into the dominion of God's dear Son. It is to such a calling that all are to be equipped to walk as children of the light in the midst of the cultural darkness. Finally, it is against such communal demonstration of the light that Satan will employ all his wiles to render it less than that.

---

5. To be sure, in oppressive and anti-Christian societies such as exist in many nations today, this might involve imprisonment, concentration camps, and even torture. Such have become rather remarkable breeding grounds for a vigorous new missionary movement, and a reinvigorated witness of the light, with much fruit. Our Western world tends to indulge the church, or respond to its presence with a yawn.

And so we proceed.

Writing a letter (such as this one) in Paul's day was no minor accomplishment. He didn't have all of the instant access we so take for granted—no twitter, or email, no post office drop box. To write was to compose such a letter and then, at no small cost and effort, to send it by human courier to its destination. The church at Ephesus (and Asia Minor) was very dear to Paul in that he had essentially given birth to it, and spent an intense three years there making disciples. In public and from house to house, he had poured himself out into the lives of those believers, equipping them, that new community, for their mission in a decidedly non-friendly social and cultural and religious context . . . which meant that the church was a decidedly *countercultural* community in Ephesus.

In this letter, Paul is intent on encapsulating those essentials required for them to have integrity as such, i.e., the church: the glory of God. Or again: it is to be the church that makes known to the rulers and authorities in heavenly places the manifold wisdom of God. (Try that one on for size in many of our present day Christendom churches, and it is not even comprehensible.)

To say that Paul wants to *evangelize* (or maybe re-evangelize) the church, is to understate it. Reflecting on all of the extravagant language that Paul properly uses to describe the "unsearchable riches of Christ" brings one to the inevitable conclusion that Paul's purpose is to literally *enflame* them—or maybe *consume* them—with the message of Christ . . . to make them absolutely contagious about who they are in the design of God, which design includes destroying the works of darkness. He wants to remind them of all that they possess in the gospel.

He wants them to never grow indifferent to this huge reality: that they have been made alive from their former spiritual death, and that they have been called out of darkness and into God's marvelous light. He wants them to be thrilled at what it means for them to be the "missionary arm of the Holy Trinity" right there in that great city of Ephesus.

What he finds, in attempting to do this, is that the language is inadequate to the message. The very content of the message is so inexpressible in ordinary terms . . . that it beggars the language. He employs terms such as *unsearchable, immeasurable, unimaginable*, and *beyond asking or imagining*, to assist in communicating the (to use the currently over-used word) *awesome*, all-consuming reality of what God has done in Christ.

A FATHOMLESS GREETING: GRACE AND PEACE

After a very typical identification of the sender and the recipients, Paul gives to these folk in Ephesus a greeting, which we absolutely must not skip over mindlessly. I love these two words: *grace* and *peace*. They are both fathomless in richness and meaning. "Grace to you and peace from God our Father and the Lord Jesus Christ" (1:2).

No bland liturgical greeting here. Not at all!

Here, at the very threshold of this letter, Paul reminds them that the sovereign, eternal God has poured himself out in all of his fullness on their behalf, and that this was accomplished through Christ, in whom "the whole fullness of deity dwells bodily" (Col 2:9). This was done in order to redeem God's rebel creation from its blindness and captivity to the dominion of darkness. All of this has all been accomplished by Christ's cross. The design of the cross is that of restoring the cosmic *shalom* to God's creation. By that cross, heaven and earth are reconciled. This design, this grace and peace, this infinite love of God, by the cross of Christ reconciling the world unto God, gives definition and cosmic scope to our term *salvation*.

"Who can explore his strange design?"[6]

THE PLAN OF THE MYSTERY HIDDEN FOR AGES

The Greek word *gospel* conveys the notion of a "thrilling announcement" of some sort. If that word, then, is to have any such meaning for Paul, then his use of it illustrates from this beginning in his letter that he is thrilled. From the start it is a breathless accolade of praise and instruction sent to his spiritual children in Ephesus. And, please note: it is all focused on Jesus Christ. Paul illustrates here both the primary Christocentric necessity of the *belt of truth*, but also unpacks the content of the *helmet of salvation*, i.e., the knowledge of the eschatological gospel of the kingdom of God.

From the foundation of the world God has designed that we should be totally *in sync* with himself, i.e., "holy and without blemish" (Eph 5:27). God, at infinite cost, comes to us in Christ to be the very "light of the world" (John 8:12), in order to destroy the works of darkness. We, in turn, are called to that light in order to also be "the light of the world" (Matt 5:14), so that Paul reminds the Ephesians that they are to "walk as

6. From Charles Wesley's hymn "And Can It Be."

children of the light" (Eph 5:8). In all of this letter Paul will be explicating both the light, and how we as children of the light learn how to walk in that light, to faithfully live into that light, and in so doing to always be putting on "the armor of light" (Rom 13:12) . . . and in so doing we are to be engaging the forces of darkness and irresistibly pushing those forces back, since the darkness is not able to overcome the light.[7]

THE DEFAULT GOOD NEWS: THE HIDDEN MYSTERY NOW MADE KNOWN

Just think how incredible this is. *In Christ* the mystery of the overarching purpose of our individual lives, of the human community, of history of the world, of the destiny of all creation, is made known.

Hey! Think of it: we know the answer. God's irresistible purpose is nothing less than to unite all things, and to make all things new in Christ, things in heaven and things on earth.

No small design here. God's now-revealed purpose, in love, is that we should become those who inherit all of the extravagant blessings of his now-inaugurated new creation, and this according to the riches of his grace toward us in Christ Jesus.

Now, dear reader, please take note that it is right here that Satan will employ every conceivable scheme, and will seek in every clandestine way to reduce all of this to one more merely human religion (as we have noted elsewhere, it is what some have aptly designated as *religious Christianity*).

When the human community rebelled against its creator, it left a void that humans have been seeking to fill with religions, and schemes of spirituality, of their own making ever since, . . . right downs to this day.

Paul is not talking about religion, however. What Paul is reminding those Ephesian folk of is: that God absolutely did *not* come in Christ to institute a new religion. No! Christ came with a huge and much grander and ultimate (eschatological) purpose: that of making us new after the image of Christ, and to seal that new creation in us with his own Spirit, so that his new humanity is animated by the Spirit of the Father and the Son: "the Spirit of wisdom and revelation in the knowledge of him" (Eph 1:17).

In seeking to communicate such a gospel, Paul also demonstrates to them something of the content and purpose of that weapon about

7. John 1:5.

which he will speak in the sixth chapter: " . . . praying at all times in the Spirit" (6:18). He does this by including in this letter at least two of his own prayers on their behalf, prayers of awesome and transformational importance.

This brief digest gives us a window into the use of the *belt of truth* and the *helmet of salvation* in living into our calling to be the faithful presence of the light. Then, right in the middle of this unfolding of the immeasurable greatness of God's power in Christ . . . Paul segues into the necessity of repentance and faith . . . or as I have chosen to interpret the *shield of faith*: as including *repentance* as a vital component of true faith, i.e., a faith that sees both the darkness and the light, and deliberately and intentionally turns from the darkness and to the light.

See how he does this: after praying that these believers at Ephesus might know "the immeasurable greatness of his power toward us who believe" (1:19), Paul, without skipping a beat, tells them that this power given to us is the same power as that power that God exercised "when he raised him [Jesus] from the dead and seated him at his right hand in the heavenly places, far above all rule and authority and power and dominion . . ." (1:20–21).

Question: What's he talking about? Who are these rulers and authorities and powers?

Who, or what, did Jesus put under his feet when he was raised from the dead? Who did God make head over all things to the church?

There's something of cosmic importance going on here, and it's too important to skip over it mindlessly. And the answers to these questions begins to come out in the passage that follows in which Paul reminds them of their own deliverance out of darkness and into God's marvelous light.

Watch how he explicates the dynamic of their conversion of mind and will:

> And you were *dead* in the trespasses and sins in which you once walked, following the course of this world, *following the prince of the power of the air*, the spirit that is now at work in the sons of disobedience—among whom we all once lived in the passions of our flesh, carrying out the desires of *the body and mind*, and were by nature *children of wrath*, like the rest of mankind. But God being rich in mercy, because of his great love with which he loved us, even when we were dead in our trespasses, *made us alive together with Christ*—by grace you have been *saved*—and raised

us up with him and seated us with him in the heavenly places in Christ Jesus, so that in the coming ages he might show the immeasurable riches of his grace in kindness toward us in Christ Jesus. *For by grace you have been saved through faith*. And this is not your own doing; it is the gift of God, not a result of works, so that no one may boast. For we are his workmanship, *created in Christ Jesus for good works*, which God prepared beforehand, that we should walk in them. (2:1–10)

This passage isn't as harmless as it might look.

If we are made alive in Christ, and delivered from captivity, then it follows that we are somehow residing still in rebel-held territory . . . a fact that Paul is seeking to underscore in the whole letter. Gregory Boyd has spelled this out quite clearly in his magisterial work on the subject,[8] namely, that Satan is a fatally wounded and desperate archenemy of God who still rules upon the earth knowing that his ultimate destruction is inevitable. He is the illegitimate tyrant whose doom was sealed on the cross. Meanwhile the battle belongs to the church, as Paul will say again in this letter.

On the one hand Paul wants the Ephesian Christians, and us, to rejoice and give thanks for such grace and peace, for such a rescue as has come to us in Christ. But on the other hand, there is that which becomes too often dim, if not totally obscured in the church's consciousness, namely, that this very deliverance from captivity makes us *subversives*, i.e., a countercultural folk in this present world. As I have quoted earlier, we are always in missionary confrontation with the dominant culture of darkness in all of its ramifications (even inside of the church), and this is the daily, and inescapable, context for all of us.

Read this passage again, and remember that Paul's commission from the risen Christ was to turn us "from darkness to light and from the power of Satan to God" (Acts 26:18). In such a description of our salvation there is an unmistakably powerful deliverance by Christ, which produces life out of death, which creates us new in body and mind. Such is not some

8. See Gregory A. Boyd, *God at War: The Bible & Spiritual Conflict* (Downers Grove, IL: InterVarsity, 1997), 258ff.

casual and convenient profession of belief in Christ required in order to be a part of the church—not at all. It is, rather, a radical decision of mind and will that embraces Jesus and his dominion with such passion that the whole of life is transformed, and continually being transformed, into that new creation and verified by its good works. And note: these good works, for which we are created in Christ Jesus, also find significant definition in the seven pieces of the whole armor with which we are dealing in this book.

That understanding begins to define for us the necessity of the *shield of faith*. When Satan's assaults of doubt and fear and accusation come against the people of God (which they inevitably do), the believer takes the shield of faith and says to Satan: "No! I have renounced your dominion, and I belong to Jesus Christ and have chosen him and his dominion. I belong to Christ, and though you use all of your devices, even death, you cannot separate me from that love and grace."

To no small degree the drift that Alan has asked about begins here. When *repentance* and *faith* are diminished, obfuscated, or made somehow an elective in the Christian community, then the church begins again to be conformed to (or becomes comfortable with) the darkness. The ostensible community of faith, then, becomes only the religious expression of the dominion of darkness.

So-called "church membership" then replaces the call for radical discipleship.

It all becomes something much less than our intentional and purposeful entrance in to the community of the kingdom of God . . . and something much more humanly explainable. The light is diminished. Darkness inhabits the church.

Dietrich Bonhoeffer gave the church a great gift when he chided the church for preaching *cheap grace*, which he defined thusly: "Cheap grace is the preaching of forgiveness without requiring repentance, baptism without Church discipline, Communion without confession, absolution without contrition. Cheap grace is grace without discipleship, grace without the Cross, grace without Jesus Christ, living and incarnate."[9] As I have noted, a more recent set of writers have designated this same phenomenon as *religious Christianity*, which is so very prevalent in all too much of the church of our experience. Bonhoeffer witnessed this

9. Dietrich Bonhoeffer, *The Cost of Discipleship*, translated by R. H. Fuller (New York: Macmillan, 1956), 38.

in the church in Germany as well as in North America in the twentieth century,[10] and Søren Kierkegaard witnessed it in his experience with the Danish church in the nineteenth century.[11]

Our calling to be children of the light, and to wear the armor of light, does not allow for such cheap grace or casual discipleship (which is an oxymoron). Rather, our lives are to be daily, perennially, and deliberately expressions of such repentance and faith, and it is by such that we quench the fiery darts of the wicked adversary.

THE CHURCH: THE DWELLING PLACE FOR GOD
BY THE SPIRIT

It is at this point in the letter (2:11–22) that Paul begins to give some definition to what is the essence this new creation community, this church, into which the Ephesian folk had been called. It is that community in which God's reconciling grace is manifested in human relationships, and most immediately for them between ethnic Jews and their Gentile neighbors. The antagonisms and barriers that had always existed between these groups were a contradiction to the essence of God's new humanity. Ultimately, in the church's mission, there must be that "one new man" demonstration between every kindred, tongue, tribe, and nation, i.e., a new humanity in Christ.

The church is a community where all are reconciled to God and to one another in Christ. Such a reconciled community is intended to be a significant witness to the reconciling power of the gospel before the watching world. It is intended to be the visible community in which God's love for us would be demonstrated in our reconciling, redemptive, and edifying servant-love relationships with each other.

". . . a dwelling place for God by the Spirit" (Eph 2:22).

What an incredibly wonderful definition of the church.

Then Paul returns to the cosmic dimension of Christ's work—or maybe to the *eschatological* dimension of Christ's work. He is again over-

10. The recent biography of Bonhoeffer by Erik Metaxas, *Bonhoeffer: Pastor, Martyr, Prophet, Spy* (Nashville: T. Nelson, 2010), makes Bonhoeffer's agony over this quite explicit.

11. See Soren Kierkegaard, *Attach upon Christendom*, translated by Walter Lowrie (Boston: Beacon, 1956).

whelmed by the magnitude of what he describes as the *unimaginable* and *unsearchable* riches of what has been made known in Christ: ". . . the plan of the mystery hidden for ages."

EXCURSUS

Why is this awesome and overarching and cosmic understanding of the work of Christ, which should be a default understanding for us, so generally *unrecognized* within all too many of our present church scenes (such as North Park and its counterparts)? Even in those church communities that do profess to take the gospel seriously, the proclivity is to always define the gospel primarily in terms of our individual or personal deliverance (salvation, forgiveness, heaven when we die, etc.). Such a personal dimension is surely an enormously necessary and wonderfully critical one for those of us who are believers. Yet in Paul's mind, as expressed here, the personal deliverance is always within the larger cosmic context of Christ coming to deal with the problem behind the problem, namely, with the great archenemy of God: "the prince of the power of the air" (Eph 2:2), and the evil he foments in the world.

The "*I was blind, but now I see*" joy that we individually experience in Christ is but a single facet of the cosmic whole of our reconciling gospel of peace. Jesus came to destroy the dominion of darkness, and in so doing to provide for us the grace and peace of being reconciled to God. That such a default understanding is so obscure in the mind and understanding of so many is, inescapably, another of Satan's schemes, i.e., to hide his own darkening work of diminishing the church's effectiveness in exercising the weapons of its warfare.

TO PRINCIPALITIES AND POWERS . . . THROUGH THE CHURCH

As we move into Ephesians 3, again, Paul paints his whole ministry against the background of the mystery of Christ, the mystery hidden for ages, into which ministry he (Paul) has been called to bring to light (3:9). There are at least several interrelated pieces to this that we need to flag.

Again, the first of these is: that it is his own ministry to bring to light this "mystery hidden for ages in God." The next is another (satanically?) obscured understanding of the church, namely, that it is *through the church* that the manifold wisdom of God is to be made known to the rulers and authorities in the heavenly places. From that understanding of the church's mission we need to lift up a specific component, which is precisely: that the church is to intentionally make known the manifold wisdom of God. Lest we mindlessly read through this, we need to stop and realize that this says to both the Ephesian believers and to us what is the eternal purpose of God in Christ.

In answer to Alan's initial inquiry about the *drift* and *drag* that seems to afflict and emasculate the church of his experience, this unique passage gives definition to the church's mission, purpose, and essence, which is to *encounter* the cosmic powers . . . the spiritual forces of evil in the heavenly places, the dominion of darkness . . . with the light of the glorious gospel of Christ that is to be incarnate in both the lives of the sons and daughters of light.

But don't stop there. Such is to be accomplished through the church as the very incarnation of the *community of light* in every existential setting in which it finds itself. This incarnation is multifaceted.

Here, I want to insist that such an incarnation is significantly defined by the whole armor of God, which we have been looking at, and especially by the *helmet of salvation*, the mind of Christ. Let me interpret this (with others) as: the people of God *thinking Christianly*. Yes, the church is not to be mindless.[12] God's people are to be "renewed in knowledge after the image of their creator" (Col 3:10). The church is to be formed by the whole counsel of God,[13] or the word of Christ dwelling richly among its participants.[14]

Personally, Paul is breathlessly excited and altogether convinced about being called to herald such a message. In this, he is modeling for them (and us) something of both the wielding of the *sword of the Spirit* and also of having on his feet the *readiness of the gospel of peace*. Take note.

Beginning with 6:14, again, he models for us another piece of the armor, which is that of *praying at all times in the Spirit with all prayer and supplication*. It is wonderful to know what the substance of such prayers

---

12. It has been said (by someone of impressive credentials, whose name I have been unable to retrieve) that the ancient church was so effective because it out-lived, out-thought, and out-died its pagan counterparts.

13. Acts 20:27.

14. Col 3:16.

might be, and this is the second prayer in this brief letter that helps those of us living today in exercising such a weapon.

Talk about extravagant and humanly impossible prayers!

They are so beyond our merely human grasp. Paul actually prays that they may be able to comprehend the incomprehensible. It is presuppositional with Paul that there is the necessary and dynamic presence of the Spirit given to the church. The Spirit is given to them, not only to strengthen them, rooting and grounding them in love, but the Spirit is given so that they will be able to comprehend how vast is the love of Christ, which surpasses knowledge. And can we grasp that we are actually to be filled with that same fullness of God?

Paul then concludes this first section of his letter with an ascription of praise in which he gives us one more piece to lift our eyes to the ultimate and exalted calling of the church. The church is to be the radiant display of the divine nature (glory), just as Christ Jesus is the radiant display of the divine nature: ". . . to him be *glory in the church* and in Christ Jesus throughout all generations, forever and ever. Amen" (3:21, emphasis added). As Christ Jesus is the light of the world, so the church, as the dwelling place of God by the Spirit, is to be the light of the world, . . . as it wears the armor of light, as it is always and everywhere putting on the whole armor of God.

He insists that through God we are able to actually do far more abundantly than all that we ask or think according to the power at work in us. Just think of it. Fathomless. It takes away all of our pitiful excuses . . .

Then, as we come to chapter 4, Paul shifts gears. To do an interpretive summary through the lens of our metaphor of the armor of God: the first three chapters of Ephesians are descriptive of the helmet of salvation in that they inform us how to *think Christianly*, how to have the mind of Christ; then what follows in most of the rest of the letter will assist in understanding the breastplate of righteous, or how to live and *behave Christianly*, both individually, and especially in the new creation community, i.e., how we visibly display the *praxis* of the divine nature in our daily lives, and so counter the relentless darkness.

SPECIFIC DEFINITION ON THE INNER LIFE
OF THE NEW CREATION COMMUNITY

Thus, as in chapter 3 of Ephesians Paul affirms that "*by the church*, the manifold wisdom of God shall be made known to the rulers and authorities in heavenly places" (3:10, emphasis added), so in chapter 4 he moves to give specific definition to the inner life of that church, through which God will make known God's manifold wisdom to such powers of darkness.

How is such a calling to be accomplished?

We know that we are to be the children of light, or the "light of the world," as Jesus taught us. We also know that God's kingdom grows and permeates the human community like leaven permeates a lump of dough. Our response might well be one of total unworthiness for such a calling. Even Paul frequently acknowledges his own weakness and, as in this discourse, confesses that he is "the very least of all the saints," i.e., he is not part of the original twelve apostles, nor is he a part of the Jerusalem "mother church" leadership.

Even so, he has insisted that we, the church, are to be the glory of God, and that this church is the "dwelling place for God by the Spirit" (2:22). Remember, also, that Jesus had said that it was *he*, not we, who would build his church, and that the gates of hell would not be able to prevail against it. The very use of the word "church," *ekklesia* in Greek, carries its own implications, since it is a common word that refers to an assembly of persons *called out* of one context in order to be engaged, or *called into*, another. That being so, it follows that those whom Jesus *calls out* to be his church are to be self-consciously called from the dominion of darkness, and so *called into* this new community of light, which Jesus is building (which, as we have said over and over, is intended to be the missionary arm of the Holy Trinity). This would also mean that they (or *we*) are, in Peter's terms: aliens and exiles in this dominion of darkness (of Satan) no matter who or where they (we) are.

It's an understatement to say that such is not your ordinary understanding of church involvement among most traditional church folk, isn't it?

But even that is all a bit theoretical. Our question is still: How does such a *glory-church*[15] (cf. Eph 3:21) where Paul speaks of the glory of God in the church) come into flesh and blood reality among ordinary people such as we? What are the dynamics? How is it equipped for such a calling? What is its inner life to display? How does it demonstrate new creation? What is it that makes it that expression of the manifold wisdom of God? These are the questions that bring it all down to earth.

15. Cf. Eph 3:21, where Paul speaks of the glory of God in the church.

We need, then, to look very carefully at chapters 4–6, because it is here that Paul speaks to these questions, and what he says is critical to our understanding of how it is that, existentially, practically, visibly, and among ordinary men and women, God purposes to make known his manifold wisdom.

This, in turn, brings us to a very delicate point in seriously engaging the questions of Alan and his bunch. It will require that we take a step back and engage in a critique of, or at least acknowledge, the *Christendom* filters (or paradigms) that prevent us from seeing and hearing the practical implications for North Park Church, and that large swath of its counterparts across the ecclesiastical scene, especially here in North America. It will be necessary for us to see how the church institutions with which we are so familiar tend to *depersonalize* the church, and inadvertently create something like convocations of friendly, and religious, and congenial strangers, who may share many convictions, and are comfortable with the Christian jargon—but in which we may participate without really having a clue as to who these other nice people are.

I think we will want to tread very lightly here, on the one hand, lest we offend some who are weak. But on the other hand, I think it necessary to be quite deliberate in setting Paul's lucid teaching on the church in this letter over against that pattern that has come to be accepted uncritically by generations of traditional church folk.

What I'm insisting is that, if we are even to begin to see what lies before us in chapters 4–6, it will be necessary for us to be delivered from that dominant pattern of the church which defines the church in terms of (forgive the alliteration): *place, pastor-priest, performance* (familiarly designated, rightly or wrongly, as a "worship service"), and a *pervasive passivity* on the part of its membership regarding their responsibility for the mission of God.

Such bland, often mindless (though sincere) identification with a church society is at total odds with the prevalence of the "one another" references throughout these coming chapters (and, indeed, the whole of the New Testament). They give us a picture of the *essential* form of the church, in which all of God's people (saints) have names, and faces, and stories. It gives us the form of the church in which all are responsible for one another, in which all accountable to one other, and in which all are *ministers*.

REFLECTION

Too often, the church has seriously compromised itself at this point (drifted?). This gets delicate because it is so *other* than the experience of so many church participants. One can be on friendly terms with other participants in a church society, sit in study groups with them, wear the church nametag, laugh, tell stories, etc. . . . yet have no idea who they are, no real *one another* knowledge of, or sense of responsibility for, or accountability to such friends. Conversely, from the beginning of the church in Acts, the word *fellowship* (κοινωνία) is used to convey the intimate, sharing, participatory nature of the communal relationships that existed among believers.

Which means, of course, that the essential form of the church must be communal, small enough for such interdependence, and a context in which the love of God in and between believers is tangible. There is a place for larger convocations, assemblies, and societies, which may be helpful in the mission of the church, but such are always supplemental and not the essential form. This is a critical distinction, and what follows in Paul's letter is only understandable in this light.

This next section of Paul's letter gives us help in knowing how this was formed.

Rather than a somewhat depersonalized society, chapters 4–6 require, or presuppose, a very intimate, mutual, personal and interpersonal set of relationships, i.e., a true *community*.[16] These chapters also require our presuppositional understanding of the very real and dynamic presence of the Holy Spirit as dwelling in and creating and empowering this church. Without the supernatural working of the Spirit of the Father and the Son, such an extraordinary life and ministry as God's new creation

---

16. I cannot resist making reference here to the marvelous theological concept of *perichoresis*, which I have used elsewhere to describe the relationships that exist within and between the three persons of the Holy Trinity: "Perichoresis conveys the picture of divine love expressing itself as those three Persons are *in* each other, *making room for each other, interpenetrating* and *interanimating* each other, *drawing life from* and *pouring life into* each other, *rejoicing in* each other, and *seeking the glory* of each other. '. . . In eternity Father, Son, and Spirit share a dynamic and mutual reciprocity'" (quoted from my earlier book, *Enchanted Community*, 26, and digested from a larger work by Colin Gunton). The church's understanding of true community should derive from this description of the Trinitarian community.

in Christ is impossible. Only by such divine presence can it in any sense be that community which makes manifest the manifold wisdom of God to the powers and authorities.

Such a concept of the church has essentially nothing (or at least very little) to do with ecclesiastical hierarchies, impressive sanctuaries, huge assemblies, marvelous music, efficient organization, or skilled church professionals—though all or any of these could be (by some salvific and missional redefinition of their self-understanding and place within God's design) useful (maybe).

Indulge me in a *non sequitur* here. I find that it is very helpful, in giving me perspective and motivation in our calling, to retrieve another divine intent for such a calling, and that is in order to prepare the church as a *beautiful bride for the Lamb* (as per Rev 21:02). I was first blessed with this insight by some of my Pentecostal brothers and sisters, but you will notice that it is also wonderfully set forth in the fifth chapter of this letter (vv. 25–27). I like it. It motivates me when it all looks a bit mundane and humanly hopeless.

" WORTHY OF THE CALLING TO WHICH YOU HAVE BEEN CALLED"

With the fourth chapter of his letter, Paul turns to the *how* question: How is such a calling created in flesh and blood persons and communities?

Right away, he describes the relationships that are to exist with *one another*,[17] and those relationships, in turn, are reflective of the divine nature, which is being created in us by the Holy Spirit.[18] Here, our daily walk with and before one another is to be "with all humility and gentleness, with patience, bearing with one another in love, eager to maintain the unity of the Spirit" (4:2–3) as God's new creation people. This becomes the more significant as it defines something of the Christlike

---

17. The single Greek word Ἀλλήλων translated as "one another" in English is a key to understanding the relationships within the community. It is everywhere present in Paul's teachings about our relationships with each other, all of which are edifying, and require some intentional intimacy of accountability to and responsibility for *one another*.

18. Cf. Rom 8:29.

aroma of our lives, even as we are, by virtue of our calling into Christ, a countercultural and essentially *radical* and *subversive* new humanity.

I love it! We are to be *Christ* to one another in love. Our calling (to borrow from Henri Nouwen) is a calling to "littleness," i.e., making of ourselves those of no reputation, but deliberately taking on ourselves the form of being servants to one another (cf. Phil 2:7). What follows in this chapter begins with this articulation of our demeanor to one another.

Let's look at this pragmatically, and discern in practical terms how it is that Christ builds his church.

Verses 4:4–16 are actually one of the very few passages in the whole of the New Testament that give us practical and significant clues as to the formation of Christian community. The ascended Lord, Paul writes, gives equipping gifts to his church. The goal of Christ's *gifting* of the church is for the express purpose of *every believer* being equipped for maturity in his or her daily walk and ministry amidst the realties of whatever time, or place, or circumstance in which they find themselves.

All are to be equipped so that they are able to think, and speak, and function as those who are mature in Christ, and so enabled to engage in the ministry and mission of the church: "the measure of the stature of the fullness of Christ" (4:13). God's people are not to be vulnerable to every negative intellectual, doctrinal, moral, and spiritual aberration, i.e., every "wind of doctrine" (4:14).

We need to underscore this: *every believer* is to be so equipped . . . and when this equipping is neglected, or obscured, or made the privilege of a few, then the *relentless darkness* again effectively inhabits the church, and in so doing emasculates it. It also leads to the lame and indefensible excuse: "Oh, I'm only a layperson."

These verses say so much more than they say. The goal of Christ's gifting of the church is to the end that every believer is gifted to be a significant part of the mission of God. That church is to be the functional and effective agent of God to make known to the authorities and powers the manifold wisdom of God, and that by always being an authentic demonstration of the love of God wrought out in the community of light, building itself up in love.

And, it is so encouraging that Christ does this awesome thing with ordinary folk, with "nobodies," with garden-variety believers such as we, who become, by his grace, the very light of the world (cf. 1 Cor 1:26–31).

FOUR EQUIPPING GIFTS TO EQUIP THE SAINTS FOR MINISTRY

To this end, then, Paul teaches us that the ascended Lord Jesus gives to the church four equipping gifts, and these gifts are in the form of persons within the community especially equipped themselves to serve as examples (models) and mentors, and teachers of the rest. These four gifts are: *apostle, prophet, evangelist,* and *pastor-teacher* (or teaching shepherd). Please note that *all* of these are of a different genre, and have no necessary connection with what Christendom designates as: the "ordained minister of word and sacrament." Such a Christendom designation tends to be an enormous and troublesome filter, even a subversion . . . *unless, of course, such a designation may be reconceived in terms of these four gifts,* whose purpose is that of producing mature folk who are *all* "working properly" (4:16).

Got it?

Every believer is to be equipped . . . each a part of the ministry, each responsible for others within the community, and each accountable. Be reminded, also, that this is impossible in a large and impersonal assembly of those who are essentially unknown to one another.[19] To this end I want to venture an interpretation of these four gifts, and to do it in the light of other scriptures, since they are not here (nor elsewhere in the New Testament) explicitly explained. It is my conclusion that all four of these gifts are required for the effective equipping of God's people.

Whether the four gifts may be present in the community in several specific persons, or whether a single individual may possess all of these gifts, is not spelled out here. In my own career I have found myself responsible for mentoring in each of these areas, but there are individuals who are uniquely gifted in one of these areas. I also know of growing missional communities that have called, or designated, individuals with these specific gifts to assist in the equipping ministry of their community in these specific areas. But what they indicate is that there are the strategic areas of ministry in which every believer is to have some degree of maturity and competence.

---

19. In Part 2 of this work we shall seek to provide some provocation on how this might be architected for the future of the church.

Apostle

I interpret this gift as that of the missionary church planter.

Strange as it may sound to our institutional orientation, it appears that in the New Testament the church did not see itself as static, or rooted, but was actually to grow spontaneously, permeating the neighborhoods and cities like leaven in a lump. Every believer was a potential church planter. Every home was a potential meeting place for a community of believers. Every believer was to be contagious with the message and, as such, engaged deliberately. The ministry of hospitality (an open home) was a key factor. Paul repeatedly speaks of the churches in people's homes.

This is a learned capacity. Believers are to be mentored by being with someone who has engaged effectively in this part of the mission of God. Some have termed this: *organic church growth*. Sound strange? To those formed by the static institutional focus and orientation of our North Park type churches, yes, it sounds strange . . . but to New Testament Christianity, not at all.

Prophet

God's people certainly need to know their cultural setting. They need to be able to exegete the context of their ministry. They need to discern the times in which they live. They need to have a larger view of who they are, and where they are going, and what some of the consequences are of their kingdom-of-God presence as the children of light in this dominion of darkness.

The New Testament documents are replete with the presence of prophets, who appear to be a vital part of the Holy Spirit's presence in the church. God's people are not to be naïve or innocent with regard to what is going on around them. And, please note: this awareness has frequently been in terms of their confrontation with principalities and powers that are ominous, and could cost them their lives, or reputations, or jobs, or security.

There are, of course, those more prominent prophetic voices such as Dietrich Bonhoeffer, Martin Luther King Jr., John Perkins, Lesslie Newbigin, Jacques Ellul, etc. But the ascended Lord gives to the vital church those local prophetic gifts to help them and us (sometimes to warn us) in the midst of the political, economic, social, cultural, environmental, and other realities and zeitgeists that are the dominant social order of our place and moment.

Evangelist

Again, we have to fight our way through familiar distorting caricatures as we take a look at this gift. But consider that in the whole armor of God, the feet are shod with the readiness of the gospel of peace. At the very least, such a part of our necessary armor is that every believer be a communicator of what God has done in Christ. Every believer needs to be somewhat articulate in who he or she is in Christ, and to have a healthy freedom in engaging in significant conversation with those still in the darkness, meeting them where they are. "How beautiful are the feet of those who preach good news" (Rom 10:15). This particular gift of persons who assist new believers in achieving this capacity is not to be exceptional, but rather the very joyous and contagious readiness to communicate to those with whom we are in contact day by day. God's ordinary people are the cutting edge of the mission of God in their 24/7 lives. Put this together with the previously mentioned gifts of *apostle* and *prophet*, and you catch something of the missional DNA of God's sons and daughters.

This gift is not learned or exercised in church meetings. One learns the gift of life-giving conversation by actual engagement with those folk who are our neighbors, friends, working partners, seatmates on international flights, beer-drinking buddies, colleagues in various projects, or on teams of one sort or another. Such equipping requires mentors who have this skill, and who enable others to see and hear and learn in real settings. In the book of Acts, Luke records that "the word went everywhere," and it did this as every contagious believer became the presence of the light, became those demonstrations of the beautiful feet of the gospel in flesh and blood.

Pastor-Teacher

There must also, and of necessity, be those in the community who are mature enough in the word (teachings) of Christ, and in wisdom, so that they can equip the novices in the "whole counsel of God" and form in them the mind of Christ—to form them in kingdom *praxis* and thinking out of the teachings of Christ and the apostles.

If the word of Christ is to dwell richly[20] among those in the Christian community, then it stands that someone must, of necessity, equip God's

---

20. Col 3:16.

people (saints) in such knowledge so that they are able to minister to one another. Paul spent two years with the Ephesian folk doing exactly that. They learned and received and heard and saw the gospel in Paul. Again, this gift is to be reproduced in *every believer* so that each one becomes a well-informed practitioner and communicator of the manifold wisdom of God, in whatever context.

One of the most tragic evidences of the darkness inhabiting our own churches is when the folk become biblically and theologically il- literate, or mindless . . . when the word of Christ does *not* dwell richly in and among the company of believers. In such churches the relentless darkness prevails, and inhabits the church, and utterly debilitates it in its God-given purpose.

≈ ≈ ≈

These four gifts also become a significant part of our understanding of the seven components that Paul names as the whole armor of God, which we looked at in an earlier chapter. Paul fills out the end result of the faithful exercising of these gifts by giving us the picture of God's sons and daughters taking on the stature of Christ. As such they speak the truth in love . . . as they are not tripped-up by "deceitful schemes" . . . as they grow "into him who is the head, into Christ" . . . as "every joint," each part of the body, functions so that the whole body grows and "builds itself up in love" (4:14–16).

The church can never become comfortable inhabiting the darkness so long as these four gifts are being exercised. Conversely, the darkness begins to inhabit the church when these gifts are relegated to the re- sponsibility of someone else, perhaps some ecclesiastical elites, or some professionals, rather than being expressed by every one of God's people. These four gifts also give us some substantive understanding of how the commission of Christ to "make disciples" is accomplished.

And, alas! This is where Alan's observation about the *drift* and *drag* find their explanation in all too much of the church that he and we have experienced. Tragically, such churches are all that many sincere folk have ever known. They cannot even imagine anything other than what they have experienced (or have not experienced)—and, sadly, probably are not interested in anything other.

THE SHAPE AND FLAVOR OF THE NEW LIFE IN CHRIST

In the remainder of his letter, Paul reminds the Ephesian believers of their own decision to turn from darkness to light. This is presuppositional and essential for them to always keep clearly in their minds, and it also calls forth a continual act of will, as this new life in Christ works itself out in the realities of their daily existence. There is an *ongoing discipline* of repentance and faith, not at all a one-time thing. One is always confronted with new and demanding challenges from the darkness when being faithful to one's calling to be the incarnation of God's new creation in Christ. And so Paul, beginning with 4:17, spells out the contrast: "you must no longer walk as the Gentiles do, in the futility of their minds. They are darkened . . ."

Please note that those Gentiles (or *sojourners*—however you want to designate them[21]) were not some ominous and unfamiliar personalities. Paul is talking about their very real, and frequently much-appreciated, family members, friends, and neighbors. Not that there weren't those who were, in fact, hostile to the gospel and to the believing community. There were and are those. Still, there are spiritual characteristics of blindness, hardness of heart, sensuousness, and all kinds of behavior that are alien to the purpose of God for humanity, i.e., all sin and "fall short of the glory of God" (Rom 3:23).

Those who have heard and believed the truth that is in Jesus are, therefore, always to be putting off the *old self* (4:22), their former way of life, and putting on the *new self*, created after the likeness of God. They are to put on the armor of light. God's people (that's who we are) are to be the very presence of the divine nature in flesh and blood. That new nature, as Paul describes it here, is being flavored by true righteousness and holiness. God's new creation folk are to self-consciously display something that is joyous and liberating and creative and loving—they are to incarnate the nature of God and the will of God. Such new life incarnates truth telling. It incarnates the forthright dealing with legitimate anger, because anger can result in destructive behavior . . . which, Paul notes, allows the devil to insinuate his darkness into the community.

---

21. Again, some of the refreshing missional church proponents (especially those from Australia) resist using such designations as: *outsiders, unbelievers, pagans*, etc., choosing rather the term *sojourners*, which they describe as "spiritually confused God-seekers." I like that and have adopted it. That describes many of my very real and much loved neighbors.

Yes, the new life is a life of profound, Christlike, self-giving love that shows itself in generosity, in conversation and communication that builds up others, in Spirit-derived and life-producing kindness, tenderheartedness, forgiveness . . . simply because that is the way God loves us. As if that did not say it clearly enough, this is all followed (5:1ff.) with Paul's remarkable word to us: precisely, that you and I, as God's children, are to be *imitators of God* as his dear children. The family DNA of God is to be visible in the lives of God's children (he gives illustrations of this in the next section). By way of contrast, the old life was profaned by all kinds of corrupt communication and behavior. He names covetousness (greed) and sexual promiscuousness as two examples. He is explicit that this kind of very common behavior doesn't have a place with God's kingdom people. (In our own day, this is much of the menu of popular television programming and news sources, alas!).

WALK AS CHILDREN OF LIGHT

"Therefore . . . at one time you were darkness, but now you are light in the Lord. Walk as children of light . . . and try to discern what is pleasing to the Lord" (5:7–10). Yes, the bottom line is that we actually destroy the works of darkness by walking as children of light, by putting on the armor of light in the ordinary, everyday vicissitudes of our lives. We push back the darkness by being the light of the world, by living into our calling. That doesn't sound dramatic, but it is enormously effective.

It is in an attempt to erode this very new creation demonstration of the light that Satan employs his wiles.

We need to take note of the fact that this section begins with the focus on the life of love that we, as imitators of God, are to display—Christlike, self-sacrificing love, which is a fragrant aroma to God. Jesus had taught the disciples that "all men shall know that you are my disciples, if you have love for one another" (John 13:35). I say we need to take note because after one generation the ascended Lord spoke to the church at Ephesus, and after commending them for their good expressions, he rebuked them for abandoning the love they had at first, and threatened to remove their lamp from the lampstand . . . or discount them as an agent of the mission of God, until they repented (cf. Rev 2:4–5). That's serious, and speaks to us about the aroma of authentic love that is to suffuse the community of the kingdom of God.

If you think back to the equipping of all of God's people (which we saw in the fourth chapter of Ephesians), you will realize that equipping for such a countercultural formation, in both the behavior and thinking of God's children, is a paramount and ongoing discipline for the Christian community. It obviously does not come easily, when folk such as we are so prone to be conformed to behavior patterns of the dominant social order. Paul makes this evident when he continues: "Look carefully then how you walk . . . the days are evil" (5:16). Yes, the darkness is relentless inside of the church—it may be "religious" darkness, or "spiritual" darkness, but it is darkness all the same.

Those who were at one time darkness, but are now light in the Lord, are apt to still reflect pieces of their former life, even though they are now children of light.

The formation of those who are the children of light, as they are together in community, has both a celebrative and a constructive (edifying) focus: God's children are to engage in singing "psalms and hymns and spiritual songs." They are to be "making melody to the Lord" with all of their hearts (5:19). They are to be always and for everything giving thanks to God the Father, in the name of Jesus.

Got it?

SUBMITTING TO ONE ANOTHER OUT OF REVERENCE FOR CHRIST

Perhaps this next section should more properly be titled: "Becoming *Christ* to One Another."

There is a subtle nuance in the transition from their celebrative ministry to and with each other, and their life of total thanksgiving, to this: " . . . submitting to one another out of reverence for Christ" (5:21).

Fleshing out what he means by this, Paul gives three *for-instances* of so becoming *Christ* to one another: 1) husbands and wives; 2) children and parents; and 3) slaves and masters. These are all, you will notice, relational. They are incarnational. They are familiar and practical. They speak to what it means to walk in love, and to be the children of light.

All require a holy submission, even as Christ submitted himself to being a servant to all. There is no indication or guarantee that such relationships will be without conflict, or without difficulty, or fair. In whichever of these roles we find ourselves, we are to model Christ to the other(s). Remember that it is in such faithful incarnation of the light that we engage the darkness and roll it back.

The first of these is the submission "out of our reverence for Christ" that is called for in the most intimate of relationships: between husband and wife. One must note that Paul concludes this with a (humorous?) note that marriage is something of a profound mystery, but that he is saying that it teaches us about Christ and his church. The implication, then, is that within the community of God's new creation we are all to model Christ's self-giving, sanctifying love in our relationships. We are all, likewise, to model submissiveness in our relationships with each other out of love.

However one defines submissiveness, it at least renounces that behavior that is born out of pride, or self-importance and self-promotion. There is always a price to pay in such behavior. But Paul made clear earlier that humility and gentleness and patience and mutual forbearing in love were to be our *modus operandi* as those called by Christ. We are to be *Christ* to one another, which mutual ministry is to be visible to the watching world, and as such a rebuke to the culture of darkness.

We are likewise to be *Christ* to our parents as children, and to our children as parents. Children are to see Christ in their parents loving and purposeful and healthy disciplines and instruction, which are the parent's responsibility. But even when parents are, perhaps, unwise and abusive, children are to respond respectfully to them in a fashion that models Christ, always with the understanding that God is able to use their godly behavior to effect change in the parents. This passage also indicates that the primary agents for making disciples out of one's children are the parents. You can't farm this responsibility out to someone else. Children need to see and hear and have models of beautiful faith in their parents and in the home, first of all (Phil 4:9).

The third area of mutual submission has to do within the relationships that exist between masters and slaves,[22] which were a common

---

22. In our modern society, the counterpart might be that of employers and employees, or executives and all the staff that operate under them, or perhaps the independent and the dependent in corporate life.

domestic reality in Paul's world. Slaves were more like household stewards or servants, purchased by more prosperous folk. The slaves were frequently very talented persons, highly intelligent and responsible, but they were the property of their masters. The slaves were also segregated socially, so that for the Christian community to model a whole new kind of inclusive set of relationships could be quite countercultural. Again, Paul addresses both the owner and the servants as those who are to model *Christ* to one another out of love.

With these very practical teachings and clarifications about the reconciled relationships within Christ's new creation community, Paul brings to an end this section of his letter. He immediately follows it with the concluding passage on which we spent time in our chapter 3 above on the whole armor of God.

Again, it is no *non sequitur*, nor an afterthought, that Paul introduces here. All the breathtaking teaching about the mystery of the ages now unfolded in Christ, and the resulting deliverance of these Ephesian believers out of their captivity into a whole new individual and corporate life as the dwelling place of God by the Spirit . . . takes place in the midst of the reality of the dominion of darkness and of the god of this world, Satan.

The goal of Paul's letter, and of this sobering conclusion, is that of a contagious, practicing, well-informed, Spirit-empowered community composed of agents of the gospel of the kingdom of God, i.e., children of the light ever pushing back and overcoming the satanic darkness, what with all of its schemes. It is this that is behind Paul's insistent word of caution, namely, that it will all revert to the darkness unless these believers are *continually* putting on the whole armor. Any piece of the armor neglected, forgotten, diminished, or reduced in importance . . . leaves them vulnerable to a drift into complacency, and a comfortable church . . . and passive members without expectation.

They are to live with a very joyous, yet sober, *warfare worldview* that eschews passivity in their mutual calling into the dominion of God's dear Son. Likewise, they must resist neglect in the daily putting on of the armor of light, as they are intentionally ministers in the mission of God—yes, the missionary arm of the Holy Trinity. Not only so, but they are to be always engaging in prayer for all of the others who are part of God's new creation in Christ as they, along with Paul, become the beautiful feet that bring the mystery of gospel to all with whom they have occasion to declare it.

With a few personal notes of greeting, Paul concludes this awesome letter with another of his blessings: "Grace be with all who love our Lord Jesus Christ with love incorruptible" (6:24).[23]

REFLECTION

The appropriation of Paul's understanding of the church in the mission of God, as given in this letter, is difficult for us, and perhaps a bit delicate to express since it requires a context of relational intimacy and mutuality that is so *other* than so much of what we often experience as church participants. One can be on friendly terms with other participants, sit in study groups with them, wear the church nametag, go to the same meetings . . . and have no idea who they really are, no real *one another* knowledge of, or accountability to, or responsibility for such, other than a theoretical kind. So, in a real sense, the human community is not re-created into that new creation community which God intends, and which is visible to the watching world.

Think what a *coup* for the devil it is if these communal disciplines and realities are eclipsed, and allowed to drift into commendable institutional identification, but without the incarnational intimacy and tangible love that this letter sets before us. And what if no one notices? Apparently something like this actually happened with this very Ephesian church, which after one generation has forgotten the love they had at first . . . the *relentless darkness.*

Also, as we approach Part 2 of this discussion, a whole other dimension of complexity opens up as we contemplate that this letter was written to *first-generation* believers, who actually experienced the captivity to the darkness, and deliverance into the glorious liberty of the children of God by God's grace in Christ.

But, what of the second generation? What of those who have no remembrance of the darkness, only of the context of the family of

---

23. It is worth noting again at this point that only a generation later the church at Ephesus was rebuked for having forsaken the love they had at first. Commentators debate over whether this was love for God in Christ or love for one another. That's hardly a worthwhile debate, since love for God and love for neighbor are both within the command to love given by Christ. It is love that binds everything together in perfect harmony (Col 3:14), therefore God's saints are to "walk in love, as Christ loved us and gave himself up for us" (Eph 5:2).

light? How are the second and third generations to be wholesomely and knowledgeably *evangelized*? That's a whole study in itself.[24]

But for now we must move on to the response of Alan and his friends in Part 2.

---

24. The short-lived Pope John Paul I is reported to have commented in a speech that the primary task of the church today is that of evangelizing those already baptized.

PART 2

"Now May the God of Hope . . ."
Seeing beyond the Horizons

7

Archaeologists and Architects

BACK AT TRACKSIDE TAVERN

Aʟʟ ᴏꜰ ᴡʜᴀᴛ ꜰᴏʟʟᴏᴡꜱ in this chapter and the next is the response of Alan and his "church around the table" bunch to what has constituted Part 1 of this discussion. What had transpired, evidently, was that these ten friends had taken this whole discussion quite seriously as their personal project. They had met as a whole and in smaller meetings . . . they had discussed, twittered, and totally processed the material, and were eager to report back to me where they had landed.

This time the whole bunch of them came with Alan to the Trackside Tavern for their reporting to me. We had all ensconced ourselves around a big table in a balcony room, ordered drinks, and settled in for an interesting evening together. Their report had a sort of "Where do we go from here?" or "What do we do with all of this?" flavor. What follows is my attempt to record the gist of their conclusions, from my own written notes and from a brief digest of the report that they had prepared for me. Those whom I had mentored now became my teachers. It had purpose and hope written all over it.

DISCOVERING SYSTEMIC DARKNESS

You need to know that within our "church around the table" bunch there are included a couple of guys who are into systems, and systems-analysis stuff. We mention this because these guys are the ones who finally surfaced our problem. Add to their gifts the fact that our bunch had on their iPads some pretty impressive resources by way of biblical commentaries and theological essays dealing with the subject we're looking at. Their insights all became a fascinating factor about midway into our processing of the data you sent along (in Part I).

We kept tripping over a sort of an elusive something, best described as a very resistant and just-out-of-sight reality, that kept making our whole quest seem a bit unreal to us. We were, admittedly, frustrated because we simply could not be completely satisfied with what we were trying to accomplish, nor with what we were observing. The initiating question that started this whole conversation with you was about how to explain the *drift* and *drag* that is perennially at work in the church subtly conforming it again the darkness out of which it had been called . . . and what possibility is there to reverse such.

Then came the epiphany.

What about a totally inadequate concept of the *gospel*, a gospel with a definition (or redefinition) truncated by the darkness?

Outrageous? Stand by.

Out of blue, we realized that we were looking at virile *systemic darkness*. One of our systems guys saw it first. Here's how it works: You have a *core concept* that determines the whole purpose and practice of an organic entity, such as the church. Okay? And if that core concept is somehow subtly redefined, or reduced, or distorted, or even eviscerated . . . then everything else that is determined by that core concept organically follows in its wake.

Question: What, then, would be the core concept with which we are dealing in New Testament Christianity? In those schemes, or wiles, of the prince of darkness, what would you need to so redefine, or truncate, or somehow do a reductionist job on (like the core concept) . . . in order to distort and emasculate everything else? Where is the systemic darkness rooted?

Simple: redefine the heart concept and meaning of *gospel* into something much less.

DISPLACE OR REDEFINE THE GOSPEL
OF THE KINGDOM OF GOD

Don't go away. This answer is huge. It's awesome. It redefines our whole discussion.

In the New Testament, the word *gospel* has well-defined content. It is primarily referred to as: the gospel of the kingdom of God. That's not just *churchy* talk. That has enormous (and we mean *enormous*) content.

It is what Paul was so excited about in writing to the Ephesians: ". . . the unsearchable riches of Christ, to bring to light for everyone what is the plan of the mystery hidden from the ages, in God . . . that through the church the manifold wisdom of God might be made known to the rulers and authorities in heavenly places" (3:8–11). Paul is breathless with his calling and message. He is formed by a concept of what God has done in Christ that is so big, so overwhelming, that he can't even find words to describe it. He uses terms like: *unimaginable, beyond understanding,* and *unsearchable riches.*

Hey! He's not talking about some "dink-definition" of gospel here. We ran that one down in our research into some of our biblical studies. That's a mind-boggling concept. At the very least is says that if Jesus has come to fulfill the promises made through the Old Testament prophets that would make all things new. He has come to reconcile heaven and earth by the blood of his cross. He has come, in short, to inaugurate his kingdom, his new creation, his "all things new." That being so, then, that also means that there is another alien kingdom already present that has to be defeated and displaced. Jesus did not come into neutral territory. He came to destroy the dominion of darkness. That is so obvious in New Testament writings that we were surprised that it hadn't become obvious to us before.

Paul's sheer thrill in what he had been sent to proclaim spills over in all of his writings.

Yet, it is even more obvious in Jesus himself. From the beginning of his ministry, "he went throughout all Galilee, teaching in their synagogues and proclaiming the *gospel of the kingdom . . .*" (Matt 4:23). The very word *gospel* carries the flavor of a thrilling and urgent announcement.

Jesus is heralding a reality that is both new and breathtaking.

The concept of the *kingdom of God* becomes the heart of the content of that thrilled, and thrilling, announcement. His call to his hearers to "repent and believe" for "the kingdom of God [or kingdom of heaven] is at hand" (Mark 1:15) is loaded with content. Jesus' hearers are called to forsake one way of understanding life, and to embrace a totally other and *totalitarian* embrace by God's new reality in Christ.

Right away, in what we know as the Sermon on the Mount,[1] Jesus spells out what that kingdom looks like, what it involves in attitudes, in

---

1. Or the Sermon on the Plain, as recorded in Luke 6.

lifestyle, in values, in relationships, in ethics—all flowing out of their response to the gospel of the kingdom. No passive "church membership" here, no mere "religion," but quite the contrary: a radically new and different way of thinking and behaving, growing out of our involvement by faith in the life of the Son of God.

(By the way, we found that there are several nearly synonymous terms used for this awesome reality of the kingdom of God, such as: new creation, salvation, the age to come, eternal life, or . . . sometimes even righteousness. They all seem to express this same eschatological gospel.)

It is this core concept that is to "be proclaimed throughout the whole world as a testimony to all nations" (Matt 24:14) before all things are consummated at the end of this age. But it is also this very core concept that has been so cleverly displaced by a redefinition of the common understanding of *gospel*. The very word has become so truncated and made "religious" and ecclesiastically acceptable . . . that one hardly discerns or notices what has taken place. The thrilling, huge, awesome, overwhelming announcement of the inauguration of the kingdom of God . . . has been hijacked by a very popular minimalist definition that refers to an individualistic, subjective religion in which I ostensibly gain forgiveness of sins and the hope of heaven (both true, of course), and which uses Christian vocabulary, but which misses the point of God's new creation in Christ.

We hasten to explain that the subversion, or reduction into such subjective definition, isn't in itself at all untrue. It is just incomplete. By repentance toward God, and faith in Jesus Christ, we are assured of the forgiveness of our sins, of justification, of peace with God, of reconciliation, of adoption into God's family, of the very great and precious promises that include our participation in the divine nature.[2]

This in itself is both beautiful and thrilling news. But this is not the whole of the gospel of the kingdom. The gospel of the kingdom of God that Jesus proclaimed, and that Paul taught, also mandates that those who come to Jesus by faith live into Jesus' own passion for the poor, the naked, the prisoners, the hungry, and the blind. Jesus calls upon those who will follow him to, like him, be peacemakers, to be willing to suffer, to engage in a life of obedience to his teaching . . . and so much, much more of a calling into a whole radically countercultural way of living

---

2. 2 Pet 1:3–4 states so much of this wonderfully.

and thinking. It is a call to obedience to his teachings. This is all encompassed in the concept of discipleship.

It is these *demands* of the gospel that get redefined, and devotionalized, and reduced into a subjective experience of salvation.

But the gospel of the kingdom is total. It leaves no part of our lives, or of our participation in the life of the world, untouched. "This is my Father's world." Everything we touch and influence, ultimately, becomes part of our stewardship of the gospel.

The church is, to be sure, not itself the kingdom of God. But the church is, all the same, the community where that kingdom is demonstrated in a new and true humanity created by the Holy Spirit—it is the community of the kingdom of God. It is the community of God's new humanity in Christ. And, just as Jesus came to "storm the gates of hell" by dethroning and disarming Satan, that prince of darkness, by his cross and resurrection . . . so also his people are called to continue to storm the gates of hell, and destroy Satan's works: "by the word of their testimony, by the blood of the Lamb, and they do it even if it costs them their lives" (Rev 12:11).

Such an awesome reality, as taught by Christ and the apostles, leaves no one uninvolved or passive. It defines what the church is to be and to do. It becomes the passion of the church. Thus, by such a subtle redefinition, such a reductionism, the prince of darkness relentlessly seeks to introduce a *systemic darkness* into the church scene . . . then what follows is that everything else is also redefined and reduced and truncated, or displaced and forgotten: faith, discipleship, church, church leadership, mission, liturgy . . . everything. It is all reduced to *religious Christianity*, to a comfortable spiritual redefinition of the gospel of God.

Missing from such a distortion is the church's responsibility, and thus every believer's responsibility, to be proclaiming this gospel of the kingdom to every people group, or nation, in the world.[3]

Is that enough?

Systemic darkness. Relentless darkness. Schemes of the devil.

It all began to come clear from that point in our process.

Distort that core concept and you can emasculate (or sterilize) the church and make it something entirely other than it is intended to be. The church, rather, becomes a witness to a subjectivized gospel, a partial and minimalized gospel—a religion, if you will—in which I am

---

3. Matt 24:14.

forgiven my sins and get to go to heaven when I die, and am comforted and religiously entertained with church activities meanwhile. It too often requires no radical repentance or faith. We are only called upon to "go to church," do what church members do, and remain oblivious to the radical calling of the gospel of the kingdom, its demands, and its transformational power.

But, in Christ's church, by his calling of us out of the dominion of darkness and into the kingdom of God, and by our baptism, every believer is enlisted in that alternative humanity—that very eschatological community, that counter-cultural body of aliens and exiles, and in its God-given mission—whose it is task is to make this gospel of peace known to the whole world.

And the *whole armor* of God metaphor, employed by Paul, gives definition to how all of God's people are to be equipped to do this, i.e., how they are to walk as children of the light in the midst of the darkness of this world, and be enabled to "stand in the evil day." Paul's teaching about the essential function of the whole armor is invaluable as a guide, a punch list if you will, to enable us to be faithful in that calling.

When our bunch we saw this, then all of our experiences and observations about the church began to make some sense to us. And, as we will spell out later on, we began to see our role as *architects* to be that of the necessity to literally reconceive many components of the church, as we have known it, from such a gospel-of-the-kingdom perspective— from the core concept of the gospel of the kingdom of God.

It is this gospel of the kingdom of God that informs us about the design of the church, its function, its purpose, and so also enables us to discern its drift away from its intended essence and purpose.

Now, back to our responses.

A WHOLE POTPOURRI OF RESPONSES

Having reported that systemic pathology, we need to give you the rest of our potpourri of responses.

But first, we'll revisit a couple of images or metaphors that you, and we, have used that probably need some clarification, just so we're all on the same page here.

Archaeologists and Architects

First, the ten of us have often used, with you, our own self-definition that we see ourselves somehow as both *archaeologists* and as *architects* in our grappling with the phenomenon of the church. There are so many riches of faith, so many episodes of obedience, of communal life, of missionary vision, and of kingdom incarnation from the past centuries that we dare not neglect in our own quest. In our role as (how to say it?) ecclesial archaeologists we are continually digging up such treasures of the past that help us in our own pilgrimage.

At the same time, these are different times. There are new cultural forces at work, and the future that is ineluctably encroaching on us does not always respond to past patterns and forms. Inescapably, in this cultural "whitewater," the church inevitably becomes the victim of the very drift and drag that started this whole discussion.

For that reason we see ourselves also as ecclesial *architects*, exploring new possibilities, seeing beyond the horizons of *what is*, to a freed-up understanding of the church that is rooted in the New Testament documents, and fulfills the church's purpose of being the missionary arm of the Holy Trinity as it incarnates the gospel of the kingdom of God in this present scene in which we live and operate.

Staging Areas and Base Camps

The other image, which you introduced to us, has also been quite helpful to in evaluating the church's purpose, form, and function. You found this somewhere, and it has to do with those daring souls who aspire to tackle the ascent of high mountains—mountain climbers, alpinists, or whatever. You described two different types of communities engaged in enabling these mountain climbers. One would be a larger community in which experienced veterans of mountaineering instructed, prepared, warned, described, and explained the equipment, the disciplines, the physical challenges, the dangers, and the ultimate joy of such a climb to those who were new to this whole thing. Those assemblies could be larger communities, and are called: *staging areas.*

We likened these to larger church assemblies, whose purpose *should be* that of equipping God's people with the biblical foundations for their engagement with the mission of God in the realities of their 24/7 daily lives, their engagement with the very real Monday morning world, and doing so by giving them the basics of the challenge, and the dynamics of the chaos they will often confront. So: *staging areas.*

But then there was the other much more immediate and necessary form, which would be those several other persons in whose company you would actually be making the climb, and with whom you were all mutually accountable to, and responsible for, each other's welfare. This has to be a group who trust and depend upon each other, and who know each other's strengths and weaknesses reasonably well. No one would (or should) initiate such a hazardous climb without such a support group (though there are always going to be the "lone rangers" who think they are self-sufficient). Such a group would also be open to receiving others who needed such. It would collaborate in helping other groups engaged in the ascent.

The New Testament's repetitive references to "one another" is the divinely inspired testimony to the fact that disciples need just such an intimate group of friends with whom to pray, have support, give encouragement, and share the joys and dangers, the triumphs and tragedies of their pilgrimage in discipleship and in their engagement with an often hostile environment. These smaller communities you called *base camps*—those fellow disciples with whom you make the journey.[4]

And, by the way, we consider our "church around the table"-bunch just such a *base camp.* We are dependent on the support of each other in our various callings, even as we are also accountable to each other. We may do it inadequately, and stumble in our efforts at times, but we are basically there for one another along the way.

We found these two images, or metaphors, not perfect but certainly helpful.

STARTING POINT: THE EPHESIANS TRIP

This whole discussion, from the start, was initiated with the inquiry about why the church seems to drift away from its intended design, and what energizes that *drift* and *drag.* We began by processing those questions in the light of Ephesians trip you gave us (Part 1), and it became obvious that we had not been seeing what was clearly before us in these

---

4. The New Testament frequently employs the Greek word *koinonia* to describe that kind of intimate, mutually engaged fellowship. Such a text as Acts 2:42 is such, and in context seems to describe the post-Pentecost growth as also engaging the believers in intimate household groups of learning and mutual caring.

writings. Paul doesn't begin his teaching to that community in Ephesus by focusing on them and their faithfulness—though he does get to that, certainly. Rather, he begins with the huge—call it what you will—cosmic or eschatological reality of what God's mind-boggling (and comprehensible only by the enabling of the Holy Spirit) design for his whole creation is, and out of this then what is God's design for his church.

Big question: What is the church to be in and through Jesus Christ? What is its true purpose?

It's like a big, "Wow! Can you believe what God has done in Christ? Awesome!"

Like: right away, Paul is contagious with the gospel, overwhelmed with the sheer magnitude of what a huge display of grace God has given us by making known the mystery of his will . . . set forth in Christ as a plan for the fullness of time, to unite all things in him, things in heaven and things on earth.[5] He speaks to those believers about their inheritance in all of this, and about what an unbelievably new and hope-filled existence is theirs through what Jesus has accomplished.

Then, after reminding them of their own deliverance from captivity to Satan's alien dominion, and darkness, and of their own calling into the whole new creation that is the that new dominion of God's dear Son . . . he again returns to exult in that which boggles the imagination, namely, the mystery hidden for ages that has now been brought to light through Christ . . . *and* (take note) that it is to be accomplished through the *church*—really, that it is actually through the church that this is to be accomplished. This manifold wisdom of God, previously hidden, is now to be made known to the rulers and authorities, to those very real forces of darkness in heavenly places, and it is to be done by the church.[6]

As if that weren't enough (and we finally slapped our corporate foreheads and took notice), then comes the instruction to put on the whole armor of God, which Paul insists is an absolute necessity if we are to be able to withstand the assaults and schemes of these same cosmic powers, whose goal is to seduce them back into the darkness with religious counterfeits in the evil day.

We had never stopped to look at that, and, as with most undiscerning readers, we had just zoomed right past it, never stopping to realize that the evil day is actually the present landscape of our own lives, what

5. Eph 1:8–10.
6. Eph 3:8–11.

with all the social, cultural, environmental, political, economic, and psychological (to name a few) realities in which we live *now*.

Big-time reality check!

How could we ever, with any integrity, conceive of our own calling to be Christ's faithful disciples . . . or how could of any of the church communities, with which we are familiar, have integrity as true expressions of God's design . . . apart from God's *eschatological* (there's that word again) purpose for the church, its God-ordained design?

How can we even approach this discussion regarding the church's *drift* apart from a clear understanding of the church's calling to make known to the powers of darkness the manifold wisdom of God in Christ—or apart from the church's incarnation in the midst of the evil day, with all of the implications inherent in such a concept? How?

Boy! Does that ever open the door to all kinds of implications as we looked into this enigmatic phenomenon called: *the church*, especially as we have experienced it. It certainly helps us sort through all of the ecclesiastical rubble and institutional clutter that we frequently encounter looking at this subject. Those implications also surface as we reconsider the dimensions of Christian discipleship . . . not to mention the whole armor of God.

What is the church called to be in this great eschatological design—this mystery hidden from previous ages, but now made known through Christ?

What has the church become? How did it get from there to here? What's the problem?

Everything else in Ephesians can only be understood in the light of this grand, and extravagant, and overarching purpose of God in Christ, and of how the church is so very critical in that design.

The problem is that such an understanding of the church's purpose has been so basically obscured, so relegated to forgetfulness, that the church has made peace with the darkness, and has thereby become little more that the religious expression of that same darkness.

What we find both distressing and sad is that a considerable part of the church phenomenon of our experience could hardly be considered any threat at all to that darkness, since its light burns so dimly, if at all. Okay?

When that reality grows dim in the consciousness of the Christian community, its participants, and its leaders . . . then the darkness again takes up habitation *inside the church.* To the degree that a particular church community forgets its calling, then that community also becomes less of a community of the light, and thus less the church. This is so because a church is only truly the church as it incarnates this very mystery, as it is the very glory of God, and as it demonstrates in community the unsearchable riches of Christ in itself as God's eschatological new creation.

Our study of Revelation 2–3 (and the letters to the seven churches) reinforced this disturbing conviction for us. In that passage, several named particular churches (the church at Ephesus among them) had, in fact, drifted and were at risk of having their lamp removed from the golden lampstand, i.e., becoming *non-churches . . .* unless they repented, and got their act together. It doesn't say they ceased in some sense to be the church, but it does say that in their drift they were essentially useless in the mission of God, and so could be shelved as the missionary arm of the Holy Trinity.

[STOP]What that says to us is that a particular community which identifies itself as a church—may not, in fact, actually be a church!

What a dangerous thought!

Like: when is a church less than a church? Traditionally the church has covered its backside here by saying that the church is only *provisionally* a community of the kingdom, and never perfect. True enough. But the letters to the churches in Asian Minor indicate that there are times when the churches have so inhabited the darkness that they are no longer viable as missional communities.

We don't take this lightly. We'll come back to this later on.

And, to add one more facet of our deliberations around the table: To the degree that our present church institutions—perhaps prestigious parts of our cultural landscape—grow dim about, or forget, who they are in this grand design of God . . . then these venerable old established churches (or even many new church plants) themselves may have become the habitation of what the mission folk designate as an "unreached people group." They become a mission field in themselves—communities of (as someone described them) "unconverted believers," who are no longer consciously formed by God's purpose for them to be in missionary confrontation with the darkness.[7]

7. Lesslie Newbigin insists that the church is always in such a missionary confrontation with the world, so that to be comfortable, or even "religiou" or "spiritual," in the

Talk about *schemes* or *wiles* of devil.

Or consider, again, as we did, that a major *scheme* of the devil would be all of those churches that have so drifted and become so locked in to patterns of congregational life that don't go anywhere. They exist to exist. They have no other expectation than institutional survival and (hopefully) prosperity. They are willing to be content with just doing the same thing over and over, while being somewhat oblivious, if not impotent, in making disciples—and even more so, unconcerned about equipping those disciples to reproduce.

How many typical church members would be appalled at the very suggestion that at some point they needed to be kicked out of the nest, so that they could learn how to fly, and to function as witnesses to the light, and to reproduce themselves as obedient disciples of Jesus Christ?

If it weren't so tragic, it would be funny.

This all becomes a tragic reality when the church is so out of focus in the perception of so many of its participants.

No compelling gospel. No compelling *raison d'être*. No eschatological or missional self-awareness. No passion for their incarnation as a community of the kingdom of God. No redemptive interest in those still captive to the darkness. Just: church—static, comfortable, impotent, and very religious!

No mountains to climb. Just endless reruns of familiar information in the staging area.

This being so, it is only possible for us to evaluate such existential phenomena, who designate themselves as *churches*, in the light of God's design for them, namely in their calling to be authentic and self-aware communities of (and formed by) the light.

So, here we are, the ten of us, looking at this, and wondering: where do we fit?

What do we do with all this? We cannot escape our responsibilities as those called out of darkness into God's new creation in Christ. We are ourselves, somehow, the church. So we had to stop and process our own self-understanding.

---

darkness is to render the church part of the darkness.

How do we see ourselves? Who are we? What do we see? How do we respond?

We're not someone else, or some other real or imagined saints . . . and we don't live in some other time or place . . . but here and now. We are where are, so what do we do? Or, better still: How does this reality work itself out in our own very real encounters with the church (in whatever ancient or contemporary, traditional or innovative form)? What is our responsibility to the church here and now?

After all, our calling to Christ is a calling *out of* the dominion of Satan, and *into* the kingdom of God's dear Son—that whole new creation inaugurated by Jesus through his cross and resurrection. Because of that calling, then, we cannot be passive in our role as the children of the light (Christ), right? By virtue of that calling we are to become the very agents of the "Thy kingdom come, thy will be done, as in heaven, so on earth" prayer.

The inescapable implication of this, then, is that we are called to expose and overcome Satan, and all of his malignant schemes . . . his subtle, deceptive, and blinding works in whatever context—both in church and world. We are thus to be calling men and women out of that darkness, and into the light. But to do this, we need to know what the darkness looks like, which raises the question: How are we to know and discern the darkness?

That calling becomes doubly difficult in this post-Christian, postmodern, neo-pagan (or whatever) culture in which we live, what with all of the caricatures of—not to mention grotesque expressions of—what pertains to be the Christian faith. Unbelief, in its religious form, dwells comfortably inside so many churches, along with a pervasive biblical and theological illiteracy.

There really aren't any patterns for the form of the church this cultural whitewater in which we live, as this culture rushes on into some unknown future.

All of these pieces are evidences of the most effective scheme of the darkness, namely, that of truncating the gospel, so that you have gospel words without gospel substance, or content. Or, perhaps you have half-a-gospel that is concerned only about "me and my experience of salvation." This produces churches without any true meaning, i.e., churches quite content with *religious Christianity*. So, when one of the particular church entities of our experience succumbs to such a scheme (unconsciously, or inadvertently perhaps), it is quite possible that it may appear to be prospering institutionally, while at the same time being essentially impotent as a faithful witness.

With all this as our context, and with our discussion of the material you gave us (Part 1), we find the implications either thrilling, or frightening . . . or both . . . but inescapable. We are just ten ordinary, thoughtful followers of Christ. We have various relationships with churches, and responses to churches. Some of us have found the church an encouragement. Some us have found it a distraction from our sense of calling and discipleship—some even a stumbling block. Most of us have questions about the role of the church in our lives since it is enigmatic in so many ways.

What becomes obvious is—whether a *base camp* community, or *staging area* community—that when the church fails to fulfill its role in our calling to discipleship, then to some degree it loses its integrity and reverts to something purposeless—to darkness. When the church's missional purpose—its contagiousness with its gospel, its *eschatological* self-consciousness about its role in God's plan for the ages—becomes obscured, or non-distinct in the community's mind . . . then the *relentless darkness* has scored a telling accomplishment.

Having said that . . . it gets a bit delicate again, since we are challenging a whole host of venerable traditions and definitions . . . but, then, harking back to our previous discussions, and the Ephesians document . . . there was that gift of *prophecy.* By prophecy God's people are to be discerning not only of their context in the light of their calling, but also of their true identity, of their faithfulness, or unfaithfulness, in their calling, and of their potential assimilation by the culture of the darkness.

Prophecy is discerning (or *exegeting*) the landscape, which necessarily requires discerning the dwelling places and influences of the darkness, not only in the social-cultural context, but also within the communities of those of us who bear the name of Jesus Christ. Such a prophetic capacity is necessary for us, which is why *prophecy* is one of the four equipping gifts mentioned in the Ephesians letter. Prophecy, we can assume, has (as per Jeremiah's example)[8] both a negative-destructive dimension—"to pluck up and break down, to destroy and overthrow"— and a positive-constructive dimension—"to build and to plant."

8. Jer 1:10.

Such was true of all of our Old Testament models. Theirs was to rebuke Israel's failure to live out of their calling and covenant, and to set before them "a future and a hope" (Jer 29:11) Israel had drifted back into the darkness, to conformity to the nations around them so that they were no longer a "light to the nations" (Isa 49:6) while maintaining all of the accoutrements of temple worship.

So much of the church with which we are familiar, and which we read about, disappointingly drifts back into the darkness, while maintaining an impressive institutional presence of religious Christianity.

Those Old Testament prophets could blaze with holy indignation at Israel's forgetfulness . . . and they could weep over this same people. So also Jesus could become angry at Israel's hardness of heart . . . and then weep over Jerusalem.

We can identify with that.

The ultimate function of the prophets was to call God's people to faithfulness and blessing in the midst of the always-complex culture in which they lived . . . and in the always-complex culture of a different sort where we live.

And then there's us!

Our response?

We really do not want all of this to sound arrogant or elitist in any way (though it could easily be construed as such). Rather, we want our priorities to be upon those involvements that enhance our role as agents of the light . . . those that are purposeful in encouraging the fruitfulness of (what the writer of Revelation terms) "the word of our testimony" (Rev 12:10) . . . and in all of our responses remembering: "And above all these put on love, which binds everything together in perfect harmony" (Col 3:14). This being so, church activities, which detract us from such, we simply reserve the right to bypass.

THE CHURCH AS MISSION FIELD

Yet that very intention raises for us the uncomfortable question about those same institutions that seem often to be so fuzzy about their purpose in the mission of God. Neither do we in any way intend to be cavalier in our attitude, especially toward those who inhabit such scenes.

In Jesus' sermon on the congregation[9] (which has to do with the ethics of life in the congregation of his kingdom folk) he makes "these little ones," i.e., the weak and vulnerable, to be a special responsibility for us.

In this post-Christian, postmodern, neo-pagan culture, and with so many of its remaining institutions of religious Christianity, it is more common than not to find that very few of its membership have ever, *ever* been equipped to be thoughtful, obedient disciples of Jesus Christ. They know little more than to be the passive recipients of whatever the clergy and church leadership passes down to them.

In our discussions with so many of our dear friends who fit such a description, we find that they are trapped within the horizons of *what is*, i.e., within a familiar custodial church . . . which is all that they have ever known. They have nothing with which to compare them. They were never taught what is Christ's purpose for his church, and how it is to demonstrate the kingdom of God (the new creation of God in Christ) in itself . . . nor do they possess the imagination to conceive of something other than what they have always known, especially to conceive their calling to engage the darkness. They are, thereby, for all practical purposes still captive to the darkness.[10]

The tragedy is that so many of these folk have come sincerely looking for the light, and so fit the definition of the weak, the little ones . . . or the sojourners sincerely seeking God, only to be given something much less. Many of them are "good soil" that would be receptive to the gospel of the kingdom.[11] It is those hungry sheep in existing drifting congregations that weigh heavily on our hearts as we have discussed this whole thesis.

Which brings us back to our conclusion that much of the church, as such, is itself a true mission field. For so many of our friends, with whom we interact in our workplaces, and who are not followers of Jesus, the church is nothing more or less than a playground for religious types. In their observation it is anything but a dynamic community of God's new humanity.

9. Matthew 18.

10. This drift into the darkness is not just the lot of older and more traditional Christendom congregations. New church plants frequently have a good focus on the purpose to equip God's people, but their goal of achieving an attractive new church can easily become an idol, or institution-keeping, and the equipping for discipleship can be diluted or displaced by the excitement of creating something new.

11. Matt 13:8.

So, in addition to Alan's initial question about the source of the *drift* and *drag*, we've found the whole larger church phenomenon of our experience to be somewhat enigmatic, often confusing, and frequently something of a stumbling block in our intention of being faithful in our lives of discipleship (not to mention, a stumbling block to so many of our neighbors).

These mission field churches are doubly difficult. When religious darkness entrenches itself inside of a church, then that church becomes doubly resistant to the light, very assured that it is all as it should be, and restive with any suggestion otherwise. Somehow a systemic and reactive darkness lurks in its traditions and structure and leadership . . . and resists the light.

Our response, then, is just that: it is *our* response. We can't speak for anyone else, though we would hope that that our coming to grips with such an awesome subject, and our example might be helpful and encouraging to others.

Not to mention that we are, admittedly, a bit impatient.

We are not willing to sit around hoping that someone else will come along with some resolution for us. So that (what?): We're seeking to articulate our own resolve, and our explication, not only to our own conscientious coming to grips with our dilemma over the church, its drift and all . . . but our resolve to incarnate a positive (and hopefully) fruitful response in our own lives. Yes, and we know that we will probably "rattle some chains," and challenge some venerable traditions, and undoubtedly offend many, since we intentionally *do not hold as sacrosanct* much of the ecclesiastical baggage that others see as necessities.

FIVE BASIC ASSUMPTIONS THAT WE REITERATE CONTINUALLY TO OURSELVES

First, we need to state our affirmative response to the thesis that we're working on, namely: that of the *everywhere presence of the darkness*, and its energizer, who is the prince of darkness. We don't take lightly the concluding petition of Jesus' prayer: "Deliver us from the evil one." We take our stand on the affirmation that the reason the Son of God appeared was to destroy the works of the devil (1 John 3:8). At the same time, we hold in juxtaposition with that the blessing given by Paul which is full of hope and joy and peace in the midst of our confrontation with the everywhere darkness: "May the God of hope fill you with all joy and peace in believing, so that by the power of the Holy Spirit you may abound in hope" (Rom 15:13).

Secondly, it seems obvious to us that if Jesus says of the church he will be building that "the gates of hell shall not prevail against it," then the clear implication is that the gates of hell will, in fact, surely seek to withstand the church that Jesus is building. Add to that Paul's teaching in Ephesians about the role of the church in the mission of God—". . . that through the church the manifold witness wisdom might now be known to the rulers and authorities in heavenly places" (Eph 3:10)—and the implications are awesome.

But, here's a fascinating implication, which we came up with in our discussions: *If the gates of hell cannot prevail against the church, then it's *not* the church that is to be in a defensive mode against the aggressive assaults of hell. Rather, it is quite the opposite. The clear implication is that the church is to be (to borrow a phrase)[12] "storming the gates of hell." This "storming" should be the goal of every member and every Christian community: that of being equipped into maturity for their works of ministry (see Eph 4:11–16), precisely so that we can be effective in the daily ministry of "storming."

And how is this to be implemented? To begin with it can be implemented by incarnating the seven components of the whole armor, which were unpacked in Part 1.

We got really excited by thinking of the church, not as some sterile religious club, but rather as that dynamic new creation community, that incarnation of the kingdom of God in which the presence of those fruits of the Holy Spirit (which Paul named elsewhere) would create a community that was itself: *gospel*. Rather than being a stumbling block, or an enigma, or some religious enclave, as seen by so many of our friends, the church would actually be in itself the joyous news, the aroma of Christ unto God, the living visible expression of God's intent for the human community he created it to be. Such a community has the element of true personhood, for every individual within it, written all over it, i.e., it is anything but a depersonalized society.

---

12. This is a chapter title in Gregory Boyd's book *God at War: The Bible & Spiritual Conflict* (Downers Grove, IL: InterVarsity, 1997).

It is such an authentic church as kingdom community, such a community of the light, that by its faithful living into its calling . . . effectively storms the gates of hell, in whatever circumstances or cultural realities it finds itself.

Got it?

That got our juices flowing.

That being so, it should not be surprising to us, then, that the prince of darkness will primarily focus his subtle and malignant schemes on the church itself in order to render it impotent, to neuter it, so that it does not, or is not able to, incarnate the kingdom of God. Such an impotent church institution is certainly no threat to his dominion, to the gates of hell.

Make sense?

Then, *third*, the references we discussed earlier—those from the early chapters of Revelation—illustrate this very reality. Within a generation or so from their apostolic founding, those churches of Asia Minor (with the exception of the two under persecution: Philadelphia and Smyrna) are already beginning to drift, and to compromise their calling, so that after some affirmations of their good works by the risen Lord, come the stern warnings to the effect that they risk being shelved (having their lamp removed from the golden lampstand) and thus becoming *non-factors in the mission of God*.

The ascended Lord gave stern warnings. Their driftings were of various sorts: lovelessness, doctrinal compromise, cultural conformity, ethical aberrations, etc. All of the listed aberrations derive from an inadequate comprehension of, and equipping for, the purpose of the church as the gospel community.

Whatever the driftings of those churches were, we were sobered at how quickly this had happened to churches that had started so well. It would seem that the charges that the risen Lord makes against them would certainly have been recognized by them *if*, in fact and in practice, they had been faithful in the daily disciplines of putting on the whole armor of God, as they approached their daily encounter with the culture of darkness . . . *and* if they had "ears to hear" what the Spirit was saying to them.

Fourth . . . all of which says to us that so many of those entities that presently call themselves "churches" may, in fact, be so only marginally . . . or possibly even be impediments to the mission of God. They bid fair to being counterfeits, or stumbling blocks in the path of discipleship. Such potential calls us to be very discerning (while chari-table) in itself as we, here and now, view the ecclesiastical scene with which we are in contact, and which can become such a contradiction, such a confusion, and the topic of non-flattering jokes to so many of our friends in this post-Christian environment.

And *fifth*, this all leads us to the inevitable conclusion to which Paul comes in the conclusion of the Ephesian letter: Specifically, that both individually and communally we are always in an encounter with the darkness—with the existential realities of our own "evil day." Our encounter may not be at all dramatic, or immediately obvious in the familiarities of our everyday lives—but it is very real. It says to us that we are quite vulnerable apart from this necessary armor, and that we will not make it (be able to stand) without a clear grasp of the weapons of our warfare, of the whole armor of God. A clear implication of this calling is that we can never be indifferent to those around us who are still captive to, and spiritually blinded by, the dominion of darkness.

OUR ATTITUDE

We have also observed that there is frequently a sort of unhealthy paranoia that surrounds even any mention, or discussion, of such an understanding of our engagement with the *devil*, with the dominion of darkness as the children of the light—spiritual conflict, and spiritual warfare, what with all of the conspiracy theories, and all that sort of thing. For whatever reason folk who seem to understand these implications about our encounter with the darkness, also tend to assume a grim defensive attitude that certainly doesn't reflect the high joy that is Jesus' legacy to his followers.[13] It certainly doesn't reflect the ecstatic liberty[14] that comes to those who have been set free by Jesus.[15] When we have, occasionally, found those persons in the churches of our experience who seem to have some grasp on the reality of this warfare, there seems to be an accompanying unhealthy cautiousness, and something of a fortress mentality.

13. John 17:13.
14. John 8:36.
15. Eph 2:4–10.

We have noted this, and it is our intention to seek to avoid such an attitude, while not minimizing the cosmic reality. Our persuasion is that such an attitude is counterproductive, or inimical, to our calling into the joyous Easter hope that belongs to the dominion of God's dear Son.

We rather think that our calling into the dominion of God's dear Son should create in us anticipation—even a genuine enthusiasm—for these very engagements with expressions of the darkness, with our high calling to daily storm the gates of hell. Paul's own obvious awareness of the cosmic battle certainly does not give him any such grim attitude. He is suffused with hope as he tells the folk in Rome (we repeat): "May the God of hope fill you with all joy and peace in believing, so that by the power of the Holy Spirit you may abound in hope" (Rom 15:13)." We have adopted this passage as our own mandate to be agents of abounding hope as we seek to be children of light in church, however we find it. Okay?[16]

And, if we understand the intent of the whole armor of God correctly, it certainly has the fascinating component to it of our feet being "shod with the *readiness* of the gospel of peace." This inescapably indicates that we are to move deliberately toward all of that which needs to be liberated from the blindness and captivity to the darkness, which includes so many of the persons with whom we rub elbows every day. To all of these persons, and to all of the vicissitudes of each, we are called to incarnate the light, to be the display of God's new creation in Christ.

In our *architect* mode we have also discovered that back through the annals of the church's missionary faithfulness, God has seemed to delight to work the most dramatically in the most unexpected places, and settings where the darkness was the greatest, and seemed the most intractable!

Which brings us back to *us*.

EXCURSUS: REMOVING THE CHURCHY FILTERS

Here's one for you.

16. New Testament scholar Gordon Fee gives a commentary on this text that is worth repeating: "Such future oriented people live in the present in such a way, different from the rest . . . as so confident in the future that they can pour themselves into the present with utter abandon, full of joy and peace, because nothing in the resent can ultimately overwhelm them. Such people make the Christian faith a truly attractive alternative" (*God's Empowering Presence: The Holy Spirit in the Letters of Paul* [Peabody, MA: Hendrickson, 1994], 623).

It is our opinion that, all too much, the concepts of *darkness* and *light* have been hijacked and somehow made captive to the church's in-house jargon . . . you know: celebrated in theological formulae and hymns, and all of that . . . but not the dynamic realities and understandings that transform God's people into those contagious folk who move with anticipation toward the cultural darkness—that darkness that holds our *sojourner* friends captive. For ourselves, we've designated all that sort of jargon as: *churchy filters*, i.e., the domesticating of those cosmic realities into some kind of otherworldly spiritual talk that seems out of touch with the everyday realities with which we live.

So we can sing about darkness and light, and we can incorporate it into our creeds . . . and then go about our lives as though that spiritual battle might be real out-there-somewhere . . . but as though the context of our own Monday morning world were basically neutral. With such an attitude we can look upon our *sojourner* friends as simply the product of their own personal decisions, or their DNA, or their circumstances that are far removed from any such category as the presence of any pernicious dominion of darkness.

We can look upon our workplace, our social contacts, our school, our laboratory, our office, our rehab center, or whatever . . . as having nothing much to do with our *church jargon*, which talks about the dominion of darkness, or with a warfare understanding of what's going on around us and in the world.

Such an impression of neutrality could only be imposed upon God's new creation people by the god of this world.

Make sense?

We'd really like to remove those filters. Our reflections on Ephesians should have taught us that.

WHERE DO WE GO WITH ALL OF THIS?

We've discussed where we go with all of this, and how realistic it is.

For starts, we have covenanted to seek to be ourselves a contagious community of the light composed of sons and daughters of the light, wherever we find ourselves. We've got to start somewhere. We want to be a *base camp* for each other—that primary community of encouragement and accountability. We hope that some living waters can flow from this so that we can, in turn, refresh and encourage others, and begin to reverse the *drift* and *drag*, and roll back whatever are the expressions of the darkness in which we find ourselves, both inside and outside of the church.

Yes, and we *do* want to stay clearly focused on Jesus, who is the light, and as such came into this world's darkness—but that pernicious darkness could not overcome the incarnation of the light.

God loves this very world in which we live. It belongs to God our Father. And that means, for us, that it is in this here-and-now world with all of its pleasant and tragic, destructive and creative forces, dismal and exciting experiences, just and unjust forces, beautiful and hostile realities—the world that our Father loves—that we live. This means that if Jesus is the light and the darkness could not overcome him, then we as his followers, who are the children of the light, are also those whom the darkness also cannot overcome. Remember: "You are the light of the world" (Matt 5:14)."

That always brings us back to Christ and his cross. We don't want to lose that focus. In our *archaeologist* mode we have noted that such a loss of focus on Christ and his cross seems always complicit in the church's drift. We would like to be like Paul, who said: "But far be it from me to boast except in the cross of our Lord Jesus Christ, by which the world has been crucified to me, and I to the world" (Gal 6:14). That may sound like an aside to our discussion, but we kept coming back to the realization that whenever the church allows such a focus to grow dim, then the darkness intrudes and reduces it all to mere religion.

That means for us that even as Christ has called us to himself, and called us to be the children of light, we roll back and destroy the works of the devil by living into our calling precisely *as that calling is defined by those seven components of the whole armor of God*—that for starts.

Have we said that often enough?

SOJOURNERS AND EXILES

We also know that we can't make this a rule for anybody else, nor do we intend to make of all of this some kind of a program for others. Primarily, we're doing this for ourselves. But we do trust that, maybe, we can be a model for others, and help equip (or make disciples of) others, so that our bunch can become contagious, and organically grow and spawn other colonies of light.

We also do not see our present "church around the table" bunch as permanent or exclusive, but rather as reproductive, versatile, mobile, and flexible in being a colony of light, and to be such in the realities of our engagement with daily responsibilities, as well as within various expressions of the church in which we find ourselves.

ARCHITECTS AND RECONCEIVERS

We would also like to be thinking fresh. We've found a whole lot of *tired thinking* out there.

We believe that the Holy Spirit can provoke creativity, can provoke the capacity to reconceive, and to reimagine, and to suspend the horizons of our biblical understanding of the church and its mission, which understanding so often seems trapped within the horizons of what is, and with no expectation that anything else is possible. That's our sense of being those *architects* of a church that we would love to engage.

How can we reconceive the church incarnating itself as: an effective missional communities here in this post-Christian setting? How can it do this, perhaps in forms that are true to the church's calling, but reconceived to be colonies of light in some and new expressions, maybe even emerging out of the old?[17]

But then we also know that our Lord Jesus has been faithfully building his church for two millennia, and we want to be aware and discern the lessons and resources that we can retrieve from the missional faithfulness of all those generations that have gone before us. Some of us have already delved into lessons to be learned from the awesome faithfulness in mission by so many of our predecessors, in often frightening, and ugly, and humanly impossible circumstances.

We read with amazement of the fruit of monastic communities, of Celtic spirituality, of classical liturgical forms, of incredible stories of faithful discipleship and missionary obedience carried out against all human odds, and in the most distressing situations. And this is not to mention the rich treasury of hymns that come down to us from the very

---

17. As I write this I think of the High Line in New York City. This was a rusting old elevated train track that ran through a deteriorating urban neighborhood. That ugly eyesore was scheduled to be demolished, until some visionary young architects saw the possibility of an elevated public park, a green space, and an urban walkway. Their vision found traction, it became a reality, and the High Line is now one of the most popular attractions in New York, with gardens, walkways, benches, and beauty. What's more, its presence has caused the beginning of the renewal of the whole neighborhood setting. Such visionary developments inspire me.

beginning. That's our *archaeologist* role, and we are already being blessed by it.

It will come up again later as we tell you about our vision of re-conceiving the role of *liturgy* (that form of ritual or worship that equips us for mission) in our life together, as one required discipline by which we maintain our integrity as children of the light. It is through such a reconceived liturgical discipline that we will be encouraged to live into our calling to be the faithful presence of that light. It will re-energize us with awesomeness of the gospel of the kingdom of God right here in the midst of the realities of our daily *existence* . . . that is to say: in our daily marketplace incarnation, what with all of its domestic, social, economic, and political, environmental, and ecclesiastical implications, along with the challenges and contradictions (not to mention difficult, and some-times pathological, personalities that go along with these).

By the way, we see our table bunch as our own wonderful context in which to process these realities of our incarnation together in the light of our calling, in the light of Scripture, in the honest awareness of how complex life can often be. We really do need one another in this journey as aliens and exiles. We almost desperately depend upon each other as our *base camp*.

THE FORM OF THE CHURCH

The *base camp* analogy brings us back to what kept surfacing, over and over, in our discussions: that of the *form* of the church. The *base camp* and *staging area* analogies speak more to function than to form. Given the myriad of forms that ostensible church communities take, it is al-together conceivable to us that there is not really any *given* form that becomes *the* model for us.

The church creates its own forms as it moves out in mission. We know from Jesus' teaching that the new wine of the gospel requires a new wineskin, one that is sufficiently flexible to handle the dynamic ferment of the new wine of the gospel. The church is, by definition, a community *called out* for a specific purpose.

Yet, the inspired writers of the New Testament never see fit to de-scribe its form. They give us information about its purpose, and about its necessary gifts for equipping, leadership, and charismatic function-ing—but no teaching about its form. Our examples are that it met where it could: in the temple precincts, in homes (primarily), by the riverside, in rented halls . . . yet, all the while, its was a mobile and versatile and flexible.

The church either fulfills its purpose of equipping and mutually encouraging one another in contagious missional obedience—in the capacity of each believer to live into his or her calling to be a child of the light—or it doesn't. A case has been made by many that those institutional expressions of the church, as are most common among us— buildings, professional staff, and all of that—tend to refocus the church's attention to permanence, maintenance, image, and other subversions of the church from its intended missional essence.

That becomes part of the dilemma our bunch has been chewing on. Some of us are, for various reasons, embedded in just such a venerable church institution. Such institutions tend to be focused on their institutional survival and *hubris*, while also frequently having within them small "villages" of faithful believers who have never known anything else, while at the same time always longing for something they know is missing. This makes our quest more than a little delicate (and purposeful).

In our weekly communications with our many contacts from many different church expressions in personal conversations (through social media, and such), we are reminded that there are those in such captive churches that long for the "pure spiritual milk" (1 Pet 2:2). You find, in the most moribund church expressions, those hungry to know the word of God who are not being helped or fed. You find those present counterparts of the ancient Anna and Simeon, who waited patiently over the years in the temple for the fulfillment of the promise.[18]

Our unanswered but continual question becomes: How are we responsible for such dear people?

Others of us are part of a new church plant that because it is new and has not acquired all of the institutional accouterments, and so can stay focused on its purpose more intentionally. Then there are some of us who are not convinced that such larger expressions of the church are worth the effort. And, to be honest, some of us actually participate in two or more such church expressions, as we find resources that meet needs. That seems to be not all that unusual with our generation.

In our reading of the New Testament documents, Paul taught publicly, first in the synagogue in Ephesus, and then in the Hall of Tyrannus.

18. Luke 2:25–38.

That says to us that there is a distinct role for larger gatherings as *staging areas*, and that there is a place for gifted and experienced teachers and disciple-makers who can assist in forming and equipping believers into maturity in the image of Christ. Such purposeful assemblies, or staging areas, then will give us some clues as to what church leadership should look like, what the church's liturgies and disciplines should include, and how such larger gatherings should conceive of themselves as the church that storms the gates of hell, rolls back the darkness, overcomes the works of the devil, and delivers men and women from darkness to light, and from the power of Satan to God.

Yet, when existing church entities forget this primary role as staging areas for mission, when they forget that there are mountains to be climbed, a mission to be accomplished, a dominion of darkness to be assaulted by the children of the light—when they have only a concern for their own institutional *hubris*, continuance, reputation, and prosperity—then the relentless darkness has prevailed. This is our conclusion, notwithstanding the many good and commendable activities in which they may be engaged.

As we have said before, we see such church expressions, in a very real sense, as mission fields in themselves. It reminds us of the reputed comment by the short-lived Pope John Paul I to the effect that the chief task of the church today is "the evangelizing of those already baptized."

There are so many unreached people who are comfortably at home in such scenes of the darkness of religious Christianity. In such churches, for those who are part of them, as God gives us grace, we want to be the faithful presence of the light, but we will have to depend upon our table bunch to help us make decisions about such, since it is so easy to get trapped into church activities that may be good but don't go anywhere.

And . . . please note: In our accountability to our calling, we reserve the right to *selectively boycott* involvements and activities of the larger church that do not contribute to our calling to be the children of light—to engage in the mission of God in our 24/7 incarnations.

This brings us back to what a necessity our smaller *base camp*, our "church around the table," will be for us. Such responsible engagement in helping each other, edifying each other, "teaching and admonishing one another" (Col 3:16), loving each other, and holding each other accountable becomes critical, and is for us the *primary form of the church*. In sort of a reverse of this image, we can hope that our *base camp* will be an agent in both reversing the drift and in refounding some larger churches that seem to have lost their way—maybe refound them as dynamic *staging areas.*

Got it?

And, by the way, our being around this table here in this tavern, because of our mutual faith in Jesus Christ, and our mutual love and respect for each other, and our common desire to be faithful in the mission to which we are called . . . constitutes us a church. It's not the place that makes the church, but the calling and purpose. We can remember Jesus Christ in the bread and wine of the Eucharist here as well as anywhere.

We are, after all, a pilgrim people!

8

The Core Discipline: Disciple Making[1]

STICK WITH US, BOB, because we're coming down to the final stretch in our attempt to report back to you. And, honestly, we're absolutely thrilled at how clarifying this discipline has been for us. So here's where we find ourselves: It is through the church that the manifold wisdom of God is made known to the rulers and authorities, yet somehow there is that *relentless darkness* that is always at work to keep this from being realized. Okay?

As we reported earlier, we discovered, systemically, that there was an almost frightening absence of understanding of the whole *gospel of the kingdom of God*, which is the core concept upon which Jesus' ministry and the essence of the church are based. So we have insisted that this core concept has to be reclaimed, if the church is to fulfill its very calling to be the community of that kingdom . . . of God's new creation in Christ.

Having said that, though, brings us back to the reality that this very church is made up of real persons, who must also be formed by that same gospel of the kingdom. They are each to be re-created into those living, breathing demonstrations of that same gospel of the kingdom. Jesus calls men and women to be *disciples*, and that designation requires definition. Discipleship must not be vague, or "dumbed down" into something much less than its true intent. (You will note that there isn't any reference to anything called *church members* in the New Testament documents. Does that tell us something we need to hear?)

No, disciples are those formed by the same gospel of the kingdom, which formation has as its goal that each disciple is to be conformed to the image of God's Son (Rom 8:29). Each disciple is so formed and

1. Admittedly, this report is an admixture of the actual response of my ten younger friends and my own additions and clarifications.

equipped that he or she attains "to the unity of the faith and of the knowledge of the Son of God, to mature manhood, to the measure of the stature of the fullness of Christ . . ." Each is to be one who, ". . . speaking the truth in love, [is] to grow up in every way into him who is the head, into Christ . . ." (Eph 4:13, 15).

This maturity, one would assume, also gives us some insights into those who understand why the seven components of the whole armor of God would be essential to their being able to stand in the evil day. More than that, the seven pieces of the armor give us one of the very best insights into the components of discipleship that we have in the whole of the New Testament.[2]

Or, a *disciple* would be one who, by the Spirit's working, finds freedom, and ". . . with unveiled face, beholding the glory of the Lord, [is] being transformed into the same image from one degree of glory to another to another" (2 Cor 3:18). That's not for some imaginary super-Christians, out there somewhere . . . but is God's intent for every one of his children. So, we can't "wimp out" with some lame excuse about only being sinners saved by grace. If we are saved by God's grace, then we are to in the process of being transformed by that same grace into demonstrations of the glory of God . . . and that's what discipleship is all about.

Such Spirit-created discipleship, also, is what makes the church to be a demonstration of the love that exists within the Trinitarian community. Jesus told his disciples that they were to love one another as the Father loved him, and as he had loved them. Discipleship makes the church more than a merely human community. It's purpose is to form the believers, and hence the church, into the dwelling place of God by the Spirit.

BUT DISCIPLES DON'T JUST "HAPPEN"—THEY ARE MADE

If you're still tracking with us, Bob, then know that we're beginning to conceive—as a key component in our calling to be *architects* for the church—of reclaiming and reconceiving our own role as *disciple makers*.

Disciples don't just happen. Disciples are made.

The word *disciple* has content. And, disciple making is written all over the New Testament, but this description of Christ's followers has gotten so obfuscated by the darkness that disciple making is an almost unknown discipline for all too much of the church scene.

---

2. Cf. ch. 3 above.

We want to say it as clearly as we can: The critical (and essential) discipline for the mission of God through the church is *disciple making*.

That's not just our opinion. Remember that Jesus gave to us the oft-repeated commission: "Go therefore and make disciples of all nations [translate: people groups], baptizing them in the name of the Father and of the Son and of the Holy Spirit . . ." But then, note that he doesn't stop there, but explicates some of the content of that mission by what follows: ". . . teaching them to observe all that I have commanded you . . ." (Matt 19–20) (followed by his own promise to accompany them in every circumstance and always).

Making disciples is that formation by which men and women are brought to repentance and faith through heralding God's great good news in Christ, then baptizing them into that radical new way of living and behaving, which then includes forming them by the teachings of Jesus (and the apostles of Jesus). Knowledge of, and obedience to, the teachings of Jesus is of the essence of discipleship. Jesus had said previously that those who had his word and did it were like the man who built his house on a rock. In that same teaching, Jesus teaches that those who are his are not his because of some orthodoxy of their profession, or of their proliferation of good works done in his name . . . but they are his because of lives that grow out of an intimate identification with himself.

The kingdom of God, the dominion of God, the new creation of God, the salvation of God, are realized through those persons responding to God in Christ, and being transformed by Jesus into his new humanity.

Again: this doesn't just happen!

To be "conformed to the image of God's Son," . . . or to be "created in Christ Jesus unto good works," . . . or to be equipped into maturity, i.e., "to the measure of the stature of Christ," . . . points to that transformation that makes God's new creation visible through the church. Only such a church is able to make known to the rulers and authorities the manifold wisdom of God.

HOW DOES THIS HAPPEN?

We know how it happens. It happens, first of all, by watching the ministry of Jesus, who invited (or commanded) interested folk to follow him, to watch him demonstrate the priorities of the kingdom of God, and to hear his teachings. "Come be with me!" He modeled a new kind of life—the kind of life that is to be lived by his kingdom people. He taught them publicly and privately. He sent them out on their own missions to preach, heal, and exorcise demons in his name, and then he called them back and processed their experience with them. He refined them in the process. He listened patiently to their questions and their doubts, sometimes rebuking them for their unbelief.

But he always put an ultimate trust in them, and always encouraged them, knowing that the church he was creating would begin with them. It was frequently painful, and they struggled to comprehend what he was presenting to them—it was beyond their merely human capacity to understand or see. Only after the resurrection did much of it become clear.

The disciple making demonstrated by Jesus had built strong foundations in them for the impossible task that was given them in the Great Commission.

And in terms of our discussions here, Jesus always reminded his followers that this was taking place against all of the efforts of the prince of darkness to keep it from happening. Jesus knew that he had come to destroy the works of the devil, and so submitted himself to the cross by which he would ultimately disarm and dethrone Satan. Exorcisms seemed to be a regular part of their kingdom mission. Jesus modeled and taught them. He formed them into his own image.

Paul, obviously, picked right up on this discipline as he taught the believers in Corinth: "Be imitators of me, as I am of Christ" (1 Cor 11:1). Or: "What you have learned and received and heard and seen in me—practice these things, and the God of peace will be with you" (Phil 4:9). Or again: ". . . what you have heard from me in the presence of many witnesses entrust to faithful men who will be able to teach others also" (2 Tim 2:2).

It seems to us that one of Satan's primary schemes is to displace this whole concept, so that it is not uncommon today to find folk who are baptized, but only into something called: *church membership*, in which they may be passive, or anonymous, or affirmed only because of their faithfulness to the institution—yet where radical discipleship is an unknown, where there are no disciple makers modeling, teaching, forming them into the image of Christ.

Real persons, for whatever reasons, take a step toward the light, but they have been formed by the dominion of darkness in their thinking and behavior, so that if they are never engaged in the transformational disciplines that teach them to think and respond to the light, to God's new creation design . . . then in a sense they are still unreached . . . they are, for all practical purposes, unevangelized.

Without significant disciple making, in some one-on-one formative engagement with mentors who teach and model . . . it tends to be all "dumbed down" into a merely human religious Christianity—certainly not New Testament Christianity. And so the relentless darkness prevails.

True baptism is baptism into a self-conscious turning from one way of thinking and behaving . . . and into another dominion, with a radically different way of thinking and behaving. Disciples embrace Christ's new dominion with its formation, and its mission, by the grace of God and the power of the Spirit of God. God's people are only able to effectively be in missionary confrontation with the dominion of darkness when by their calling they live into that new creation calling, no matter what the context of their lives might be. After all, we are *always* in missionary confrontation with the dominion of darkness, with the rulers and authorities, with the world.

Always!

So we are persuaded that for us, the schemes of the devil that constitute "the evil day," in which we live, are those schemes that leave men and women and (hence, the church) vulnerable by diluting, or displacing, or forgetting, or "dumbing down" this critical discipline of disciple making.

WHO DOES THIS DISCIPLE MAKING?

For us, the answer to that question is: *us*!

Yes, the obvious design for the fulfillment of the mission of God is to proclaim the gospel of the kingdom throughout the whole world.[3] How does that happen? Who are the agents of such a global strategy? For us, the answer begins with us. We are not some others of God's people, in some other place or time. We are his people here and now and in this place. And what is quite obvious in the New Testament is that the gospel enterprise, that of heralding God's love in Christ to every people group in the world begins with us, here and now. The design of God is that the growth of his kingdom is to be organic, and natural. The design of God is disciples making disciples, who in turn make disciples.

---

3. Matt 24:14.

That means that the ten of us cannot be passive. We are responsible to be part of that leaven that is to grow until the whole is leavened.[4] What is indicated in Jesus' teaching is that the kingdom grows spontaneously as disciples make disciples, who then make disciples . . . until the gospel of the kingdom is heralded to the entire world. The people of God in Christ are to be evangelized, and contagious, and reproductive. Their disciple-making nature is always intentional, but may well be (and frequently is) unplanned and spontaneous with the sons and daughters of the light.

When this is *not* so, when the church becomes static, then the relentless darkness has prevailed.

But, again, the gospel of the kingdom of God is by its very nature is dynamic, and is in a very real sense: out of control. The gospel of the kingdom is going to be heralded to every nation no matter what. That's not the question. The question is whether we, as God's people, are faithful or unfaithful, obedient or disobedient, in the disciple-making mandate. The question is whether a particular church community is so formed as to be the incarnation of the missionary passion of the Holy Trinity.

The question is whether a church community is so formed in discipleship that, individually and communally, they are a rebuke to the darkness, whether they are able to storm the gates of hell in their daily faithful presence, whether they are able to conquer the devil ". . . by the blood of the Lamb and by the word of their testimony, for they loved not their lives even unto death" (Rev 12:11)?

The *drift* and *drag* (that Alan had observed) finds its origins somewhere in this neighborhood. The relentless darkness inhabits the church when disciple making is displaced, or so redefined, as to allow for passive, consumer-oriented church membership, in which faithfulness is determined only by one's participation in church activities, and contributions to the budget.

Children of the light, and communities of the light, on the other hand, are to be reproducing sons and daughters of light, who are equipped to live out the light in all of the everyday relationships, conversations, and the vicissitudes of each day's incarnation, and displaying the divine nature within them through their knowledge of Christ.

That's where we come down. We know that life can be messy. We know that we live in a culture too often formed by dissatisfaction, cyni-

4. Cf. Luke 13:18–21.

cism, discontent, moral confusion, and gross materialism . . . but that is the very darkness into which Jesus came as the light, and into which he calls us also to be the faithful presence of the light. Those men and women who are captive to that darkness are those who need to know God's good news. We see the calling of the children of light to be messengers of the truth of God, the hope that comes in Christ, and the love of God for the world.

Okay, Bob, we know . . . we're preaching to the choir . . . but we've really gotten charged up with the magnitude of God's great design in Christ.

DISCIPLE MAKING: IMPLICATIONS FOR RECONCEIVING THE COMMUNITY'S INCARNATION

Now it gets serious. When disciple making is embraced as the critical and essential discipline for the mission of the kingdom community, it has some (probably disruptive) implications.

Disciple Making and the Form of the Church

In reconceiving the church out of its core principle, and its core discipline, we came inevitably to the question: What does that look like? There is no question that Jesus intends the community of his followers to be *visible*, but that visibility has to do with the display of the divine nature in the lives of his followers, both individually and when together. Those outside of the community of faith, those *sojourners* who are still walking in darkness, are to see something in those lives that, for them, is humanly beyond explanation.[5] This has to do with *kingdom praxis.*

But, it is in the relationships that flow out of self-giving love and so dominate the community that those watching from outside can see the new life in Christ at its most intriguing. Jesus said that all men would know that they were his disciples because of the way they loved each other. Paul told the Ephesian believers: "And walk in love, as Christ loved us and gave himself up for us, a fragrant offering and sacrifice to God" (Eph 5:2). The reality is, however, that such relationships of self-giving love can be hardly visible, or barely present, in large institutions of religious Christianity. To be sure, there are always those within such institutions who practice such love, but it is generally relegated to

5. Cf. Matt 5:14–16; 1 Pet 2:11–12.

a pastoral care committee, or to the church professionals. It is quite easy to be anonymous, and hardly know others with any degree of intimacy necessary for such love in such large religious assemblies.

Not so in small colonies of disciples! House churches, for instance, do not allow anyone to be a stranger, or anonymous, or unaccountable, or overlooked. Which means that the *primary* form of the church, of the kingdom community, must be small enough so that everyone is known, everyone has a face, everyone has a story known by the rest. When life is shared, in and by the Spirit's presence, there is a demonstration of God's new humanity in Christ. Our study of Ephesians, especially chapters 4–6, underscores this necessity.

This brings us back to disciple making. Such new life in Christ, and the resulting life in the new creation communities, does not just happen. Such communities grow out of, and are continually being formed into, their calling as a demonstrations of the light by a mutual disciple-making process. "Let the word of Christ dwell among you richly, teaching and admonishing one another in all wisdom, singing psalms and hymns and spiritual songs, with thankfulness in your hearts to God" (Col 3:16). The primary form must be small enough for this to take place. We ten have experienced this in our "church around the table" life with each other. Those who have been invited (or wandered in) to our gatherings are nearly always impressed at the depth of the relationships, and the intimacy of honest interaction between us. This is as it should be.

But there is no *one* form of the church. It is quite possible, and often the practice, for large communities of believers to insist that all of the participants be part of such a small support and accountability community. We're back to the *staging area* and *base camp* metaphors.

It becomes more apparent that we all need such a community to remind us of the actualities, the practical expressions, of the evil day. We need each other to remind us, and to engage with us in the disciplines of the whole armor of God. Discipleship and disciple making, the mentoring and modeling process, find healthy soil in such smaller communities.

Such a reconceiving of the form of the church is more easily realized in the formation of new church plants, where such principles are built in from the beginning. Older and more institutional forms can easily become idolatrous of their size and prestige and traditions and their continuance, to the obscuring of these primary disciple-making principles.

When such obscuring takes place, the darkness dwells more comfortably within the church.

What we have discovered, however, in our experience, is that within these older, distracted, forgetful, "light burns dimly" church communities . . . there are nearly always those small cohorts of disciples who remember, and are agents of hope and love and gospel . . . there is that remnant of patient, gentle, faithful, and long-suffering practitioners of true discipleship—God's witnesses of light within the ecclesiastical darkness.

Disciple Making and the Mission of the Church

Disciple making equips the individual believer, and the community of believers, to live out their calling as the incarnations of the light, of the gospel of the kingdom of God, in the context of all of the realities that compose the daily life within this culture of darkness. It is not an escapist community. There is always the *empire*: the so-called *dominant social order*, what with its cultural, economic, interpersonal, political, environmental, ethical, and often intractable eruptions within the neighborhoods in which we are to be the incarnations of the divine nature in Christ.

This means that we need desperately to reclaim and reconceive the mission in terms of formation for Christian discipleship in terms of the Monday morning world in which we find ourselves. Sometimes, by the common grace of God, such a daily environment can be pleasant to the point of being seductive. At other times it can be ugly and irrational and expressive of the brokenness and malice of the darkness. All of this forces us back to the urgency of habitually putting on the whole armor, and seeing to it that we understand the hopeful purpose of each piece of that armor so that we may "stand in the evil day."

Disciple making not only equips us to discern the times, it also equips us to reproduce ourselves in making of other disciples. It is a discipline that equips us to plant new Christian communities. It is a discipline that refines the meaning of having on our feet the shoes of the readiness given by the gospel of peace. Disciple making makes us eager to engage in conversation with those who still do not know, or are indifferent, or are hostile to God's love in Christ. This doesn't just happen. It is to be the continual communal equipping of one another to be engaged in our small part of heralding the gospel of the kingdom to the whole world, beginning with the guy next door.

Disciple Making and the Liturgy of the Church

What are we (as a community of disciples) to do when we come together? The Colossians passage that we referred to just now gives us clues. We find the New Testament churches (especially in the Acts accounts) spending huge amounts of time praying. What does it all amount to? The word *liturgy* literally has to do with service given to someone, or something, such as a state or organization. The church has appropriated the word to speak of a service rendered to God that becomes a reminder of who God is, what God has done and is doing in Christ, the wonder of his grace and love, an occasion to render true adoration and praise.

So, if disciple making is the core discipline of the new creation community, the church, then how does disciple making reclaim and reconceive of that which the church does when it comes together in the presence of Father, Son, and Holy Spirit? How does it determine the liturgy? How does our time spent together thrill us again and again with the wonder of who God is, and of the "mystery hidden from the ages" now revealed and realized in Christ Jesus, our Lord?

Our coming together is to (literally) *re-evangelize* us again and again by rehearsing the gospel message. Our coming together is to equip us unto maturity so that we can engage in our daily missionary confrontation with the world. Our coming together is to be a time of refocusing, of cleansing and refining, of confession and repentance, so that we are free and bold in our calling to be disciples. Our times together are occasions to publicly renew our vows of faith and devotion of the God of our salvation. Our times together are to remind us of those seven critical pieces of our daily clothing, which is the whole armor of God.

Our times together are to remind us again and again that Jesus didn't come to save the religious, but to seek and to save those who are lost, and to imbue us afresh week by week with his own passion so that we each become incarnations of that passion. Our times together are to be an ongoing disciple-making formation to equip us to walk as children of light. Our times together are to be those precious moments when the word of Christ dwells richly among us.

In our *archaeologist* role we discovered that behind the beautiful formal and written liturgies, such as the Roman Catholic Mass, or the Anglican Prayer Book, is the model from which they are fashioned, namely, Isaiah's encounter with the Holy God recorded in Isaiah 6. Isaiah was in the temple and saw a vision of the thrice-holy God that just blew him away. The result was that he fell on his face in confession of how totally unworthy and unclean he was. In grace, God sent an angel with a live coal and placed it on Isaiah's mouth and declared him forgiven, and his sins atoned for. Then came an invitation to engage in the mission of God to Israel, and Isaiah affirmed his readiness. Thereupon, God instructed him on what he was to do and say, and also what the response would be.

We like that: adoration, confession, absolution, invitation, and instruction. There are all kinds of ways that any group, large or small, formal or informal, can include that progression in their times together—but note: God was calling Isaiah to a life in response to God, and to God's mission in the world.

Jesus gave his followers only one simple instruction, and that had to do with a meal, which included bread eaten and wine consumed: "in remembrance of me." In the simplest terms it means that whenever his people are together they are to rehearse who Jesus is, what he has done, what he has called us to be and to do, and he promises his presence in that observance. The church has developed an elaborate (and sometimes laborious) theology around this, but the ten of us are of a mind that the simplicity, yet profundity, of this *Eucharist* is its beauty and meaning.

We also do not see in the New Testament any reference to certain sacralized persons required for its celebration. Jesus simply said: "When you are together . . . do this in remembrance of me." He gives them the visible observance so that they will be continually reminded and re-evangelized in the rehearsal of the thrilling announcement of his own life, teachings, death, resurrection, and coming again. It was always assumed that at the Eucharist the community rehearsed its own baptismal vows and renewed them at the table.

Those recorded baptismal vows, incidentally (we discovered in our archaeologist role), contain a renunciation of Satan and his dominion of darkness. Such a renunciation needs to be reclaimed as a significant pare of our *Eucharistic* observance, i.e., a renewal of one's renunciation of the dominion of darkness, of Satan's domain and workings . . . and a renewal of one's faith and repentance and deliberate choice of the dominion of God's dear Son. We like that. It fits what we are looking for here. It gives a continual reminder that the context in which we live is not neutral.

The critical discipline of disciple making and the community's liturgical response go hand in hand. The liturgy is to be a continual refresher course in discipleship.

Disciple Making and Church Leadership

This brings us to the strategic topic of who gives the community its leadership. What are the qualifications for leadership? And, what does disciple making have to do with this?

The simple answer is: leaders are to be examples of mature discipleship and are to be, themselves, disciple makers—they are to be reproductive of other disciples. They are to be those who epitomize the mature and equipped believer described in Ephesians 4. They are to be the faithful men and women of whom Paul spoke in his letter to young Timothy, who have responded to and received the teachings of the apostles, and are then to be engaged in teaching others.[6]

Or they are to be the examples to the flock spoken of by Peter in his epistle. The writer of the Hebrews adds that they are those whom the community can imitate, and that they are those who keep watch over the souls of the believers in the community, and are accountable to God for the welfare of those believers.[7]

Leaders in the new creation community are those who are the practitioners of the radical discipleship that is of the essence of our calling out of darkness and into God's marvelous light. The leaders are to be those who are disciple makers, even church planters. They are those formed by the word of Christ and who can cause it to be taught richly within the community. They are those who are formed by the four essential gifts mentioned in Ephesians 4.

One of the tragic subversions of the whole Christian enterprise was the redefinition of leadership into some kind of a priestly class of sacralized persons, who might have no disciple-making qualifications, who are hardly wholesome flesh-and-blood examples of discipleship, but who are somehow set apart to be church leaders by other church leaders, who may even be strangers to the whole design of God.

The very notion that an academic degree in theology qualifies one for church leadership is enormously questionable, in our view. This is not to say that well-equipped and well-qualified models and mentors should not have access to good resources themselves. Quite the contrary, leaders should always be growing and enriching themselves so as to be more fruitful in their disciple-making role in the community (which may have some reconceiving potential for our theological training schools—but that's a whole other subject).

6. Cf. 2 Tim 2:2.
7. Heb 13:7, 17.

For our discussion here, the bottom line is: wholesome leaders should be models and mentors of all that we have been discussing over these months, i.e., they should be those who know what they have been called out of, and they should know what they have been called into. They should know of the ever-present malice of the prince of darkness to render the church impotent, and what the *evil day* is all about. They should be those who both know and wear the whole armor of God, and assist others in the disciplines of wearing that armor. They should be those who, in their faithful presence as children of light, storm the gates of hell in the ordinariness of each day.

Disciple making exposes the relentless darkness, which is ever at work to cause the church to drift. Disciple makers are models and mentors in the mission of God. They are those people of hope and joy and love—those who spread the fragrance of the knowledge of Christ everywhere. Against such communities of disciples, the church as Christ intends it, the gates of hell cannot prevail. The relentless darkness, the dominion of darkness, is overcome by the faithful presence of God's people, living out their kingdom calling in the ordinariness of each day's life, and that with excellence—disciples who overcome ". . . by the blood of the Lamb and the word of their testimony, for they loved not their own lives even unto death" (Rev 12:11).

That's our conclusion, and the final word of our report to you— except for our thanks to you for engaging with us in this quest. We ten friends are not initiating any program for anyone else, but only clarifying our own role in God's mission. If others find our reflections and us helpful, praise God! We are who we are, and where we are, and our engagement with this darkness theme for these months has been formative for us, and . . . awesome!

The long and incredible evening came to a close. We had been God's people refreshing and refining each other as a "church around the table" in the balcony of the Trackside Tavern. We join that innumerable company of other aliens and exiles who have struggled with their own incarnation as the children of light over these past two millennia. We are indebted to their contributions to us, and trust that we may also leave an example and a legacy of faithfulness to generations yet to come, nearby and around the globe.

9

Conclusion: Reconceiving Holiness

Two centuries ago, a remarkable young Scottish preacher by the name of Robert Murray McCheyne is said to have made the telling comment: "A holy man is a terrible weapon in the hand of God." It is with that comment that I want to begin to bring this entire discussion to its conclusion, simply because there are those followers of Christ, those holy men and women, who make a difference and who are the light that rolls back the darkness wherever they find themselves. These are those who stem the drift back into the darkness that Alan noted in our first conversation.

Holiness is a very difficult word to put one's finger on. On the one hand, God is *holy*. What does that mean? On the other hand, we who belong to Jesus Christ are called to be holy, as his followers.[1] What does that look like? Does that simply mean that Christ's people are weird somehow, or does it have a wonderfully positive and re-creating connotation? Or, what do we do with the statement by the author of Hebrews: "Strive for peace with everyone, and for the *holiness* without which no one shall see the Lord" (Heb 12:14)?

That should get our attention!

There really doesn't appear to be a nice, succinct single definition of holiness in Scripture. At the same time the concept permeates Scripture and so must not remain nebulous in our minds. Holiness is to be present and observable in our lives, and when suffused with hope, should (to quote, once again from Gordon Fee) ". . . make the Christian faith a truly attractive alternative."[2]

In the absence of a single biblical definition of holiness, I will take the liberty of extrapolating one from the broader biblical source for our

1. 1 Pet 1:15; 2:9.
2. For the fuller quote and citation, see fn. 16 in ch. 7.

purposes here. When speaking of God, the term *holy* speaks, first of all, of the uniqueness of his attributes, and of their infinite perfection. But then it also speaks of the fact that God's attributes are all interanimating and complementary of each other. They inform each other, and there is an inner harmony—something of an integratedness (or integrity) among them. Love and justice, wrath and mercy, longsuffering and calls for obedience, along with all of those other attributes ascribed to God in the biblical narrative, dwell together in perfect harmony in God's being. His attributes enhance each other. They create in God an overwhelming and awesome revelation of the God of infinite perfection.

For us, holiness speaks to our identification, and oneness, with that same holy God. It speaks of those who know that once we were enemies of God, but have been delivered by him from our captivity to the darkness, and have become adopted has his sons and daughters of light through Jesus Christ. We know that, as such, we have been welcomed into God's new humanity, the dominion of God's dear Son. That being so, it with robust joy and thanksgiving that we cherish and nurture our identity with the holy God, who has called us through Jesus, who with that calling has purposed to conform us to the image of his dear Son, i.e., to form us in holiness.

We become, through Jesus Christ, the dwelling place of God by the Holy Spirit of God, who takes up residence within us. We are called to be that present incarnation, and that radiant display of the divine nature, right here in the midst of the darkness—in the midst of whatever might be the complexion of our present *evil day*. It is as such that we are the light of the world. We, in Christ, become a "holy nation" (1 Pet 2:9).

For our purposes here, also, I would like to offer to my readers the proposal that to "bind on the whole armor of God" is then, for us, a marvelous guideline for what constitutes our daily walk in holiness. More than that: I would like to use Paul's metaphor of the whole armor of God as a very succinct definition of the several facets of the holy life.

Knowing our calling, we therefore robustly and joyously focus our whole lives on Jesus Christ the *Truth*: who he is, what he came to do, what he taught, what he commanded, what he did by his death and resurrection, and how he is the Alpha and Omega of all things. We are those who know that in him the mystery hidden for the ages has now been made known. We know that he is the one who has inaugurated the plan for the ages to make all things new, and that we are to be demonstrations of that new creation.

The first principle of the life of holiness begins, then, by fastening on the *belt of truth*. It is Christ in us who is our hope of glory. That determines all else that pertains to ours lives as a holy people. It is the foundation of our calling to holiness.

Out of that Spirit-created new life in Christ comes our passion to be the radiant display of the divine character of the one who calls us, demonstrated in lives of true *righteousness*.[3] The *breastplate of righteousness* is the visible character of God's people—it is the *praxis* of God's new creation folk. The breastplate of righteousness bespeaks our passion to live out, in flesh and blood, the Sermon on the Mount, with its beatitudes, and its explication of what the kingdom life is to include . . . our passion to know and practice all of those teachings of Christ in his eschatological purpose of creating all things new.

Every new day presents to us a new occasion (sometimes in seductively peaceful settings, and sometimes in the most vile and distasteful of circumstances) to be those children of light who walk in righteousness. Holiness is putting on the breastplate of righteousness faithfully each day of our lives.

Our oneness with God, in Christ, also imbues us with Christ's own spontaneous and contagious love for the world. That divine missionary passion becomes ours. His own missionary nature, which moves in love toward those who still walk in darkness, to be the "beautiful feet," becomes our nature. We become the flesh-and-blood expressions of the gospel of peace as we have *on our feet the readiness of the gospel of peace*.

Our lives of holiness require that we, with joy, take our place in every day's life as the missionary arm of the Holy Trinity, as those consumed with Jesus' own passion to seek and to save those who are lost. Having on our feet the gospel of peace is not some grim responsibility assigned to us, but is our highest joy—it is what we were made for, and is essential to our walk as a holy people. With anticipation, day by day, we put on those shoes essential to the purpose of the whole armor.

The *shield of faith* is that act of will by those called by God whereby they renounce the dominion of darkness, and by faith enter into the dominion of God's dear Son. The shield of faith is our daily renewal of our vows of the embrace of Christ's invitation to become his. As we said

3. Eph 4:24.

earlier (chapter 3), it always has the component of repentance within it. We are always to be those who want the sin within us to be exposed and forsaken. It is the shield of faith with which we take our place in God, and in his holy calling.

Faith speaks of our confidence and assurance that all of God's promises are true and trustworthy. It is the act of will whereby we identify with the mind and heart and will of the Holy God. It is by faith that we appropriate both the promises and the demands of the gospel of the kingdom of God, and so is foundational for our walk in *holiness*.

Holy men and women have the mind of Christ. They are always being transformed into holiness by the renewal of their minds, and being in continual formation by the "whole counsel of God." Holiness is not mindless. God's holy people put on the *helmet of salvation*, which has to do with *thinking Christianly*. Just as the breastplate of righteousness has to do with *living and behaving Christianly,* so the helmet says that the use of the mind in the service of Christ is essential to holiness. Putting on the helmet of salvation is the implication of our being ". . . renewed in knowledge after the image of its creator" (Col 3:10).

When Paul wrote to the Ephesians, he opened up to them the awesome grandeur, the eternal consequence, and the eschatological design of God's revelation in Christ. The implications of that are total, and are fathomless in their meaning. To say that Jesus Christ is the center of time and eternity sounds true enough, but to begin to comprehend why and how this is so is of the essence of the renewal of the mind. So the helmet of salvation is a critical component of the life of holiness. The whole biblical narrative speaks to this.

Closely related to the helmet is the *sword of the Spirit*, which is the spoken word of God. God's holy sons and daughters are those who both know and communicate what God has revealed in the words of Holy Scripture, and in the incarnation of the new creation of God in Jesus Christ.[4] Then too, this designation reminds us that it is not *our* sword, but the *Spirit's* sword. We exercise the sword, but the Spirit empowers and animates it. Note how this is related to all of the other pieces of the armor: thinking, living, mission . . . all of the pieces of the armor complement and enable all of the others, and so present a holistic understanding of the life of holiness.

4. Heb 1:1–2.

But the life of holiness is not possible apart from what has been called "the trustiest weapon: prayer."[5] More accurately, it is "praying at all times in the Spirit" (Eph 6:18). We are taught in the New Testament that the Spirit enables us to know how to pray, and prays in us and through us. This speaks to our relationship. It reminds us that we "have access in one Spirit to the Father" (Eph 2:18). It tells us that in our lives of holiness, our identification with the Holy God, our being indwelt by the Spirit of the Father and the Son . . . we have access to, and communion with, the Lord of all. We live within the embrace of our Father, the holy God, so that continually and everywhere: "While I breathe, I pray."[6]

The communion of God's people with the holy God through Jesus Christ is a life of prayer. Such prayer energizes all of the other facets, or components, of the whole armor. It is to be noted that the description of this weapon is: ". . . praying at all times in the Spirit." Holiness and prayer are inextricably linked, and interanimating.

All of this tells us why McCheyne's word about a holy man being a terrible weapon in the hand of God is so inescapable. Holiness is given such awesome substance and confirmation when described in terms of the whole armor of God. Such holy lives are a continual demonstration of the Light, and a continual rebuke to the darkness, however and wherever that darkness expresses its malignant presence—in the vicissitudes of our daily context, and even inside the church. It is such lives that are spoken of in Revelation 12:11: those that have conquered Satan ". . . by the blood of the Lamb and by the word of their testimony [translate: *holy lives*], for they loved not their lives even unto death."

My readers will notice that I have defined both *discipleship* and *holiness* out of Paul's metaphor of the whole armor of God—this is quite deliberate. I am proposing that the two terms are, if not synonymous, at least nearly synonymous. It also begins to give answer to Alan's initial question about the reasons behind the church's drift back into the darkness.

---

5. From James Montgomery's hymn "Behold the Christian Warrior Stand" (1825).

6. This line is from one of the oldest hymns known to the Christian church: "Christian, Dost Thou See Them," ascribed to Andrew of Crete in the seventh century, and having to do with our warfare with the powers of darkness.

~ ~ ~

In answer to Alan's initial question about the proclivity of the church to drift, my response is: Yes, particular churches do drift, and do die, and for a reason. While that reality remains undeniable, be assured that Christ's church, which he is building, does not die, but ever grows, taking on new forms, re-emerging in colonies of Light in unexpected places and expressions.

Particular churches drift and die because the darkness, and the prince of darkness, are relentless and ever present. The "evil day" is Paul's description of this age in which we live. The darkness is subtle, clandestine, very clever, and so too frequently takes up residence inside of a church unnoticed.

But also, take note: such drift takes place one by one. With any one of those of us who make up the church community, and when we are not alert and watchful, the darkness will subtly preoccupy us with good, even religious, distractions. Such preoccupation or distraction has a way of causing us to overlook or minimize one or several pieces of the whole armor, and leaves us vulnerable. The Light grows dim, we become less and less focused on (what Alan and his friends designated as) the *core principle* and the *core discipline* of God's new creation community: the church. Not surprisingly, we drift into an *ecclesiocentric* preoccupation, in which the church institution and its activities and prosperity become our focus.

This drift is always accompanied by an inadvertent minimizing of the crucial and daily necessity of putting on the whole armor of God.

Such drift begins with one person, then two . . . and it continues until the darkness has taken up habitation in the community, so much so that the very suggestion of such a drift is usually met with offended denial. Such a discerning insight as that the church has displaced, or diluted, or forgotten the purpose of its calling is hardly conceivable by such a community.

One by one, the relentless darkness energizes the drift until the whole community is hardly more than an impotent institution of religious Christianity.[7]

---

7. Bonhoeffer's description of Christless Christianity.

~ ~ ~

Conversely, that darkness can be exposed and overcome one by one, by those who have stayed alert and watchful, who have remembered and been formed by the *core principle* and *core discipline* of the church as the community of the kingdom of God—of God's new creation in Christ. These take their place as sons and daughters of the Light in the midst of the ecclesiastical darkness . . . and each becomes, then, a "terrible weapon in the hand of God."

One holy man or woman, one son or daughter of the Light, finds another, or several others, and so a colony of Light comes into being, and becomes the dwelling place of God by the Holy Spirit within the precincts of the forgetful, drifting church.

Sometime such colonies of holiness, of Light, become a *critical mass* so much that the whole forgetful church is refounded into a community of Light. At other times, such colonies become the emerging sprouts of new life as the older communities die and cease to exist. Someone has likened these to the example of the giant Sequoia redwoods of California, which die and fall to the ground and rot . . . but out of the rotting trunk new redwood saplings spring up to guarantee the ongoing existence of such marvels. Church history is replete with such episodes.

Such colonies of holiness, i.e., those small colonies, or cohorts, of two, or three, or a dozen have played a huge role in the church's spread over the centuries. They find their residence closer to the grassroots: in homes, or around a supper table, or in a coffee shop or tavern. There these folk "teach and admonish one another" (Col 3:16), share the pilgrimage, hold each other accountable for their walk of faith; they also take responsibility for one another's faithfulness to their mutual calling.

Holy men and women stay alert. They know how critical is every piece of the whole armor, and so wear it intentionally day by day. Holy women and men are contagious with the word of Christ. Holy men and women are inveterate disciple makers.[8] They are the present-day practitioners of Paul's instruction to become models and mentors: "What you have learned and received and heard and seen in me—practice these

---

8. They remind us of the instruction given to the Israelites about equipping their children in the Law: "You shall teach them diligently to your children, and shall talk of them when you sit in your house, when you walk by the way, and when you lie down, and when you rise" (Deut 6:7).

things, and the God of peace will be with you" (Phil 4:9). They are the joyous, sensitive, self-effacing demonstrations of the Light.

They are so equipped that they are able to be the evangelists inside, and outside, of the church. They are equipped for the prophetic task of discerning the complexion of the evil day as it expresses itself where they live. As such (as per Jeremiah's commission), they know how to "root up, pull down and destroy" the expressions of the darkness . . . and know how to "build and plant" (Jer 1:10) authentic kingdom communities of Light. As such builders they become the archaeologists and architects of new church communities—missionary church planters—in the complex and ambiguous emerging culture of our day.

Holy men and women find each other.

Holy men and women encourage each other.

Holy men and women minister the word of Christ to each other.

Holy men and women are incarnate in the realities of the evil day, both inside and outside of the church. In the various neighborhoods of the daily incarnations, they are the glory of God; they are "terrible weapons in the hand of God" . . . those who with their Lord Jesus "storm the gates of hell." All of this is often hidden and out of sight, but by their faithful presence as the sons and daughters of the Light they expose the darkness and become the Light of the world. They do this with hope and anticipation and utter confidence in the promises of God.

It is as such that we exercise the weapons of our warfare, and so, by the blood of the Lamb, the word of our testimonies, loving not our lives unto death, we overcome the devil.[9]

May God be with my friends in the emerging generation, such as Alan and his bunch, who are called to faithfulness in the unknowns of the emerging post-Christian culture, with all of its unknowns, and its evident resident hostility to much that is called: *Christian*, or *church*. Humanly, it is impossible, and the darkness may be much more aggressive, but darkness is no match for the community of the kingdom of God, the church, as it heralds the gospel of the kingdom unto every people group in the world before the Lord returns.

---

9. Rev 12:11.

Christian, seek not yet repose,
Hear thy guardian angel say:
Thou art in the midst of foes;
Watch and pray.
. . . .
Gird thy heavenly armor on,
Wear it ever night and day;
Ambushed lies the evil one;
Watch and pray.
. . . .
Watch, as if on that alone
Hung the issue of the day;
Pray that help may be sent down;
Watch and pray.
(Charlotte Elliott, "Christian, Seek Not Yet Repose," 1839)

Appendix: Signs of Authenticity

In previous works of mine, I have insisted that there are at least eight (of what I call) *Signs of Authenticity*.[1] These signs are essentials that I see in the New Testament documents that give to the church its authenticity as the community of the kingdom of God. They have been most helpful to me, personally, in maintaining some sense of integrity in my own church leadership. They are:

1. The Doxological Sign: The authentic church is passionately focused on and formed by its adoration of Father, Son, and Holy Spirit. "Holy, holy, holy is the Lord of hosts; the whole earth is full of his glory" (Isa 6:3).

2. The Sign of Dynamic Spirit-Presence in the church community. The whole enterprise is humanly impossible, and inauthentic, without the Spirit.

3. The Christocentric Sign: Jesus is the center and focus of the church and its mission.

4. The Sign of the Word of Christ dwelling richly in and forming the church.

5. The Sign of Christ-like love for one another within the community: ". . . love one another as I have loved you" (John 15:12).

6. The Sign of Prayer as the church's primary activity, as seen in New Testament accounts of the church encountering its environment.

7. The Sign of the Alternative and Subversive New Creation thinking and behaving.

8. The Sign of the Church incarnating the mission of God.

---

1. Actually, I originally named only seven, but in a subsequent book realized that the doxological focus of the church was not at all optional, and so I made it the first in the list of signs of authenticity thereafter.

"None of these *signs* stands alone. They are all *symbiotic, interdependent,* and *interactive.* Each points to all the others. When any one of them is muted or absent, our caution lights should go on. Because this is true, then, it isn't even possible to rank them in importance. But *signs*, if they are not visible, should at the very least be discernable and unmistakable."[2]

---

2. Quoted from my book *Enchanted Community: Journey Into the Mystery of the Church* (Eugene, OR: Wipf and Stock, 2006), 138.